CW00818952

Antiquarianisms

Joukowsky Institute Publications

1. KOINE: Mediterranean Studies in Honor of R. Ross Holloway
   Edited by Derek Counts and Anthony Tuck

2. Re-Presenting the Past: Archaeology through Text and Image
   Edited by Sheila Bonde and Stephen Houston

3. Locating the Sacred: Theoretical Approaches to the Emplacement of Religion
   Edited by Claudia Moser and Cecelia Feldman

4. Violence and Civilization: Studies of Social Violence in History and Prehistory
   Edited by Roderick Campbell

5. Of Rocks and Water: Towards an Archaeology of Place
   Edited by Ömür Harmanşah

6. Archaeologies of Text: Archaeology, Technology, and Ethics
   Edited by Matthew T. Rutz and Morag Kersel

7. Archaeology for the People: Joukowsky Institute Perspectives
   Edited by John F. Cherry and Felipe Rojas

ANTIQUARIANISMS

CONTACT, CONFLICT, COMPARISON

edited by
Benjamin Anderson and Felipe Rojas

 OXBOW | books
Oxford & Philadelphia

Joukowsky Institute Publication 8

General series editor: Prof. John F. Cherry
Joukowsky Institute for Archaeology and the Ancient World
Brown University, Box 1837/60 George Street, Providence, RI 02912, USA

Published in the United Kingdom in 2017 by
OXBOW BOOKS
The Old Music Hall, 106-108 Cowley Road, Oxford, OX4 1JE

and in the United States by
OXBOW BOOKS
1950 Lawrence Road, Havertown, PA 19083

Published by Oxbow Books on behalf of the Joukowsky Institute

© Brown University, Oxbow Books and the individual contributors 2017

Paperback Edition: ISBN 978-1-78570-684-4
Digital Edition: ISBN 978-1-78570-685-1 (epub)

A CIP record for this book is available from the British Library

All rights reserved. No part of this book may be reproduced or transmitted in any form or by
any means, electronic or mechanical including photocopying, recording or by any information
storage and retrieval system, without permission from the publisher in writing.

Printed in Malta by Melita Press

For a complete list of Oxbow titles, please contact:

UNITED KINGDOM
Oxbow Books
Telephone (01865) 241249
Fax (01865) 794449
Email: oxbow@oxbowbooks.com
www.oxbowbooks.com

UNITED STATES OF AMERICA
Oxbow Books
Telephone (800) 791-9354
Fax (610) 853-9146
Email: queries@casemateacademic.com
www.casemateacademic.com/oxbow

Oxbow Books is part of the Casemate Group

Front cover: Detail of Louis-François Cassas, view of the Acropolis of Athens from the Temple of
Olympian Zeus (see p. 190, Figure 9.1). Suna and İnan Kıraç Foundation Orientalist
Paintings Collection, Pera Museum, Istanbul.
Back cover: Detail of the ornamented façade of Mshatta (see p. 166, Figure 8.3). Woodcut after
photograph by Buxton, published in Henry Baker Tristram, *The Land of Moab: Travels and
Discoveries on the East Side of the Dead Sea and the Jordan*, Harper & Brothers, New York,
1873.

Contents

Acknowledgments   vii
List of Figures   viii
Notes on Contributors   xi
Contributor Addresses   xiii

1. Introduction: For a More Capacious History
   of Archaeology   1
   Benjamin Anderson and Felipe Rojas

Part I: Comparison and Its Limits

2. Archaeophilia: A Diagnosis and Ancient Case Studies   8
   Felipe Rojas

3. The Virtues of Oblivion: Africa and the People
   without Antiquarianism   31
   Alfredo González-Ruibal

Part II: Contact in the Americas

4. *Las Relaciones Mediterratlánticas*: Comparative
   Antiquarianism and Everyday Archaeologies in Castile
   and Spanish America, 1575–1586   49
   Byron Ellsworth Hamann

5. Ancient Artifice: The Production of Antiquity
   and the Social Roles of Ruins in the Heartland
   of the Inca Empire   72
   Steve Kosiba

6. Inventing the Antiquities of New Spain: Motolinía
   and the Mexican Antiquarian Traditions   109
   Giuseppe Marcocci

Part III: Contact in Ottoman Lands

7. RIVALING ELGIN: OTTOMAN GOVERNORS AND ARCHAEOLOGICAL AGENCY IN THE MOREA   134
Emily Neumeier

8. "… THAT WE TRUSTED NOT TO ARAB NOTIONS OF ARCHAEOLOGY": READING THE *GRAND NARRATIVE* AGAINST THE GRAIN   161
Eva-Maria Troelenberg

9. FORGETTING ATHENS   184
Benjamin Anderson

10. CODA: NOT FOR LUMPERS ONLY   210
Peter N. Miller

INDEX   220

Acknowledgments

Most of the essays collected in this volume developed from presentations at a symposium, "Antiquarianisms Across the Atlantic," which was held at Brown University on November 13–14, 2015. We wish to thank the Joukowsky Institute for Archaeology and the Ancient World, the John Carter Brown Library, and the Department of Egyptology and Assyriology, as well as their respective directors and chair, Peter van Dommelen, Neil Safier, and John Steele, for sponsoring the symposium. We would also like to thank Susan Alcock, former director of the Joukowsky Institute, for her enthusiastic encouragement during the early stages of the project; and Sarah Sharpe, Jessica Porter, and Brenda De Santiago for their expert organizational help during the event.

For adopting this volume in the Joukowsky Institute Publications, and for his advice and editorial savvy, we extend our gratitude to the General Series Editor, John Cherry. A subvention for color printing was supplied by the Fund for Ancient Art of the Cornell University Department of Classics, and the index was prepared by Ayla Çevik, with funding from Cornell's Department of the History of Art and Visual Studies—our thanks to all. Finally, we thank all symposium participants—speakers, moderators, and audience members—and volume contributors for their open-minded engagements with a still-developing discourse.

List of Figures

3.1   Fragments of an incense burner on the surface of an Anäj site (sixteenth to eighteenth century A.D.) pointed out to us by a Dats'in (author's photograph).

3.2   Test-pitting in a Gumuz village (author's photograph).

3.3   Inside the ritual house of Adam Yeme, a Sith Swala. Left of the ritual specialist there are several ancient artifacts on display, including a hippopotamus tail used as a drumstick (author's photograph).

3.4   Interviewing Itafa Fido, an old Busase with a deep knowledge of the history of his people (author's photograph).

5.1–5.2   Two views of the Ozymandias in the Texas desert, a ruin that artists and travelers from antique lands alike have painted and decorated (often with socks) since the monument's installation. Figure 5.1 (top): 2009 (AMBOO213/FLICKR [CREATIVE COMMONS]); Figure 5.2 (bottom): 2011 (NICHOLAS HENDERSON/FLICKR [CREATIVE COMMONS]).

5.3   The Ponce monolith provides an example of the stone figures of Tiahuanaco. In the early colonial era, some authors mixed indigenous and Spanish tropes of origins to tell of an original species of humans whom the creator deity had turned to stone because of their sins (photograph by John Janusek, used with permission).

5.4   Photographs of Inca *wak'as*, which could be modified environmental features such as rock outcrops or water sources (pictured here, major Inca origins *wak'as* at Lake Titicaca [left] and the volcanic rock of Puma Urco in Cusco [right], author's photographs), or unaltered things such as trees or corn cobs (*mamazara*) (not pictured).

5.5   Ollantaytambo, an extensive Inca urban landscape and agricultural system (author's photograph).

5.6   The boulder of Hatun Kancha at Pachar personified the Inca ruler Mama Ocllo. Large Inca buildings and walls adjoined the boulder, demarcating the space of the *wak'a* (author's photographs).

5.7   View from the mountaintop of Huanacauri toward the city of Cusco. The Incas recognized this place as a sacred and ancient site where their ancestors first saw, appropriated, and then founded their capital (author's photograph).

5.8   Huanacauri is divided into two sectors. Sector A (top left) features a large plaza and was likely used for theatrical feasting and beer (*chicha*) drinking ceremonies. Sector B features a jagged boulder *wak'a* enclosed within a zig-zag wall (author's photographs).

5.9   Our 2014 excavations (which are ongoing) in Sector A revealed a dense layer of *chicha* service and fermentation vessels broken *in situ* and covered with ash from the burnt roof, as well as a thin layer of red clay (author's photograph).

5.10   Excavations at Huanacauri revealed the practices by which Spaniards and Andeans put this *wak'a* to death in 1536. In the building pictured here, test excavations revealed a sequence of decommissioning, including: a false threshold (a line of rocks that closed off the doorway) (top); a smashed *chicha* storage vessel with a burnt guinea pig offering (*cuy*) (middle); and the original, burnt threshold of the door (bottom). The excavations found evidence for similar sequences in three other buildings of the site, revealing that Andean people participated in or directed the destruction of the Inca *wak'a* (author's photographs).

6.1   Boban Aztec Calendar Wheel (c. 1545–1546). Ink and colors on amatl fiber (35 cm × 38.1 cm). Codex Ind 42, The John Carter Brown Library, Providence, RI (Courtesy of the John Carter Brown Library at Brown University).

6.2   View of the Pyramid of Cholula, near Mexico. Ink on paper (21.6 cm × 12.5 cm). From Alexander von Humboldt, *Researches, Concerning the Institutions & Monuments of the Ancient Inhabitants of America ...* (London: Longman, Hurst, Rees, Orme & Brown, J. Murray & H. Colburn, 1814), vol. 1, following p. 80. J814 H919r, The John Carter Brown Library, Providence, RI (Courtesy of the John Carter Brown Library at Brown University).

6.3   Chicomoztoc, or the seven caverns, with men and women (c. 1585). Painting on leaf (21 cm × 15.2 cm). Codex Ind 2, Juan de Tovar, *Historia de la benida de los yndios apoblar a Mexico de las partes remotas de Occidente ...*, plate 1, The John Carter Brown Library, Providence, RI (Courtesy of the John Carter Brown Library at Brown University).

6.4   Prehispanic giant, or *tzocuillixeque* (second half of the sixteenth century). Painting on leaf (46 cm × 29 cm). Detail from Codex Vaticanus Latinus 3738 (also known as Codex Vaticanus A, or Ríos Codex), fol. 4v, Vatican Library, Vatican City (Courtesy of the Vatican Library).

7.1   View of the Treasury of Atreus display at the British Museum, Room 6 (photograph by Taylan Güngör).

7.2   Reconstruction drawing of the Treasury of Atreus façade from Mycenae (© Trustees of the British Museum).

7.3   Map showing sites mentioned in the text (author's image).

7.4   William Gell's cross-section and ground plan of the Treasury of Atreus, 1810, reproduced as Plate 4 in Gell 1810.

7.5   William Gell's view of the entrance to the Treasury of Atreus, 1810, reproduced as Plate 5 in Gell 1810.

7.6   Marble Kore, Hellenistic Period (© Trustees of the British Museum).

7.7   View of the Temple of Apollo Epicurius, Bassae, in Stackelberg 1826, Plate 11 (Gennadius Library, Athens).

8.1   Bedouin shepherd near the ruin of Mshatta, March 1900 (photograph by Gertrude Bell, © The Gertrude Bell Archive, Newcastle University).

8.2   Mshatta in the Islamic Department of the Pergamonmuseum, Berlin, after 1932 (ZA SMB, Archivische Sammlung).

8.3   Detail of the ornamented façade of Mshatta, woodcut after photograph by Buxton, published in Tristram 1873, pl. 38.

8.4   Reconstruction of the Mesha Stele, basalt stone, ca. 800 B.C., Musée du Louvre AO 5066 (© RMN-Grand Palais [Musée du Louvre]/ Mathieu Rabeau).

8.5   Remains of Dhiban, location of the Mesha Stele ("Moabite Stone"), woodcut after photograph by Buxton, published in Tristram 1873 (London edition), p. 133.

9.1   Louis-François Cassas, View of the Acropolis of Athens from the Temple of Olympian Zeus, 103 × 67 cm. 1790s (Suna and İnan Kıraç Foundation Orientalist Paintings Collection, Pera Museum, Istanbul).

9.2   Detail of Figure 9.1.

9.3   Detail of Figure 9.1.

9.4   View of the Acropolis of Athens from the Temple of Olympian Zeus, 2014 (author's photograph).

9.5   Excavations at Herculaneum. Reproduced from Saint-Non 1782: 3 (Universitätsbibliothek Heidelberg).

9.6   View of the Erechtheion. Reproduced from Stuart & Revett 1787: Chapter II, Plate II (Cornell University Library).

9.7   View of the "Tomb of Absalom." Reproduced from Cassas 1800: Plate 30 (Universitätsbibliothek Heidelberg).

9.8   So-called Diez Album, "Danseuse Turcque," 22 × 37 cm, ca. 1790 (British Museum, 1974,0617,0.12.2.21).

9.9   "Hamale: portefaix," 38 × 25 cm, 1786 (Médiathèque E. & R. Vailland, Bourg-en-Bresse, MS 65, No. 134).

Notes on Contributors

Benjamin Anderson (Ph.D., Bryn Mawr College, 2012) is Assistant Professor of History of Art and Visual Studies at Cornell University, and author of *Cosmos and Community in Early Medieval Art* (Yale University Press, 2017).

Alfredo González-Ruibal (Ph.D., Complutense University of Madrid, 2003) is an archaeologist with the Institute of Heritage Sciences of the Spanish National Research Council. He conducts archaeological fieldwork in Spain and the Horn of Africa and is the author of *An Archaeology of Resistance: Materiality and Time in an African Borderland* (Rowman & Littlefield, 2014).

Byron Hamann (Ph.D., University of Chicago, 2011) is Assistant Professor at The Ohio State University. He is an editor of *Grey Room* (www.greyroom.org); co-director (with Liza Bakewell) of *Mesolore: Exploring Mesoamerican Culture* (www.mesolore.org); project manager (for Dana Leibsohn and Barbara Mundy) of *Vistas: Visual Culture in Spanish America, 1520–1820* (http://vistas-visual-culture. net); and author of *The Translations of Nebrija: Language, Culture, and Circulation in the Early Modern World* (University of Massachusetts Press, 2015).

Steve Kosiba (Ph.D., University of Chicago, 2010) is Assistant Professor of Anthropology at the University of Minnesota. He is currently directing archaeological and archival research (Huanacauri Archaeological Research Project [HARP]), which is examining how the Incas constructed a landscape that manifested their historical claims to origins and sovereignty in their capital city of Cusco, Peru.

Giuseppe Marcocci (Ph.D., Scuola Normale Superiore, 2008) is Associate Professor of Early Modern History at the Università della Tuscia, Viterbo (Italy). His main field of research is the global history of the early modern Iberian empires. He is the author of *Indios, cinesi, falsari: Le storie del mondo nel Rinascimento* (Rome: Laterza, 2016).

Peter N. Miller (Ph.D., University of Cambridge, 1990) is Professor at the Bard Graduate Center in New York. His main field of research is intellectual history, more specifically the history of historical research. Recent publications include: *Peiresc's Mediterranean World* (Harvard University Press, 2015), *Peiresc's Orient: Antiquarianism as Cultural History in the Seventeenth Century* (Ashgate/Variorum, 2012), and *Antiquarianism and Intellectual Life in Europe and China, 1500–1800,* (University of Michigan Press, 2012), the last of which he edited with François Louis.

Emily Neumeier (Ph.D., University of Pennsylvania, 2016) is ACLS Postdoctoral Fellow of Islamic Art at The Ohio State University and former Research Collaborator at the Kunsthistorisches Institut—Max Planck Institut Florenz. Her research has been supported by the Fulbright-Hays Program and the American Research Institute in Turkey.

Felipe Rojas (Ph.D., University of California, Berkeley, 2010) is Assistant Professor of Archaeology at Brown University. He conducts archaeological research in Turkey and is currently finishing a book entitled *Inventing the Past in Roman Anatolia.*

Eva-Maria Troelenberg (Ph.D., LMU Munich, 2010) is an independent research group leader at the Kunsthistorisches Institut in the Florenz—Max Planck Institute. She is the author of *Mshatta in Berlin-Keystones of Islamic Art* (Kettler Dortmund, 2016). Her main fields of interest include the arts of the modern eastern Mediterranean, transcultural museum history, as well as the historiography of the arts and archaeology of Islam. She has held teaching assignments at the universities of Heidelberg and Vienna and visiting professorships at the Universities of Munich and Zürich.

Contributor Addresses

Benjamin Anderson
Department of the History of Art
GM08 Goldwin Smith Hall
Cornell University
Ithaca, NY 14853
USA
bwa32@cornell.edu

Alfredo González-Ruibal
Incipit-CSIC
Avenida de Vigo s.n.
Santiago de Compostela 15705
Spain
alfredo.gonzalez-ruibal@incipit.csic.es

Byron Hamann
Department of History of Art
The Ohio State University
5036 Smith Lab
174 W. 18th Avenue
Columbus, OH 43210
USA
byronhamann@gmail.com

Steve Kosiba
Department of Anthropology
395 Humphrey Center
301 19th Ave S
Minneapolis, MN 55455
USA
skosiba@umn.edu

Peter N. Miller
Bard Graduate Center
Bard Hall
38 West 86th Street
New York, NY 10019
USA
miller@bgc.bard.edu

Giuseppe Marcocci
Dipartimento di studi linguistico-
    letterari, storico-filosofici e giuridici
    (DISTU)
Università della Tuscia
via San Carlo 32
01100 Viterbo
Italy
g.marcocci@unitus.it

Emily Neumeier
Department of History of Art
The Ohio State University
5036 Smith Lab
174 W. 18th Avenue
Columbus, OH 43210
USA
neumeier.25@osu.edu

Felipe Rojas
Joukowsky Institute for Archaeology
    and the Ancient World
Brown University
60 George Street
Providence, RI 02912
USA
felipe_rojas@brown.edu

Eva-Maria Troelenberg
Leiterin der Max-Planck-
    Forschungsgruppe
Kunsthistorisches Institut—Max
    Planck Institut Florenz
Via Giuseppe Giusti, 44
50121 Florence
Italy
troelenberg@khi.fi.it

— 1 —

Introduction: For a More Capacious History of Archaeology

Benjamin Anderson and Felipe Rojas

This is a book about antiquarians and antiquarianisms: people who are interested in and knowledgeable about the material traces of the past, and the cultural and intellectual apparatuses that support their endeavors. Traditionally, the term "antiquarian" (or "antiquary") has denoted specifically early modern European men who turned their attention to things (such as coins, medals, and stone-cut inscriptions), as opposed to literary texts, in order to explore Greek and Roman as well as regional European antiquity (thus Momigliano 1950, a foundational essay[1]). Roughly analogous practices have existed in other times and places, for example, at various moments in Chinese history. Fittingly, scholars of China have used the term "antiquarianism" to describe the endeavors of experts such as connoisseurs and collectors of bronze vessels and rubbings of ancient inscriptions (e.g., Hung 2010). It is therefore appropriate that one of the first forays into the comparative history of antiquarianism addresses the similarities and differences between European and Chinese traditions (Miller and Louis 2012).

More recently, the word "antiquarianism" has been extended to include a much broader range of practices beyond the undertakings of literate and leisured scholars. This is how the term is employed in the volume *World Antiquarianism: Comparative Perspectives*, edited by the prominent historian of archaeology Alain Schnapp (2013). Schnapp's book covers antiquarian traditions as diverse as those of ancient Mesopotamia, pre-Columbian Mexico, medieval Egypt, and contemporary India. This is also how the term is used here. In the pages that follow the reader will encounter figures familiar from traditional accounts of early modern European interest in the past, such as Paolo Giovio (1483–1552) and James Stuart (1713–1788)[2], but also a series of people—often anonymous—who have received at best passing mention in histories of archaeology and antiquarianism. These include indigenous experts on the pre-Columbian past in colonial Mexico and Peru, and local interpreters of antiquities in the provinces of the Roman and Ottoman Empires. Additionally, multiple contributions to this volume investigate what we could call "non-antiquarian" and even "anti-antiquarian" attitudes, including those of communities and individuals in contemporary Ethiopia who maintain a conscious and deliberate indifference towards the material remains of their past, as well as inventors of "fake" antiquities in sixteenth-century Mexico and eighteenth-century France.

The scholarly conversation in which this book participates was given impetus by the magisterial histories of archaeology and antiquarianism written by Bruce Trigger (1989; 2006) and Alain Schnapp (1996 [1993]). This volume builds on that work, most directly on the model of Schnapp (2013), by offering fine-grained case studies of antiquarian practices from different parts of the world. However, whereas the essays in Schnapp's *World Antiquarianism* tend to present snapshots of discrete traditions, the contributors to this volume explore the dynamics of interaction between antiquarianisms.

We approach the study of antiquarianisms with two principles in mind. The first, we suspect, is generally accepted by contemporary archaeologists and historians. Political, financial, and other asymmetries regularly obscure alternative discourses about the past, even those that in practice directly inform the dominant discourse. A more comprehensive history of archaeology should strive to detect and recover alternative discourses (often from patchy or hostile sources), and also recognize motivations, interests, and practices that could be radically different from those of modern European antiquarians and contemporary archaeologists.

The second principle is closely related to the first, but has received less scholarly attention, especially from historians of archaeology (note however Hamilakis 2011: 63): all antiquarian traditions are, inevitably, traditions in contact. Every discourse about antiquity emerges and develops in dialogue and conflict with alternative discourses. While the notion of a discrete antiquarian tradition may be heuristically useful, its limitations should also be explicitly acknowledged. Even the hegemonic practices of modern European antiquarianism and contemporary archaeology, whose power and apparent ubiquity frequently obscure the existence of divergent approaches, are themselves influenced, informed, threatened, and energized by alternative ways of engaging with antiquity.

By now the existence of antiquarian interests in many times and places has been demonstrated, even if their universality has also been forcefully contested (as, for example, by Alfredo González-Ruibal in this volume). Therefore, instead of continuing to fill in the picture by producing further examples of antiquarian traditions from additional regions and eras, this volume proposes to explore contact and conflict between antiquarian traditions, in other words, the dynamics of antiquarianisms as they interact with each other. Fine-grained case studies of traditions in contact will allow us, first, to counteract Whiggish narratives of the history of archaeology as a secure, steady march toward the currently dominant tendencies of the discipline; and second, to appreciate the distinct contours of antiquarianisms within their specific historical and cultural contexts instead of gauging them all by the standard of European developments.

The need for finer detail is especially acute in the treatment of pre-Renaissance endeavors and in cases where texts are patchy, biased, or nonexistent. When the very long-term history of antiquarianism has been probed (as by Schnapp and Trigger), discussion of pre-Renaissance antiquarians has tended to emphasize apparent similarities to modern European practices at the expense of differences. Elite individuals whose concerns are partially commensurable with those of early modern European antiquarians come to stand in for entire periods; thus Herodotus for "Greece," Pausanias for "Rome." The result is that such figures inevitably seem "ahead of their times." And yet, as archaeologist Susan Alcock (2002) has demonstrated through close attention to material evidence from Roman Greece, conflict about the meaning of the past was endemic and pervasive in the past (see also Van Dyke and Alcock 2003, with a much wider geographic and chronological scope). As their frequently polemic tone indicates, Herodotus and Pausanias were not alone, and, in addition, when viewed in their milieu come to seem much less "like us" than before. While religious devotion has played an almost insignificant role in antiquarian and archaeological endeavors since the early modern period, for example, one should not overlook the religious dimension of Pausanias's and even some of Herodotus's antiquarian interests. Their cases can hardly be unique. The challenge, accordingly, is to imagine a history of archaeology that might explore diachronic change across the long term while preserving synchronic disagreement about and variance of approaches towards the past. Indeed, we should expect that robustly multivocal accounts of the interpretation of the material remains of the past at specific places and times will suggest new explanatory models for long-term change.

Accordingly, many of the chapters that follow attempt to place individual protagonists in a deeper and messier social field than is usually found in global histories of archaeology and antiquarianism, thereby revealing unexpected connections, dissonances, and enthusiasms. Greater historical depth and social breadth, in turn, enable us to move beyond simple dichotomies of folk and elite, vernacular and official, indigenous and colonial. We aim to trouble, if not demolish these binaries. We are convinced that this expansion of the notion of "antiquarians" will facilitate dialogue between the history of antiquarianism and both the archaeology of memory (Alcock 2002; Bradley 2002) and the study of indigenous archaeologies (e.g., Watkins 2000; Atalay 2008). These fields have remained fairly independent, but they have much to offer each other.

The core of this book deals with the Spanish colonies in the Americas (Chs. 4–6) and the provinces of the Ottoman Empire (Chs. 7–9). These regions offer ideal scenarios for exploring contact and conflict between notionally distinct antiquarian traditions. Both the "New World" and the sultan's realms were prominent arenas for the activities of European antiquaries, who upon arrival encountered—even if they did not always recognize—existing antiquarianisms. Some of those local, non-European traditions have been probed in recent literature under the rubric of "indigenous archaeologies" (for the Americas see Hamann 2002; for Ottoman Greece see Hamilakis 2007: 73–74; 2008, as well as Bahrani et al. 2011). Cultural differences of various sorts (e.g., religious, economic, and political) posed obstacles to dialogue between antiquarians of differing background, as did conceptual differences that we might call "ontological" (for example, concerning the nature of time and the agency of objects).

The two regions also exhibit salient differences. In the Americas, the activity of European antiquarians was often directly tied to the operations of a single colonial and missionary state, a point highlighted in the contributions of both Byron Hamann (Ch. 4) and Steve Kosiba (Ch. 5). In the eastern Mediterranean, by contrast, the situation was more convoluted. The gulf between European antiquaries and the state apparatus was much wider than in the Americas. During periods of weak central authority, moreover, provincial governors constituted a third, semi-independent interest group which itself existed in a complicated relationship to religiously and linguistically diverse local communities. In her study of the antiquarian activities of a governor in Ottoman Greece, Emily Neumeier (Ch. 7) demonstrates that the "colonial-indigenous" dichotomy is, at best, unable to represent the complexity of such constellations, and, at worst, misleading.

The Ottoman Empire was moreover home to those "Classical" and "Biblical" antiquities in which European antiquarians saw their own origins. European claims to superior knowledge vis-à-vis local interpreters of the material remains of the past, as well as the concomitant suppression or misidentification of local discourses, are explored in the contributions of Eva-Maria Troelenberg (Ch. 8) and Benjamin Anderson (Ch. 9). American antiquities, by contrast, do not so obviously appear in the classical texts on which learned Europeans were raised, although many of those Europeans attempted to understand American *realia* by analogy to classical models. The extent to which the histories of Classical and American "antiquities" are intertwined can be surprising: as Giuseppe Marcocci (Ch. 6) shows, the same forgeries that shaped the conceptualization of the remote past in Renaissance Viterbo also informed an influential Franciscan friar's account of pre-Columbian history in central Mexico.

Dissent and discord among antiquarian traditions are ubiquitous in this book; but what is the role of "comparison"? To begin, comparison of analogous yet distinct arenas of antiquarian interaction, along the lines of the three paragraphs above, should facilitate a more refined account of the specific cultural and historical pressures under which knowledge about the past has been and continues to be produced. Furthermore, and most crucially, comparison should make us aware of how our own assumptions, prejudices, and limitations shape our apprehension of other approaches to the past. We must examine the grounds on which the "strange" has been reflexively removed from the history of archaeology. For example, Felipe Rojas (Ch. 2) calls attention to antiquarian traditions in the Greek and Roman world that little resemble our own, but which were demonstrably familiar to those intellectuals who are usually considered forerunners of European antiquarians and archaeologists. The opposite also holds true: sometimes the apparently "familiar" is in fact radically other. As Alfredo González-Ruibal (Ch. 3) argues, there is no reason to assume that interest in the past is a human universal like language or music.[3] On the contrary, many people have had good reasons *not* to cultivate an interest in the past (cf. Connerton 2008 on the roles of forgetting, as opposed to remembering, in the shaping of community identity). In our desire to discover alternative antiquarianisms we might fundamentally misunderstand opposing and well-founded impulses to forget, ignore, or neglect the material traces of the past.

Faced with the question of radical otherness, there are at least two ways forward for the comparative study of antiquarianisms. Rojas in his contribution proposes a less historically freighted term, "archaeophilia," that might accommodate a broader range of phenomena than those customarily subsumed under "antiquarianism." Anderson, by contrast, proposes a narrower, theoretical definition of "antiquarianism" that might cut across the colonial-indigenous divide. It is no surprise that this volume's editors and the respondent, Peter Miller (Ch. 10), have most directly addressed the question of comparison. After all, we are the first to have had the benefit of reading these thoughtful and stimulating contributions all together. We are confident that subsequent readers will propose new answers of their own.

Notes

1. For Momigliano a key difference between antiquarians, on the one hand, and historians, on the other, was that the antiquarians were primarily compilers of documents (including coins and inscriptions), while the later were analytical narrators.

2. Paolo Giovio was an Italian polymath, who collected classical antiquities and also *realia* from the New World in his villa on Lake Como, which he called "Museo." James Stuart was a British antiquarian best known for his handsomely illustrated volumes on *The Antiquities of Athens*, which he produced with Nicholas Revett.

3. The universality of such interests is often assumed and sometimes even stated explicitly. Consider, for example, the following statement of archaeologist Paul Bahn (1996: 8): "Most human beings have some interest in the past: indeed, together with the fact that we know we are going to die and that we are uniquely capable of destroying our planet this may be one of humankind's distinguishing characteristics."

References Cited

Alcock, Susan E.
2002   *Archaeologies of the Greek Past: Landscape, Monuments, and Memories.* Cambridge University Press, Cambridge.

Atalay, Sonya
2008   Multivocality and Indigenous Archaeologies. In *Evaluating Multiple Narratives: Beyond Nationalist, Colonialist, Imperialist Archaeologies*, edited by Junko Habu, Clare Fawcett, and John M. Matsunaga, pp. 29–44. Springer, New York.

Bahn, Paul
1996   *Archaeology: A Very Short Introduction.* Oxford University Press, Oxford.

Bahrani, Zainab, Zeynep Çelik, and Edhem Eldem (editors)
2011   *Scramble for the Past: A Story of Archaeology in the Ottoman Empire.* SALT, Istanbul.

Bradley, Richard
2002   *The Past in Prehistoric Societies.* Routledge, London.

Connerton, Paul
2008   Seven Types of Forgetting. *Memory Studies* 1: 59–71.

Hamann, Byron
2002   The Social Life of Pre-Sunrise Things: Indigenous Mesoamerican Archaeology. *Current Anthropology* 43: 352–382.

Hamilakis, Yannis
2007   *The Nation and Its Ruins: Antiquity, Archaeology, and National Imagination in Greece.* Oxford University Press, Oxford.
2008   Decolonizing Greek Archaeology: Indigenous Archaeologies, Modernist Archaeology and the Post-Colonial Critique. In *A Singular Antiquity: Archaeological and Hellenic Identity in Twentieth-Century Greece*, edited by

Dimitris Damaskos and Dimitris Plantzos, pp. 273–284. Benaki Museum, Athens.

2011   Indigenous Archaeologies in Ottoman Greece. In *Scramble for the Past: A Story of Archaeology in the Ottoman Empire, 1753–1914*, edited by Zainab Bahrani, Zeynep Çelik, and Edhem Eldem, pp. 49–69. SALT, Istanbul.

Momigliano, Arnaldo

1950   Ancient History and the Antiquarian. *Journal of the Warburg and Courtauld Institutes* 13: 285–315.

Hung, Wu (editor)

2010   *Reinventing the Past: Archaism and Antiquarianism in Chinese Art and Visual Culture*. Center for the Art of East Asia, University of Chicago, Chicago.

Miller, Peter N., and François Louis (editors)

2012   *Antiquarianism and Intellectual Life in Europe and China, 1500–1800*. University of Michigan Press, Ann Arbor.

Schnapp, Alain

1996[1993]   *The Discovery of the Past*. The British Museum, London.

Schnapp, Alain (editor)

2013   *World Antiquarianism: Comparative Perspectives*. The Getty Research Institute, Los Angeles.

Trigger, Bruce G.

1989   *A History of Archaeological Thought*. Cambridge University Press, Cambridge.

2006   *A History of Archaeological Thought*, Second Edition. Cambridge University Press, Cambridge.

Van Dyke, Ruth M., and Susan E. Alcock (editors)

2003   *Archaeologies of Memory*. Blackwell, Oxford.

Watkins, Joe

2000   *Indigenous Archaeology: American Indian Values and Scientific Practice*. Alta Mira, Walnut Creek.

Archaeophilia: A Diagnosis and Ancient Case Studies

Felipe Rojas

This paper was incited by the suspicion that the ways in which humans throughout the world have used material remains to explore and explain the past have been—and, hopefully still are—more varied than archaeologists or historians usually recognize. Variety should be expected, since the mental processes by which one determines that the past "was" a certain way are, to say the least, multiple and complex. The hypothetical links binding things in the present to chronologically remote events involve, for example, ideas about causality, ontology, and agency that are not "natural" or self-evident, as well as agendas, practices, and social structures that, obviously, are culturally specific. Historians of archaeology have demonstrated that human interest in material remains that are old (or imagined to be old) is widespread and frequent, although perhaps not universal (as Alfredo González-Ruibal reminds his readers in Ch. 3 of this volume). Despite that recognition, there is still much to be done to investigate the heterogeneity of human interactions with the traces of the past, especially in places other than Europe and in times before the Renaissance. This paper is a contribution to that investigation.

An expansive and inclusive history of archaeology and antiquarianism could begin by asking the following three questions of specialists working in different cultural settings:

I.   Who are the "antiquaries," if we may call them such, or—if we decide to disregard the contemporary meaning of the word "archaeologist" and to attend instead to its Greek etymology—we could ask, who are the "archaeologists," i.e., those knowledgeable about ancient things?

II. What, if anything, do they consider "archaeological" evidence? Or, less anachronistically, what things do they recognize as meaningful traces of the past?

III. How do the "antiquaries" imagine themselves to be historically associated with those traces of the past in which they are interested?

As I point out below, all of these questions resonate with contemporary issues in academia and beyond. They seem especially relevant to current debates in archaeology (about, for example, cultural heritage management and the challenge of attending to local, non-specialized voices in the production of historical narratives) as well as in anthropology (especially those regarding the possibility of understanding or even studying ontologies different from modern Western ones, on which see Steve Kosiba in Ch. 5 of this volume). My expertise lies in the so-called "classical" Mediterranean so I ground my discussion of these questions using evidence from the Greek and especially the Roman period. Instead of producing lists of possible answers for each of them (by responding to the second one, for example: "coins, medals, statues, etc."), I concentrate on cases that, from our contemporary perspective, seem outlandish. My aim is not to strain the reader's belief with bizarre examples, much less to mock the perceived error of ancient investigators of the past, but rather to show that even within relatively well-studied cultures such as those of ancient Greece and Rome, the pluralism of ancient archaeological or antiquarian thought has been overlooked or at least seriously understudied. If this is true for Greece and Rome, such neglect must be even worse in the case of traditions that are less familiar to modern Western archaeologists and historians. What was considered a trace of the past in Bronze Age China or in the pre-Columbian Amazon? Who cared about antiquities in Aztec Tenochtitlan or in the Kingdom of Aksum? How did "antiquaries" in Neolithic Anatolia or in Mongol Samarkand imagine themselves to be connected to the things they recognized as antiquities?

Readers may wonder whether such questions can be answered at all, even if we narrow our scope to ancient Greece and Rome. Some may object, claiming that they involve insuperable anachronisms and cultural differences that elude translation. Luckily for those undertaking this project, similar difficulties have been confronted already by historians of other fields of knowledge who have chosen to ask themselves whether it makes sense to speak, for example, of ancient Greek "science" or of Aristotle as a "scientist" when practices that we can understand broadly as "scientific" (or, in our case, "archaeological") were part of very different social and cultural dynamics than those of science (or archaeology) today, and when the word "science" did not exist in Greece and Aristotle did not apply for grants or manage a laboratory (Lloyd 2009: 153–171).

Those wishing to ask "What was 'archaeology' in antiquity?" have several options available to them. The easiest and least interesting is to declare the entire notion an oxymoron and to ignore it, ideally after determining a more or less random moment after the European Renaissance in which archaeology purportedly begins to exist and concluding that any event before then cannot be meaningfully considered "archaeological," or even "antiquarian." The historian of science David Pingree would have deemed this option unacceptable. In a seminal essay that informs my own discussion, he argued that:

> it is the historian's task to seek out the origins of the ideas that he or she is dealing with, and these manifestly lie, for astronomy [which was Pingree's specialty], in the wedges impressed on clay tablets [in ancient Mesopotamia] as well as in the observed motions of the celestial bodies [Pingree 1992: 557].

Pingree was objecting to historians of astronomy who refused to count astrological omens, for example, as part of their remit, because they were not, by modern standards "scientific," even though it was demonstrable that some of the ideas and practices that those historians would consider properly "astronomical" found their origins precisely in such omens. I share Pingree's dissatisfaction with presentist approaches; apart from being self-centered, they are ahistorical.

Another option is for historians of archaeology and antiquarianism to try to find embryonic analogues of our present-day selves in the historical and archaeological record, in other words, to look for proto-archaeologists and proto-antiquarians in antiquity as others, such as the historian of science George Sarton, once looked for proto-scientists. (Note, for example, that Sarton organized his monumental *Introduction to the History of Science* prosopographically: Thales, Anaximander, Cleosthenes, etc.) Though slightly less reductive, this approach is also inadequate because the chances of finding our hypothetical predecessors are minimal—although, as shown in section I below—not altogether nil. The risk of anachronism, however, is enormous. If the Greek historian Thucydides cannot be considered the colleague of a modern historian, as the classicist Nicole Loreaux (1982) memorably contended, much less could he be considered the colleague of a modern archaeologist.

A third and bolder option is to define "archaeology" so generously that it does not appear as a uniquely modern western phenomenon. Pingree's words, *mutatis mutandis*, may again offer some guidance:

> … my interest lies not in judging the truth or falsehood of these or any other sciences [in our case, of ancient archaeological or antiquarian interests and practices], nor in discovering in them some part that might be useful or relevant to the present world, but simply in understanding how, why, where, and when they worked as functioning systems of thought and interacted with each other and with other systems of thought [1992: 554].

The dangers of proposing a more capacious definition of "archaeology" are many, the principal of which is diluting the specificity of the term to the point that it ends up describing almost any interaction with old things. One of its main advantages, however, is the possibility of recovering some of the variety and complexity of how humans have interpreted or manipulated things to explain or explore the past.

Perhaps what we need to do instead is to come up with a different word, a word that can describe both our own archaeology, as we understand it, and also, more generally, interactions with the traces of the past that, although attested in other times and places, are radically different from our own. I propose the neologism: "archaeophilia," which I define as *the urge to explore and explain the past by identifying, interpreting, and manipulating things that are (or are imagined to be) old.* The word has a medical ring to it, which is purposeful, but needs to be qualified. It does not designate an extreme aberration (like necrophilia or zoophilia or even Hellenophilia[1]). Instead, it describes a common "itch."

In what follows I tackle the three questions posed above using several examples of "archaeophilia" from the Greek and Roman Mediterranean.

I: Who Were the "Antiquaries"?

Throughout the twentieth century, European and American historians and archaeologists working in the Mediterranean and Near East noted similarities between their own interests and practices, and those of the people in the past whom they studied. Those scholars wrote articles with varying degrees of sympathy for their ancient subjects, using titles such as "Archaeologists in Antiquity" (Van Buren 1925), "Greeks and Romans as Archeologists" (Wace 1949), "Thucydides as Archaeologist" (Cook 1955), and the much more recent and theoretically sophisticated—note the parentheses—"Babylonian Archaeologists of the(ir) Mesopotamian Past" (Winter 2000). Much of that work was synthetic; indeed, several of the earlier pieces amount to lists of "archaeological" incidents. But even in-depth analytical studies unapologetically described people in the past as engaging in "archaeology." Take, for example, the historian Christian Habicht's assessment of Pausanias:

> In little more than one page (II.16), Pausanias describes the myths that are told of Mycenae's foundation, the destruction of the town by the Argives in 468 B.C., and the ruins as he saw them, beginning with the famous Lion Gate (II.16.3–7). This single page is the origin of what may be called professional archaeology [1986: 29].

Or consider archaeologist Susan Alcock's evaluation of the protagonist of Philostratos's *Heroikos* (an ancient literary fiction that is concerned with the relationship between present and past, especially as attested in material remains):

> From a modern perspective, even the figure of Protesilaos himself could be seen as a kind of "archaeologist," digging down into layers of tradition, exposing, retrieving, assessing. Places and things, burial and recovery—in other words a material context—are central to interpretations of the *Heroikos* [2005: 159].

The lexical problem of what to call people like Pausanias or Thucydides or even Philostratos's fictional Protesilaos—antiquaries, archaeologists, or "past-loving-creatures," as suggested by Peter N. Miller at the conference from which this volume arose—may seem inconsequential, except that it is inevitably tied up with that of whether and how to incorporate these people and their practices into an expansive and inclusive history of archaeological and antiquarian thought. It is incontrovertible that in the Greek and Roman Mediterranean there were people who were deeply interested in the material traces of the past. And yet, even if we completely set aside the admittedly anachronistic label "archaeologist," problems arise when we try to determine precisely who, if anyone, is worthy of being called an "antiquary." In a recent discussion examining the implications of classicist Arnaldo Momigliano's influential 1950 essay "Ancient History and the Antiquarian" for the study of Chinese antiquarianism, art historian Lothar von Falkenhausen defined antiquarianism as "the systematic preoccupation with the material remains of the past, motivated by an interest in the past as such, and attempting to bridge a rupture in transmission" (2015: 128). Von Falkenhausen's definition is explicit and eminently clear in the abstract, but once applied to specific cases all three of its components pose interpretative difficulties. What is systematic enough? Can any interest in the past ever be described as merely "interest in the past as such"? And, finally, what constitutes a sufficient rupture?

Von Falkenhausen's lucid essay deals with Chinese and European elite antiquarian practices and is consequently partial to literate traditions. Scholars working on such traditions can much more readily gauge such factors as systematicity, intention, and the nature of the rupture with any given past than those working without the benefit of texts. Thus, it is not surprising that many of the articles cited above deal primarily and sometimes exclusively with textual evidence, even if their authors' concerns are explicitly "archaeological." In the Greek and Roman Mediterranean, the most obvious example of an "antiquarian" is the second-century A.D. traveler and historian Pausanias, the author of a book that dealt with, among other things, the antiquities of Greece (Alcock et al. 2001). But texts are not indispensable. Alcock demonstrated in groundbreaking publications (e.g.,

1997; 2002; Alcock and Cherry 2006) that it was possible and, in fact, desirable to study Roman-period interests in the material traces of the past from an archaeological perspective. Such interests are especially conspicuous in the Roman East, a time and place in which people could be described, without exaggeration, as veritably obsessed with their own past. Borg (2004) analyzes the dynamics of such interests and I myself (2014) have explored elsewhere what antiquarianism might have looked like in a major city of Roman Anatolia. But what about the Roman West, where the texts of locals are much more scarce and, at least according to some modern scholars, there was no interest in the local past at all?

The historian Greg Woolf has stated, provocatively:

> One of the most striking features of the early Roman culture of the western provinces of the empire is the absence of any independent memory of a past before their conquest by Rome. No local coinages preserved images of founders, festivals and monuments did not celebrate historical events and no local histories or vernacular literatures were created [1996: 361].

Woolf's assessment seems to be supported by ancient opinion. The first-century A.D. geographer Strabo, for example, famously said of the pre-Roman inhabitants of Hispania Baetica (which roughly coincides with contemporary Andalucía):

> The Turdetani, and especially those who live around Baetis, have completely adopted the Roman way [of life] and do not remember even their own language. Most of them have become Latin and have received Romans as colonists, so that they are not very different from being all Roman [3.2.15].[2]

Strabo's assessment of the impact of Roman colonization on southern Spain has incited intense academic reflection, especially among scholars interested in ancient colonization and in the Iberian peninsula. It provides fertile ground also for those investigating collective memory in antiquity and in particular contact (and conflict) between local and trans-local historical and antiquarian practices. In discussions of the above passage it is often pointed out that Strabo's assessment that the Turdetani had forgotten absolutely everything contradicts what he himself reports earlier in the same book about the Turdetani's deep historical awareness: "The wisest of the Iberians are they [i.e., the Turdetani]; they use letters and they have inscriptions and poems of ancient memory and laws that are six thousand years old, as they say" (3.1.6).

These incongruous statements demand clarification. Fortunately, Spanish scholars—both archaeologists and philologists—have done much to shed light on the apparent contradiction. The historian Gonzalo

Cruz-Andreotti (1993), for example, has shown that Strabo's claims about the wisdom of the Turdetani are paradoxically in keeping with the geographer's assertion about their wholesale assimilation to Roman ways. In Cruz-Andreotti's reading, Strabo contends that the Turdetani's pre-Roman experience of "civilized" practices made them ideally suited to acknowledge the advantages of the colonizers' way of life (in contradistinction to the irredeemably barbaric people of northern Iberia). Brutally summarized: Strabo pictured the Turdetani as an eminently civilized people—endowed with writing, literature and laws (i.e., with what we could call cultural memory)—and, *because* they were already civilized, they were also fully willing to embrace Rome, even if that embrace implied forgetting what they knew about their pre-Roman selves.

Judging from the texts alone, one could perhaps argue that by Strabo's time nobody actually cared to remember anything about local antiquity in southern Spain, but mounting material evidence challenges the notion of complete forgetfulness. Archaeologist Alicia Jiménez (2016), for example, has studied the imaginative ways in which local communities responded to the exigencies of becoming Roman: these include, in addition to minting coins celebrating pre-Roman gods and heroes, sculptural traditions that are indebted partly to local Phoenician and Punic practices. Similarly, archaeologists Leonardo García Sanjuán and Marta Díaz-Guardamino (2015) have studied the re-use of prehistoric stelae (and other monuments) in southern Spain. They have shown, first, that some Late Bronze Age stelae inscribed with figurative motifs were reused during the early Iron Age by people who carved inscriptions in Iberian alphabetic scripts (including "Tartessian") on them; and, second, that during the Roman period similar Bronze Age stelae were also carved with Latin texts. In other words, from the Iron Age through the Roman period, some of the Turdetani, or rather, the people who lived in the region, re-used local Bronze Age stelae in funerary contexts.

One inevitably wonders who told Strabo (or rather, Strabo's sources) that the Turdetani were the wisest of the Iberians and that their poems and laws were six thousand years old. Could it have been the "Turdetani" themselves? Were there "Turdetani" who could point to ancient stelae inscribed in local scripts and claim that their antiquity was ciphered in those drawings and indigenous characters? Perhaps not, but it seems almost certain that there were people in south-western Iberia who knew about the local past and celebrated their own connections to it during the Roman period. Would Strabo and those of his contemporaries who visited Iberia have recognized those people as their own intellectual peers? Unlikely. Much as modern archaeologists have generally dismissed local opinions about antiquities, most ancient authors tended to elide and distort those opinions or to preserve them in ways that are woefully incomplete. In fact, even when they are recorded, they are frequently dismissed as primitive, fanciful, or the like. The result is that local traditions about antiquity were rarely recognized as "history" and that, even today, they are regularly deemed unworthy of being treated as "antiquarianism," although they do not differ substantially from those of thinkers that historians of archaeology acknowledge as "antiquarians," and even as our own intellectual predecessors.

Gauged by Von Falkenhausen's standards, then, the evidence for Roman-period interest in the local past in southern Iberia does not count as "antiquarianism." But the lack of systematicity, the opacity of motives, and the impossibility of knowing the extent of rupture with the pre-Roman past is simply a result of our fragmentary evidence and biased sources. By contrast, in the Roman East, it is sometimes possible to provide details about specific historical narratives, both local and foreign, surrounding Bronze and Iron Age objects (Rojas and Sergueenkova 2014). In Anatolia, where I have examined analogous cases of interaction with the Bronze and Iron Age monuments, it is clear that that the most noticeable difference between local and foreign perspectives was that "foreign" interpreters of the past had usually traveled whereas local people interested in their own antiquities had not. Thus, the frame of reference of someone like Strabo (or Pausanias) was pan-Mediterranean, and in fundamental ways akin to that of a modern "classical" archaeologist, whereas local interpreters had geographically narrow horizons and their frame of reference is often impossible to recover in detail.

Bruce Trigger warned that among prehistoric communities ruins and other such

> remains were explained in terms of commonly held beliefs that in their specificity are usually unknown to us. Hence, to identify such interpretations as "indigenous archaeology," or even as precursors of archaeology, is to transgress the limits of inference (2003: 43).

Indeed, there is a serious risk in assuming that any engagement with an object that we recognize as old involved ancient awareness of that object's antiquity. And yet, provided that people in the past understood or imagined an object to be old, and that archaeologists can demonstrate this, the question of our own capacity to reconstruct the details of the narratives surrounding that object should become, I think, secondary. If so, the people of southern Spain minting coins with Neo-Punic inscriptions, and perhaps also those recovering and re-inscribing Bronze Age stelae to adorn the tombs of their dead, should be considered "antiquaries."

II: What Were Considered Traces of the Past?

The Jesuit priest Matteo Ricci (1552–1610) was surprised to realize that Chinese antiquaries in the Ming court collected bronze, porcelain, and jade vessels, ink paintings, and the autograph letters of ancient authors, instead of medals, coins, and ancient marbles as did their counterparts in Europe (Clunas 1991: 95; 2010, citing a passage of Ricci's own reflections on the matter). The difference to us may seem trivial because today we recognize all of those things as deserving care and attention, but Ricci thought it noteworthy. His surprise highlights the historical and cultural specificity of archaeological and antiquarian interests (Fontana 2011: 123). It prompts us to ask hypothetical questions: What would Ricci have thought about engagements with the material traces of the past elsewhere and at other times? Could he have understood other people's "antiquities" as such, even if he did not have access to living "antiquaries" as he had in China? More importantly, can we?

Let me reflect briefly about the range of things that are usually recognized to have served as "archaeological" evidence in antiquity. Anthropologist Byron Hamann (2001: 355) has shown that in pre-Columbian Mesoamerica, for example, "fossilized bones, ancient statues, and ruined buildings … repeatedly provided tangible evidence for beliefs about a previous age and its vanished inhabitants." Remarkably, in a completely different cultural setting, the second-century A.D. traveler and historian Pausanias used precisely such things to support many of his own claims about the local past in Roman Greece (Arafat 1996: 43–80). Have bones, statues, and ruins always and everywhere been thought to provide a viable means of access to remote antiquity? Perhaps so. If one reads the chapters dealing with archaeological and antiquarian practices before the Renaissance in Bruce Trigger's *History of Archaeological Thought* (2006; first edition 1989) or in Alain Schnapp's *Discovery of the Past* (1997; French edition 1993), one comes across projectile points, stone celts, metal ornaments, fossilized bones, and shards of decorated ceramics—in other words, things that even today could be housed in a museum or at least in an excavation storeroom.

This apparent coincidence in the range of things that allegedly counted as traces of the past may seem "natural" until we consider the vast cultural differences among the protagonists of the early archaeological or antiquarian endeavors discussed by Trigger and Schnapp (i.e., Iroquoian Indians, Neo-Assyrian rulers, medieval European peasants, Greek historians, Maya queens, etc.). If we keep in mind also the chronological gaps separating those various groups from ourselves the lack of outliers is outright bizarre. Is it not surprising that in most places throughout the globe and in most times before the European Renaissance the past was found in things that we ourselves today, for the most part, recognize as archaeological evidence? Merely one hundred years ago no one would have thought that pollen, tooth enamel, microscopic seeds, much less the radioactive isotopes of carbon were meaningful indices of antiquity. Is human engagement with the material traces of the past simply a cumulative progression in which we recognize more and more things as remnants of antiquity?

The limited range of what seems to have been considered "archaeological" evidence is at least partly the result of an epistemological bias: it is easier to imagine that others have found the past where we ourselves find it. But, as the philosopher of archeology Alison Wylie has noted:

> What material archaeologists recover depends not only on what is visible, accessible, and technologically tractable but also on what archaeologists find interesting, puzzling, and relevant to current concerns, academic and popular. The retrieval and constitution of archaeologically usable facts of the record is very largely a function of what questions we know to ask and what material remains we know (how) to look for in attempting to answer them [2008: 189].

As I argue below, some people in the Greek and Roman Mediterranean identified, interpreted, and manipulated traces of the past that most modern archaeologists rarely think about and almost never consider meaningful indices of antiquity, including, for example: smell.

On Marvelous Things Heard is a miscellany compiled roughly between the second century B.C. and the second century A.D. (Vanotti 2007) and usually attributed to Aristotle—although no modern scholar has ever taken that attribution seriously. The text is a farrago of wonders (e.g., gold-digging mice on the Black Sea [§26], fertile mules in Cappadocia [§69], and an ox-like creature in northern Greece that was said, when threatened, to shoot hyper-caustic excrement "over a distance of about twenty-four feet" [§1].) It also includes the following paragraph describing various traces allegedly left behind by the Greek hero Herakles in the "heel" of the Italian peninsula:

> They say that around Cape Iapygia, there flows a powerful fetid discharge from a certain place in which—as the story goes (μυθολογοῦσιν)—Herakles battled the giants, and it is such that, because of the intensity of the smell, it is impossible to navigate the sea there. And they say that throughout Italy there are traces of Herakles on the roads on which he traveled. And around Pandosia on Iapygia the footsteps of the god are shown, upon which no one must walk. There is also around Cape Iapygia a stone the size of a wagon, which was lifted by him [i.e.,

Herakles] and transported there, and it happened that he moved it with one finger [§96–§97 = 838a27–838b1].

A skeptic could dismiss the entire paragraph as fantasy or folklore arguing that the giant stone was likely a natural formation; that the footprints—if indeed anthropogenic, which is not at all certain—were carved as votive offerings; and that the smell proves nothing else than the pitiful absence of substantial archaic remains near Cape Iapygia; in other words, that the locals pointed to these seemingly random things as traces out of abject "archaeological" poverty. But only from an anachronistic perspective can we doubt the evidentiary character of these traces. Weirdly shaped rocks were regularly invoked as proof that the past had been this or that way or that someone had done something memorable precisely where a peculiar rock was. A famous case is that of a natural rock outcropping on Mount Sipylos in Western Turkey that ancient authors including Homer *(Iliad* 24.613–619*)* and Pausanias (1.21.5) seem to have identified as the petrified Niobe (Taplin 2002). It would be impossible to argue that absence of actual "archaeological" evidence led people to believe that the rock indexed a specific event in the past since Mount Sipylos was littered with patently anthropogenic remains (Salvini and Salvini 2003). Nor does the mythological referent pose a problem: many people in antiquity detected the traces of Herakles throughout the Mediterranean and beyond. In fact, this paradigmatic civilizing hero was often thought to have left his mark in places that were considered remote from Greek and Roman civilization such as Iberia in the West and Baktria in the East.

But what about the stench? The skeptic could disregard it as nonsense and assert that olfactory associations with the past are entirely in keeping with the general outlandishness of *On Marvelous Things Heard*, which belongs to an ancient literary genre known as paradoxography that dealt with the wondrous and the abnormal. And yet, more "serious" writers than whoever wrote this passage also noted the fetid discharge and the specific association with Herakles and the giants. According to the Roman geographer Strabo, for example, there was a town near Cape Iapygia called Leuka:

> in which is shown a malodorous fountain. As the story goes (μυθεύουσι), Herakles drove out those of the giants who survived at Campanian Phlegra (the ones called Leuternian), and they fled there and were covered by earth, and so from their fetid discharge the fountain has such a flow: and for this reason they also call this coast Leuternian [6.3.5].

Strabo and the pseudonymous author of *On Marvelous Things Heard* seem to flag the report; the terms μυθολογοῦσιν and μυθεύουσι—both of which I have translated as "as the story goes"—signal doubt, but it is not clear what exactly raises their suspicion. It could be the reference to giants or, more likely, the locals' claims about the precise location of the famous battle with the giants. According to most ancient authors, the gigantomachy had taken place near modern Naples—not on Cape Iapygia (Vanotti 2007: 179). (Strabo transmits a possible solution to the problem arguing that the wounded giants had fled to the Leuternian coast from Campanian Phlegra, near Naples.)

At any rate, there is no reason to think that locals were at all incredulous about the historical origin of the smell. On the contrary, many communities and individuals throughout the Roman Mediterranean considered smells to be viable means of accessing antiquity. People were ready to explore and explain the past by pointing to powerful lingering odors, instead of insisting exclusively on hard, tangible, visible traces. I have shown, with classicist Valeria Sergueenkova, that distinctive smells in the ancient Greek landscape were variously said to be remnants of the rotting corpses of ancient giants, centaurs, and dragons. Monsters were not the only referent: in the region of Phokis in the village of Panopeus (an undistinguished settlement during the Roman period, but one with a proud ancient past), the smell of two peculiar stones in a ravine was adduced as evidence that a local archaic cult statue celebrated the mythical hero Prometheus, rather than the god Asklepios. Locals agreed that the stones in the ravine in Panopeus smelled like human flesh and said that they were the remnants of the very clay used by Prometheus to mold mankind. In fact, stench could even index chronologically remote, non-mythological events, as happened in Ozolian Lokris, whose citizens associated a local foul smell with the untanned hides allegedly worn in remote antiquity by prehistoric men (Rojas and Sergueenkova 2017, with detailed references).

The skeptic could insist that such olfactory cues are proof of the naive credulity of peasants or the uneducated populace. Even if we leave aside the problems involved in pitting the errors of the common folk against the prudence of learned intellectuals, it is still the case that "respectable" authors including Pausanias, Plutarch, and even Strabo weighed in on the various merits of such specific olfactory associations without explicitly doubting that smells could linger in the landscape over many generations. What's more, urban sophisticates were also using their senses of smell and taste to make inferences about the relationship between objects in the present and various events in the past. Even in Rome itself, there were sensorial experts who knew how to use smell and taste to determine, for example, the authenticity of antiquities: one way to tell true from fake archaic Corinthian bronzes—a prized possession among collectors in the capital—was by smelling them (Martial 9.59);[3] and according to Pliny the Elder, even in his day, the exceptional high-quality plaster used by the famous Greek sculptor Pheidias still tasted of saffron—five centuries after it had been first made (36.55). For what it's worth, the author of *On Marvelous Things Heard* records that by smell too ancient connoisseurs could recognize a special type of copper that was said to have been used to make the drinking cups of the Persian king Darius (§49).

Obviously, these are very different examples to those involving small communities in remote places. While those communities appealed to stimuli that absolutely anyone could smell—in other words, to the incontrovertible evidence of the senses—olfactory connoisseurs in Roman antiquity, like modern sommeliers and parfumiers, claimed exceptional expertise about embodied traces that almost no one could detect. At any rate, both country hicks and urban pedants thought themselves capable of recognizing the past through their noses. It is worth remembering, that "our sense of smell is so underdeveloped in the modern West that we can no more appreciate the importance of odour in the ancient world than the blind can describe a colourful scene" (Classen et al. 1994: 6 summarizing Faure 1987).

And why should anyone have doubted that smells could serve as meaningful indices of antiquity? The classicist Tim Whitmarsh has discussed Roman-period references to material remains in ancient debates involving conflicting traditions about the past. He has argued that "[t]hese appeals to physical monuments are not innocent; blocks of stone are ontologically nonnegotiable, concrete symbols of a claimed solidity in the relationship between past and present" (2013: 230). In other words, it is hard to object to the sheer reality of a rock. But are powerful, lingering smells any different from a block of stone? I would argue that few things are less negotiable than an intense fetor penetrating the nostrils, even against one's will, demanding immediate attention and explanation. Even now people disagree not only about who exactly has "left things behind," and for what reason, but also about what constitute the most meaningful "left-behind-things" in the first place. The indices by which the relationship between past and present is established are a matter of debate, whether they are a foul smell, DNA, C-14, or a block of stone.

It is worth noting that while the evidence I have presented here is literary, there is also an archaeological dimension to Greek and Roman sensory engagements with the past. In western Turkey, for example, there are caves along the Maeander River valley that expel powerful mephitic gases near the ancient cities of Hierapolis, Nysa, and Magnesia. In the Roman period, several of those caves were monumentalized. Elaborate architecture marked them as cultural hotspots in which bulls and birds were made to suffocate, while religious experts learned to control their breathing to survive descent into those caves. There one could experience the effect of powerful primeval vapors in the present. (For further details, see Rojas and Sergueenkova 2017.)

III: How Did the "Antiquaries" Imagine Themselves to be Connected to Those Traces?

In 2011, the pre-eminent Danish evolutionary geneticist Eske Willerslev confronted an ethical dilemma involving the different ways in which he and others imagined themselves to be historically associated with the material remains of antiquity. In that year, Willerslev led the international team of scientists that published the first complete genome of an aboriginal Australian (Rasmussen 2011; Callaway 2011a). They extracted DNA from hair samples obtained in the early twentieth century by a British ethnologist that are now housed at the University of Cambridge. After publication, several people, including at least one member of Willlerslev's own research team, objected to the fact that they had not sought permission from living aboriginal Australians who felt a right of possession over that material. His response was described recently by journalist Carl Zimmer: "At first, Dr. Willerslev didn't understand the fuss. 'My view was that human history belongs to all of us because we're all connected, and no people have a right to stop our understanding of human history,' he said" (2016).

Initially, Willerslev could not make sense of the aboriginal Australians' claims over the DNA and the hair samples from which it was extracted. In the geneticist's eyes, those things provided demonstrable links to a past that was everyone's. The Australians, by contrast, considered that past and its traces to be specifically their own. Various specialists on bioethical matters weighed in on the debate over the published genome, among them Hank Greely, director of the Center for Law and the Biosciences at Stanford University, who said: "In a sense, every Aboriginal Australian has had something about themselves revealed to the world without their consent" (quoted in Callaway 2011b). Eventually, Willerslev visited the aboriginal Australians, who granted him permission to continue his research (Callaway 2011b; Zimmer 2016).

This incident raises a question that every investigator of the past inevitably confronts: how are we (as, for example, archaeologists or historians) connected to the traces of the past which we (and others) care about? Obviously, the answer does not involve a simple binary determining whether the past is our own or not, but rather, a process of unraveling the different ways in which the past is and is not "ours." A middle ground of some sort can be reached even between parties making claims that appear to be in opposition, as occurred in Willerslev's case. The public and seemingly insurmountable problems of deciding what to do with, for example, the Elgin Marbles or the Pergamon Altar (now in London and Berlin, but once in what are now Greece and Turkey, respectively) are largely practical and diplomatic, and much less complicated than those concerning the Australians' hair and DNA. But there are situations in which there is disagreement over fundamental notions about how the world works.

Here I am interested specifically in cases of individuals and communities who have imagined not just ethnic or familial, but actually personal bonds between themselves and things in the world which they recognized as traces of the past. Consider the following anecdote preserved in the historian Diodoros of Sicily's biographical sketch of the sixth century B.C. sage Pythagoras:

> They say that when he [i.e. Pythagoras] was visiting Argos and he saw a shield that was one of the spoils of the Trojans hung up [on a wall], he cried. And when he was asked by the Argives he stated the cause of his affliction, namely, that he himself had owned that shield when he had been [the warrior] Euphorbos in Troy. The [Argives] did not believe him and thought he was mad, but he said that a sign would reveal the truth of this incident: for in the interior the shield had been inscribed with archaic letters [that read] "of Euphorbos." Since this seemed impossible, they said to him to take down the shield, and it turned out that they found the inscription [10.6.2–3].

It is worth pointing out that, although the outline of the Pythagoras story was known to earlier sources, Diodoros wrote in the first century A.D. and thus about half a millennium after Pythagoras. In addition, several passages concerning Pythagoras' life are notoriously difficult to study, because Greek and Roman biographies of great personages gravitate towards the spectacular or the scandalous, and, more importantly, because Pythagoras seems to have been in touch with mystical and shamanistic traditions that were not understood by many of his successors or even his contemporaries (Burkert 1972: 120–165). Even so, this anecdote highlights the fact that our own ideas about things that we consider meaningful indices of antiquity are not "natural" or universal. They are part of more or less complex systems of thought that inevitably impose limitations on the kinds of information that can be extracted from them as well as on the connections that we can imagine between those indices and ourselves.

Even if we assume that the story related by Diodoros and others was a combination of misunderstanding and fantasy, it still sheds light, obliquely, on at least two strategies of ascertaining the antiquity of objects in the "classical" Mediterranean. One is contextual: the shield's provenance was supported by the fact that it was housed in a temple, presumably along with many other antiquities. Greek and Roman temples acted as depositories for collections of objects that could be used to reconstruct and substantiate local and trans-local history, as occurred, for example, in the temple of Athena at Lindos with its detailed catalogue of votive offerings dating back to mythological time (Higbie 2003). The other is epigraphic: texts in alphabetic and other scripts were used by ancient specialists to date inscribed objects or at least to place them in historical sequences. In terms of their techniques of authentication of ancient objects, Pythagoras and the Argives were agreed. The problem, obviously, was—and is—that the sage's claims contravene our understanding of, among other things, personhood and the nature of life and death. We live, we die, we do not reincarnate—at least not in the opinion of most ancient Greeks or modern archaeologists—nor do we recognize as our own objects that were made and used about half a millennium before our time.

Although from the perspective of modern archaeology this anecdote could be easily consigned to the history of quackery, it seems much less ridiculous from the perspective of the history of religion. Pythagoras was said by several of his ancient biographers to claim to have been reincarnated many times (Gottschalk 1980: 115, with ancient references). The ideas about metempsychosis associated with Pythagoras may have had a non-Greek, perhaps Asian origin (Dodds 1951: 135–178). The recognition at Argos evidently resonates with Tibetan and Mongolian ideas about reincarnation according to which holy men were capable of remembering and recognizing their belongings from previous lives (Kingsley 2010: n.23 for references). The authenticity of a reincarnated Tibetan lama, for example, was traditionally tested by subjecting him to a series of "mnemonic" challenges in which he had to remember former lives (Zivkovic 2014: 23–25). In one such test, the future lama was presented with a series of identical objects only some of which had been his own in a previous incarnation (Aziz 1976: 349). Other lamas knew the history of the objects in question making it possible to determine whether the future lama had, in fact, successfully recognized them.

Similar "mnemonic" tests were performed also by indigenous people in North America, including the Gitksan of British Columbia who, as explained by anthropologist Antonia Mills, "would offer a series of war clubs to a child thought to be a particular high chief reborn. The purpose was to see if the child could pick out the club which had belonged to the deceased high chief" (1994: 213). (Mills notes the striking parallel with Tibetan traditions.) Do these instances of recognition concern "archaeological" or "antiquarian" thought? Not in any recognizable way. But they do involve "the deliberate use of material remains to learn more about the past," which is how Trigger (2006: 40) defined the scope of his inquiry in *A History of Archaeological*

Thought. Furthermore, they are obviously part of whole systems of thought, with their own rules and standards—even if in the case of Pythagoras the specific system is impossible to reconstruct completely.

One can imagine what Pythagoras felt upon seeing his shield in the temple at Argos. A favorite tool or a musical instrument can trigger instant, embodied recollection when its owner holds it again after many years of neglect; an old toy or a childhood bicycle can incite similar reactions. We rarely consider these moments "antiquarian," much less "archaeological." They are so intimate as to seem solipsistic. But, at its core, any attempt to interpret the traces of the past makes sense only within certain cultural and historical parameters—whether it involves a geneticist sequencing DNA order to determine the date of human dispersal into eastern Asia, aboriginal Australians claiming that their own history is entangled in an ancestor's tuft of hair, the modern Greek and Turkish states demanding back "their" monuments, or Pythagoras recognizing what had been his at the time of the Trojan War. Clearly, people have allowed for engagements with the traces of the past that are much more personal than those imagined by most modern western archaeologists, let alone most classicists. (Although, those familiar with the antics of the nineteenth-century German entrepreneur Heinrich Schliemann, excavator of Troy, may recall now the images of Schliemann's Greek wife Sophia adorned with the "jewels of Helen" extracted from a tumulus in Hısarlık, Turkey.) The problem of studying such systems of thought constitutes a major challenge for scholars who want to understand "archaeological" and "antiquarian" practices in cultures with radically different ideas of the self and of what it means to be human. For specialists in the ancient Mediterranean this fragmentary evidence should serve as a reminder that, despite how much we have lost, it is still possible to detect alternatives to those we consider the predecessors of our own ways of engaging with the material traces of the past.

Profound differences over the imagined connections with "archaeological" evidence were emphasized recently by North American Indians protesting an auction of ethnographic materials to be held at the Eve auction house in Paris. One of the Indians' leaders explained:

> When we create the objects [that would be put up for auction], we're in prayer, we're breathing life into the object. And so these objects are not just a mere object in some fancy collection. These objects are living beings to us. These objects are part of our family, these objects are part of who we are as a people, these objects have a sacred purpose within our community. At the auction coming up on Monday is one of these objects. We're hopeful that somehow, some day, that member of our community, that member of our family, will be able to return home to us and continue its lifespan within our community. The

auctions that take place around the world are deplorable. It harkens to me of the slave auctions that took place so long ago that we thought they were past [Smith 2016].

Conclusions

The cases of "archaeophilia" presented above are meant to suggest ways in which we can begin to conceive of a more expansive and inclusive, as well as a less self-centered history of archaeology and antiquarianism. As has been pointed out by archaeologist Margarita Díaz-Andreu, the history of archaeology has been written almost exclusively by practicing archaeologists (as opposed to the history of science or the history of music, which have not been the exclusive domain of scientists and musicians). This monopoly has resulted in a tendency to accept a "narrow, almost positivisitic understanding of what the writing of one's own disciplinary history represents" (Díaz-Andreu 2007: 1). And yet, as archaeologists and historians, I think, we should strive to understand ancient (and modern) human experience in spite of its heterogeneity, or rather, precisely because of it. Our investigation may show that we are one distinct—now dominant—voice in what has been a long, fractious, and continuous dialogue to make sense of the traces of the past in our midst. The dialogic aspect of this endeavor is key, although not always acknowledged. It seems almost impossible that any discourse about how the past was (or is) embedded in things has ever developed in isolation from contrasting and conflicting interpretations. If a truly comparative history of archaeological and antiquarian thought is worth undertaking at all, then it should attend also to ideas that are radically different from our own. We owe those ideas our attention not simply out of encyclopedic duty, but rather because our own archaeological and antiquarian traditions came to be as they are in tension with many others that we have sidelined, silenced, or banished to obscurity. The presentist biases of modern western archaeology should not get to determine what has counted as a trace of the past in other times and places, or who has been able to interpret such traces, and much less how people have imagined themselves to be connected with them.

Acknowledgments

I thank Susan Alcock, Benjamin Anderson, Yannis Hamilakis, Sarah Newman, Valeria Sergueenkova, and John Steele for comments on early drafts of this paper.

Notes

1. Pingree (1992: 555) explicitly intended the term to sound pathological: "I like 'Hellenophilia' as a word because it brings to mind such other terms as 'necrophilia,' a barbaric excess that erupts as a disease from the passionate rather than from the rational soul."
2. Translations from the Greek are my own.
3. This and a related passage of Petronius (50.7) have been the subject of much debate; recent discussions include Emanuele (1989) who argues that the patina of such bronzes may have been the source of the smell, and Linderski (1992), who believes that the idea of smelling the antiquity of bronzes was merely a way to mock pedants. Pedants or not, the claim was made in antiquity.

References

Alcock, Susan E.
  1997   The Heroic Past in a Hellenistic Present. In *Hellenistic Constructs: Essays in Culture, History, and Historiography,* edited by Paul Cartledge, Peter Garnsey, and Erich S. Gruen, pp. 20–34. University of California Press, Berkeley.
  2002   *Archaeologies of the Greek Past: Landscape, Monuments, and Memories.* Cambridge University Press, Cambridge.
  2005   Material Witness: An Archeological Context for the Heroikos. In *Philostratus's Heroikos: Religion and Cultural Identity in the Third Century,* edited by Ellen Bradshaw Aiken and Jennifer K. Berenson Maclean, pp. 159–68. Society of Biblical Literature, Atlanta.
Alcock, Susan E., and John F. Cherry
  2006   "No Greater Marvel": A Bronze Age Classic at Orchomenos. In *Classical Pasts: The Classical Traditions of Greece and Rome,* edited by James Porter, pp. 69–86. Princeton University Press, Princeton.
Alcock, Susan E., John F. Cherry, and Jaś Elsner (editors)
  2001   *Pausanias: Travel and Memory in Roman Greece.* Oxford University Press, Oxford.
Arafat, Karim W.
  1996   *Pausanias' Greece: Ancient Artists and Roman Rulers.* Cambridge University Press, Cambridge.
Aziz, Barbara N.
  1976   Reincarnation Reconsidered: Or the Reincarnate Lama as Shaman. In *Spirit Possession in the Nepal Himalayas,* edited by John T. Hitchcock and Rex L. Jones, pp. 343–360. Aris and Phillips, Warminster.
Borg, Barbara (editor)
  2004   *Paideia: The World of the Second Sophistic.* Walter de Gruyter, Berlin.
Burkert, Walter
  1972   *Lore and Science in Ancient Pythagoreanism.* Harvard University Press, Cambridge.
Callaway, Ewen
  2011a   First Aboriginal Genome Sequenced. *Nature,* 22 September 2011. doi:10.1038/news.2011.551.

2011b   Aboriginal Genome Analysis Comes to Grips with Ethics. *Nature*, 28 September 2011. doi:10.1038/477522a.

Classen, Constance, David Howes, and Anthony Synnott

1994   *Aroma: The Cultural History of Smell.* Routledge, London.

Clunas, Craig

1991   *Superfluous Things: Material Culture and Social Status in Early Modern China.* Polity Press, Cambridge.

2010   Antiquarian Politics and the Politics of Antiquarianism in Ming Regional Courts. In *Reinventing the Past: Archaism and Antiquarianism in Chinese Art and Visual Culture*, edited by Wu Hung, pp. 229–254. The Center for the Art of East Asia, Hong Kong.

Cook, Robert M.

1955   Thucydides as Archaeologist. *Annual of the British School at Athens* 50: 266–270.

Cruz Andreotti, Gonzalo

1993   Estrabón y el pasado turdetano: la recuperación del mito tartésico. *Geographia antiqua* 2: 13–32.

Díaz-Andreu, Margarita

2007   *A World History of Nineteenth-Century Archaeology: Nationalism, Colonialism, and the Past.* Oxford University Press, Oxford.

Dodds, Eric Robertson

1957   *The Greeks and the Irrational.* University of California Press, Berkeley.

Emanuele, Daniel

1989   "Aes Corinthium": Fact, Fiction, and Fake. *Phoenix* 43: 347–358.

Faure, Paul

1987   *Parfums et aromates de l'Antiquité.* Fayard, Paris.

Fontana, Michela

2011   *Matteo Ricci: A Jesuit in the Ming Court.* Rowman and Littlefield, Plymouth.

Galinsky, Karl, and Kenneth Lapatin (editors)

2016   *Cultural Memories in the Roman Empire.* John Paul Getty Museum, Los Angeles.

Gottschalk, Hans Benedikt

1980   *Heraclides of Pontus.* Oxford University Press, Oxford.

Habicht, Christian

1988   *Pausanias' Guide to Ancient Greece.* University of California Press, Berkeley.

Hamann, Byron

2002   The Social Life of Pre-Sunrise Things: Indigenous Mesoamerican Archaeology. *Current Anthropology* 43: 351–382.

Higbie, Carolyn

2003   *The Lindian Chronicle and the Greek Creation of Their Past.* Oxford University Press, Oxford.

Hurst Thomas, David

2000   *Skull Wars: Kennewick Man, Archaeology, And The Battle For Native American Identity.* Basic Books, New York.

Jiménez, Alicia
2015   The Western Empire and the "People without History": A Case Study from Southern Iberia. In *Cultural Memories in the Roman Empire*, edited by Karl Galinsky and Kenneth Lapatin, pp. 170–190. John Paul Getty Museum, Los Angeles.

Kingsley, Peter
2010   *A Story Waiting to Pierce You: Mongolia, Tibet, and the Destiny of the Western World*. Golden Sufi Center, Point Reyes Station, California.

Loreaux, Nicole
1980   Thucydide n'est pas un collègue. *Quaderni di storia* 12: 55–81.

Linderski, Jerzy
1992   Aes Olet: Petronius 50.7 and Martial 9.59.11. *Harvard Studies in Classical Philology* 94: 349–353.

Lloyd, Geoffrey E. R.
2009   *Disciplines in the Making: Cross-Cultural Perspectives on Elites, Learning, and Innovation*. Oxford University Press, Oxford.

Mills, Antonia
1994   Rebirth and Identity: Three Gitksan Cases of Pierced-Ear Birthmarks. In *Amerindian Rebirth: Reincarnation Belief Among North American Indians and Inuit*, edited by Antonia Curtze Mills and Richard Slobodin, pp. 211–241. University of Toronto Press, Toronto.

Momigliano, Arnaldo
1950   Ancient History and the Antiquarian. *Journal of the Warburg and Courtauld Institutes* 13: 285–315.

1990   *Classical Foundations of Modern Historiography*. University of California Press, Berkeley.

Pingree, David
1992   Hellenophilia versus the History of Science. *Isis* 83: 554–563.

Rasmussen, Morten, and Xiaosen Guo, Yong Wang, Kirk E. Lohmueller, Simon Rasmussen, Anders Albrechtsen, Line Skotte, Stinus Lindgreen, Mait Metspalu, Thibaut Jombart, Toomas Kivisild, Weiwei Zhai, Anders Eriksson, Andrea Manica, Ludovic Orlando, Francisco M. De La Vega, Silvana Tridico, Ene Metspalu, Kasper Nielsen, María C. Ávila-Arcos, J. Víctor Moreno-Mayar, Craig Muller, Joe Dortch, M. Thomas P. Gilbert, Ole Lund, Agata Wesolowska, Monika Karmin, Lucy A. Weinert, Bo Wang, Jun Li, Shuaishuai Tai, Fei Xiao, Tsunehiko Hanihara, George van Driem, Aashish R. Jha, François-Xavier Ricaut, Peter de Knijff, Andrea B Migliano, Irene Gallego Romero, Karsten Kristiansen, David M. Lambert, Søren Brunak, Peter Forster, Bernd Brinkmann, Olaf Nehlich, Michael Bunce, Michael Richards, Ramneek Gupta, Carlos D. Bustamante, Anders Krogh, Robert A. Foley, Marta M. Lahr, Francois Balloux, Thomas Sicheritz-Pontén, Richard Villems, Rasmus Nielsen, Jun Wang, Eske Willerslev.
2011   An Aboriginal Australian Genome Reveals Separate Human Dispersals Into Asia. *Science* 334(6052): 94–98.

Rojas, Felipe
2014   Antiquarianism in Roman Sardis. In *World Antiquarianism: Comparative Perspectives*, edited by Alain Schnapp, pp. 176–200. Getty Research Institute, Los Angeles.

Rojas, Felipe, and Valeria Sergueenkova
2014   Traces of Tarhuntas: Greek, Roman, and Byzantine Interaction with Hittite
                Monuments. *Journal of Mediterranean Archaeology* 27: 135–160.
2017   The Smell of Time: Olfactory Associations with the Past in Ancient Greece.
                In *Knowing Bodies, Passionate Souls: Sense Perceptions in Byzantium*, edited
                by Margaret Mullet and Susan Harvey, pp. 141–151. Dumbarton Oaks
                Publications, Washington, D.C.

Rosenberg, Daniel
2007   Marking Time. *Cabinet* 28: 96–100.

Salvini, Béatrice André, and Mirjo Salvini
2003   Il monumento rupestre della "Niobe" o "Cibele" del Sipilo. In *Licia e
                Lidia prima dell'ellenizzazione: atti del convegno internazionale, Roma, 11–12
                ottobre 1999*, edited by Mauro Giorgieri, pp. 25–36. Consiglio nazionale
                delle ricerche, Rome.

Sanjuán, Leonardo García, and Marta Díaz-Guardamino
2015   The Outstanding Biographies of Prehistoric Monuments in Iron Age,
                Roman, and Medieval Spain. In *The Lives of Prehistoric Monuments
                in Iron Age, Roman, and Medieval Europe*, edited by Marta Díaz-
                Guardamino, Leonardo García Sanjuán, and David Wheatley, pp.
                183–204. Oxford University Press, Oxford.

Sarton, George
1927   *Introduction to the History of Science 1.1.* Carnegie Institution, Washington,
                D.C.

Schnapp, Alain
1997   *The Discovery of the Past.* Harry N. Abrams, New York.

Smith, David
2016   Native Americans Implore France to Halt Artifact Sale: "It Harkens of
                Slave Auctions." *The Guardian* May 25, 2016 (published online). https://
                www.theguardian.com/us-news/2016/may/25/native-american-france-
                sacred-objects-auction-smithsonian.

Taplin, Oliver
2002   A World of Consolation in *Iliad* 24.614. *Studi italiana di filologia classica*
                20: 24–27.

Trigger, Bruce G.
2006   *A History of Archaeological Thought.* Cambridge University Press,
                Cambridge.

Vanotti, Gabriela
2007   *Aristotele: Racconti Meravigliosi.* Bompiani, Milan.

Van Buren, Elizabeth Douglas
1925   Archaeologists in Antiquity. *Folklore* 36: 69–81.

Von Falkenhausen, Lothar
2015   Antiquarianism in China and Europe: Reflections on Momigliano. In
                *Cross-Cultural Studies: China and the World—A Festschrift in Honor of
                Professor Zhang Longxi*, edited by Qian Suoqiao, pp. 127–151. Brill,
                Leiden.

Wace, Alan J. B.
1949   The Greeks and Romans as Archaeologists. *Bulletin de la société d'archéologie d'Alexandrie* 21: 21–35.

Whitmarsh, Tim
2013   *Beyond the Second Sophistic: Adventures in Greek Postclassicism.* University of California Press, Berkeley.

Winter, Irene
2000   Babylonian Archaeologists of the(ir) Mesopotamian Past. In *Proceedings of the First International Congress on the Archaeology of the Ancient Near East*, edited by Paolo Matthiae, Alessandra Enea, Luca Peyronel, and Frances Pinnock, pp. 1785–1798. Università degli studi de Roma, Rome.

Woolf, Greg
1996   The Uses of Forgetfulness in Roman Gaul. In *Vergangenheit und Lebenswelt: Soziale Kommunikation, Traditionsbildung und historisches Bewusstsein*, edited by Hans-Joachim Gehrke and Astrid Möller, pp. 361–382. Günter Narr Verlag, Tübingen.

Wylie, Alison
2008   Mapping Ignorance in Archaeology: The Advantages of Historical Hindsight. In *Agnotology: The Making and Unmaking of Ignorance*, edited by Robert N. Proctor and Londa Scheinbinger, pp. 183–208. Stanford University Press, Stanford.

Zimmer, Carl
2016   Eske Willerslev Is Rewriting History With DNA. *The New York Times* May 16, 2016 (published online).

Zivkovic, Tanya
2014   *Death and Reincarnation in Tibetan Buddhism: In-Between Bodies.* Routledge, London.

— 3 —

The Virtues of Oblivion:
Africa and the People without Antiquarianism

Alfredo González-Ruibal

In this chapter, I argue that we need to accept that some societies in the past as well as in the present might have had a relationship to the past which is incommensurable with familiar forms of historicity and historical practices, including archaeology, historiography, heritage, and antiquarianism. I surmise that those groups that reject history often do so for political reasons and therefore the rejection should not be understood as a failure. I find that the postcolonial concern with finding historical practices in non-Western communities may unwittingly end up recapitulating colonial epistemic imperialism by ultimately using modern values as the measuring rod for all humanity.

For over a hundred years, archaeologists did not have any doubt that their knowledge about past societies was superior to that produced by non-Western societies or other communities within their own society. Humility was largely reserved for their relationship with other hegemonic sciences, like history or biology. Other ways of dealing with the past, such as those of the colonized, indigenous groups, non-Western societies, marginalized communities, peasants, workers, and so on were dismissed as folk knowledge (and even superstition) of only local value, something that was, at best, worth studying in itself, but hardly to be considered equal with archaeology or any other western science. This arrogant confidence is long gone. The feminist and postcolonial critiques have demolished the universal aspirations of Eurocentric humanism and this has led to the gradual acceptance of multiple voices and forms of knowledge production (Liebmann and Rizvi 2008; Habu et al. 2008; Braidotti 2013). In the case of archaeology, the critique has produced different outcomes depending on the social context.

In the case of mainstream Western society, archaeology has become gradually perceived as just another *Geschichtskultur* (culture of history) among many others coexisting simultaneously in any Western society (Holtorf 2005: 5). Other cultures would be those of amateurs, re-enactors, neo-Druids and so on, which some consider simply alternative ways of working with the past in the present. These many ways of relating to history have their correlate in a multiplicity of heritages. Traditionally, heritage was defined by academia and the state and favored those elements that buttressed hegemonic ideas of nation, religion, class, sex, and gender. This is no longer the case. Normative heritage is equated now with authorized heritage discourses, which stand in opposition to a variety of subaltern or alternative heritages and even counter-heritages (Smith 2006; Byrne 2014).

Indigenous minorities in former European colonies have led to a different kind of postcolonial decentering of archaeology. In this case, the emergence of indigenous archaeologies has challenged the epistemic imperialism of Western science, and produced collaborative forms of knowledge in which native communities have the upper hand (Atalay 2006; Gnecco 2011). Indigenous archaeologies also imply a rethinking of the relations between archaeology and modernity. Two perspectives can be generally identified. Some argue that archaeology (and heritage) is inextricably linked to modernity; others argue that they are not and that practices that are analogous to heritage and archaeology can be found among non-Western communities. By "non-Western" I refer here to communities whose cultural core lies largely outside the modern European episteme and is characterized by different values, logics, and often ontologies. From this point of view, non-Western includes both what are usually described as "indigenous communities" within former European settler colonies (such as Australia or Argentina) and societies that have been variously labelled as traditional, preindustrial, or non-modern, and that are not necessarily indigenous or minority.

Among those who argue that archaeology is essentially modern, we can distinguish two attitudes: there are those, such as Cristóbal Gnecco (2013) or Alejandro Haber (2013) who consider that due to the strong relationship of archaeology and modernity, the former is irrevocably tarnished and has to be either abandoned (Gnecco) or "undisciplined" through a radical transformation of its foundations (Haber). In both cases, typical archaeological practices, such as excavation, are deemed epistemologically aggressive and have to be stopped. There are those, however, who, like Julian Thomas (2004) or Gavin Lucas (2004), consider archaeology essentially modern, but do not think that this renders archaeology automatically invalid as a powerful form of knowledge production. It requires critique, rather than demolition. Personally, I identify myself more with this second option: I still believe in the potential of archaeology, although I am very aware that it is a culture-specific practice, strongly related to the coloniality of power (Quijano

2000) and that it has been used to cause damage to subaltern communities and the colonized all over the world. With Haber and Gnecco, I agree that in certain contexts it is necessary to abandon conventional archaeological methods altogether and devise other approaches to the past.

Those that defend the second standpoint—namely, that archaeology is not the preserve of modernity—argue that decolonizing the discipline implies looking for alternative forms of doing archaeology (or heritage). Paul Lane, for instance, surmises that "defining archaeology as a modern, Western disciplinary practice limits its potential to non-Western contexts and, more seriously, reproduces (albeit in an unintentional manner) the kind of differential evaluation of Western and 'Other' understanding of space, time, being and materiality" (2011: 9). According to this author, "people throughout the world frequently draw on the material traces of previous inhabitants in their construction of historical narratives about their own past" (Lane 2011: 17). He considers that by regarding material memory practices that have been attested since prehistoric times as archaeology, we can involve indigenous and non-Western communities in the co-production of hybrid archaeological knowledge. Lane speaks about Africa, but similar ideas were first developed and put into practice in Australia and North America (Smith and Wobst 2004; Atalay 2006).

The search for other antiquarianisms can be understood within this postcolonial framework. If heritage and archaeology can be extended to non-Western societies of the past and present, the same can be done, and with more reason, with antiquarianism, which we know was practised outside the European world and before modernity (Schnapp 1996: 39–119). In my opinion, however, the desire to find the specific forms of relationship to the past that are antiquarianism, archaeology, and heritage in non-Western contexts and in ancient periods is problematic. In all three cases, a genuine postcolonial concern coalesces with a reluctance to accept radical Otherness. Postcolonial anthropologists, archaeologists, and historians consider that by portraying the Other as radically different, they are reiterating the colonial tropes that made the Other into an imperfect human being and justified her domination by colonial powers, if not outright extermination. This, for me, is throwing out the baby with the bathwater. It is well known that colonial science created categories of the Other as inferior, a distorted image of the Westerner (Said 1978). These categories were in place and had very real political effects from the late fifteenth to the mid-twentieth century (Quijano 2000) and they have not yet vanished.

Nevertheless, colonial science has been widely deconstructed after the 1960s. The way in which deconstruction has been carried out, however, has not allowed for a thorough evacuation of colonial categories. Thus, instead of accepting Otherness without moral judgement, scholars have rejected Otherness and accepted the moral judgment of Empire: every feature that was used to describe the Other (from the absence of abstract thinking to the refusal of history) was considered to be wrong or exaggerated, a figment of the colonial imagination. The sacred paradigm now is that there is no distinction between Us (Westerners) and Them (non-Westerners): the Other was then and is now just like us, only superficially different. It is legitimate to say that, in a reversal of Bhabha's dictum, the Other is today "almost different, but not quite" (González-Ruibal 2015). The difference that is accepted exists at the level of culture, not at the level of ontology and rationality. This is quite surprising given the passion for ontology that we experience today in the social sciences, including archaeology (Alberti et al. 2011), and the efforts deployed by the likes of Descola (2005) and Viveiros de Castro (1998) to show how radically, incommensurably different some indigenous groups are to Western cultures.

From the dominant perspective, indigenous peoples must be historical, because if they are not, they are not proper humans—that is, like Us, the measure of all things. It does not matter that they insist in denying historical change: they have to have a history.

Needless to say, all peoples have changed, but this, as Lévi-Strauss (1966: 234) rightly noted, is not the point—precisely because it is universal. The point is that some societies refuse to fit our notions of historicity, which emphasize change, movement, and connectivity. Thus, when I talk here about peoples without history I am not referring to peoples that have been marginalized from world history (Wolf 1982) and even less to any supposed community that might have remained changeless for millennia. I refer, instead, to societies who reject forms of experiencing and imagining the past that are homologous to Western historical regimes and that have mobilized their social and cultural resources to prevent transformation. The idea of history as change, despite being typical of state societies and particularly modern ones, is so ingrained in our mentality that even critical practitioners, such as Eric Wolf (1982), Sahlins (1985) or the Comaroffs (1992) consider it as the only imaginable historicity (for an extended critique see González-Ruibal 2014: 16–33).

Archaeologists have uncritically inherited the anthropological fear of Otherness and insist not only that non-Western peoples have history, but also that they have archaeology as well, practice antiquarianism, and value heritage. This is an understandable attitude, and perhaps even necessary, since a supposed lack of appreciation for the past, historical remains or antiquities has often been used as proof of the barbarity and ignorance of the Other and served to legitimize the domination and exploitation of subaltern communities (see Anderson 2015). However, for me, the real anticolonial stance is accepting that one might have a totally different relationship to the past, one that cannot be assimilated in any reasonable way to history, archaeology, heritage, or antiquarianism and still remain fully human. By insisting in finding in the Other what she is not, we accept that those colonial categories that defined people as proper humans were correct, they simply had to be extended to the colonized. This not only prevents us from understanding other ontologies, it denies also an often unrecognized but nevertheless crucial human right: the right to Otherness, the right to differ radically without being expelled from the realm of humanity. My criticism of Western historicity as a defining factor of the human can be understood as part of the larger critique to the heteronormative, patriarchal, and Eurocentric roots of Western humanism (Braidotti 2013).

Is Antiquarianism Universal?

The problem is that archaeologists are so busy finding indigenous archaeologists that they often disregard the signals sent by some indigenous communities. An excellent example is provided by a recent, atypically honest article by Bilinda Straight and co-authors (2015). They examine what could be considered folk antiquarian practices among the Samburu of Kenya in relation to an archaeological excavation of several prehistoric graves. The local community had an important role in initiating the archaeological project, showed a genuine interest in the material traces of the past, and elaborated their own theories about vestiges and artifacts. What makes this article different from most pieces on indigenous or collaborative archaeology is the conclusion: when the reader is convinced that the Samburu do have something that could be equated with heritage, archaeology, or antiquarianism and enthusiastically collaborate with archaeologists in the pursuit of the past, the elders prove us wrong. The authors include interviews with older people at the end of the paper and those people put things in perspective: "We just don't like it [the excavation] because we see it [the grave] as belonging to the dead. That's how it is, and so then you see now those people who dig up graves, we really look down on it. Yes, we despise it" (Straight et al. 2015: 411). According to one informant, it was *maendeleo* that excavated the graves. *Maendeleo* means modernity. To conclude that the Samburu have a folk antiquarian tradition because the younger generation wants to know about ancient bones and burials would be an error. Antiquarianism, here, is *maendeleo*. It does not have an indigenous genealogy, although it has become vernacular through the interaction with the modern world and the colonial and post-colonial state. The fact that the elders reject antiquarian/

archaeological practices does not detract of course from the fact that such sensibility is genuinely felt among large parts of the community today, but it is good evidence that most of the Samburu were without such sensibility in the past.

Admittedly, antiquarianism is less culture-specific than heritage or archaeology. It is difficult not to accept that archaeology and heritage as we know them and have been popularized all over the world are children of modernity and of the West. However, antiquarian practices are well documented before the sixteenth century and in non-Western contexts—particularly in the Middle East, India, China, and Japan (Schnapp 1997; 2013), but also in the Americas, as other papers in this volume demonstrate (see also examples in Schnapp 2013). That antiquarianism is less problematic does not mean that it is trouble-free. It is not necessarily an option that can replace archaeology as we strive for extending Western regimes of historicity to other societies. I argue that antiquarianism, like archaeology, is a specific form of engaging with the material traces of the past (artifacts, buildings, monuments, landscapes). I would suggest that such engagement is generally characterized by the existence of a method (which may include comparison, typology, visual or written forms of recording), a notion of calendrical chronology, a certain measure of secularization or disenchantment (the past is not understood in strictly mythical terms, although myth can play a role), the idea that the past can be subjected to critical scrutiny, individual rather than collective engagement with the past, connoisseurship as esoteric rather than social knowledge, and an interest in history *qua* history. I am aware that this can be criticized as a too restricted version of antiquarianism, but I think that such restriction is useful so as to maintain the heuristic potential of the term. Besides, antiquarianism as outlined above can be found in such different cultural contexts as the Roman Empire, medieval Japan, or ancient India.

The great majority of societies where antiquarianism, defined in this way, has been found are state societies or at least societies with marked hierarchical differences. In them, antiquarians belong to the elite: imperial officers in China, kings in Mesopotamia, aristocrats in Rome (Schnapp 1997: 41–65, 74–79). This is of course not a coincidence. On the one hand, an interest in the material past that might be deemed antiquarian is linked in those societies to a specific habitus and its concomitant notion of taste: the enjoyment of (material or immaterial) antiquities is related to a high degree of literacy and, in general, to a high symbolic, economic, and social capital. On the other hand, the interest in the material past was often a search for one's identity, which has always been a matter of concern more of the powerful than of the dispossessed. Often, there was an obvious desire to link oneself with prestigious ancestors. Thus, Frederick II, emperor of the Holy Roman Empire, was an avid collector of antiquities and even commissioned excavations in Sicily. This was part of his desire "to establish continuity between the ancient and the medieval worlds" and present himself as the descendant of Augustus (Schnapp 1997: 102–103). The duality between aristocratic and popular memory, each associated with different memory practices, is particularly clear in the case of Republican Rome. Thus, while the origins of Rome in popular memory were associated with Romulus and were played out in songs and ritual performances, the myth that linked the city and the Trojan hero Aeneas was a later aristocratic invention, which was mediated through antiquarian practices (Rodríguez-Mayorgas 2010). Although there was of course cross-breeding between aristocratic and popular engagements with the past, those practices that were more similar to what is commonly understood as antiquarian were characteristic of the elites.

Defending the idea that antiquarianism is not universal does not mean that other societies or classes lack any kind of relation or interest to the material past—far from it. There exists a diversity of cultural practices that focus on the tangible remains of the past, but that are not usefully framed, in my opinion, as antiquarianism. In fact, antiquarianism is just one among many forms of engagement with ancient materialities and not necessarily better or worse than other forms. Examples abound from prehistory (Bradley 2002), early history (Rojas and Sergeenkova 2014), and recent (Anderson 2015) and contemporary periods (Byrne 2014). These material engagements very often have a ritual content (Rojas and Sergeenkova 2014) or are associated with myths and the creation of local identities (Hamilakis 2008; Anderson 2015). At times, these material engagements share practices with antiquarianism: this is the case with practices of "reading" the landscape through storytelling (Santos-Granero 1998) or collecting.

Thus, it is well known also that peasants throughout Europe and in other parts of the world collected polished axes for various reasons—as natural marvels (thunderstones), mythical artifacts (elf arrows), or amulets (Goodrum 2008: 483). However, unlike in societies with an antiquarian tradition, collecting rarely goes hand in hand with a theory of vestiges that helps interpret the past. Thus, polished axes only became antiquarian objects when they were identified as human-made elements and thus transferred from the realm of nature or the supernatural to the realm of history (Sklenar 1983: 37; Schnapp 1997: 347–348; Trigger 1992: 58–61; Goodrum 2008): they became traces of a past Other that had to be interpreted and inserted into previous narratives. However, even when human traces of the past are identified as such (a pottery sherd as part of an old vessel), they do not have to be part of the wider historical tradition of a group. This is what happens among many sub-Saharan African societies and this is the case, in particular, with those groups that have moved many times and have little attachment to the landscape. To apply the term antiquarianism to mere collecting practices—including relics of saints—would detract from the heuristic power of the concept.

Antiquarianism, Inequality, and Historical Change

My intention is not just to point out that antiquarianism, as happens with archaeology and heritage, is a culturally-specific practice, characteristic of modernity or state societies. Rather, the interesting question is why some communities reject the idea of history, in its material or immaterial version or both. In fact, archaeologists have long known why historical practices are problematic: at least since the early 1980s, we have become aware that archaeology and heritage have been actively used to legitimize colonial expansion, capitalism, nationalism (Trigger 1984), and all the dark undertakings of modernity and the state (Gnecco 2013). We know that heritage has been put at the service of the racist, classist, and patriarchal nation-state. We know that history is written by the victors and the powerful. But for some reason, we forget all that when we deal with indigenous and subaltern groups, because they *must* have heritage, history, archaeology, and antiquarianism. Perhaps we are so naive as to think that they are not aware of the grisly relations between those forms of historicity and inequality.

However, even if they have not read a line by Trigger or Said, they do know consciously or intuitively. They know very well what history and its remains are for and they have often chosen to reject them altogether. In some cases, they know because they live in the periphery of states or hierarchical societies and may have an experience of the work of legitimation to which history is put. But this is not necessarily the case. Many egalitarian communities reject anything (surplus production, hereditary positions, monuments, or sedentarization) that may help create divisions within the social body, even if they have limited or no experience of inequality (Clastres 2001). Archaeological vestiges and written history have one point in common: they have a durable quality that is opposed to the malleability and ephemerality of the oral (Assmann 1992: 63–68). Things that remain are dangerous, because they can become normative and canonical. They are less easy to challenge and can be employed to naturalize inequalities. It is not strange that the rejection of historical practices has been attested in many egalitarian communities all over the world. James C. Scott, for instance, mentions the case of the Lisu in

Burma. He considers that their "short and truncated genealogies" are tantamount to a refusal of history:

> The purpose, after all, of most lineage histories, oral or written, is to establish a claim to distinction and rank—to establish a 'lineage' for those claims. If, then, lineage histories are abbreviated or ignored altogether, it amounts to something of a cultural discouragement, if not prohibition, of historical claims to superiority. To have little or no history is, implicitly, to put every kin group on roughly the same footing [2009: 275–276].

He concludes that "the Lisu are without history not because they are incapable of history but because they choose to avoid its inconveniences". Many other egalitarian communities, such as the Kalahari San, have been argued to be ahistorical, in that they do not have practices of inquiry into the past—not that they do not have historical consciousness (Suzman 2004). In the same vein, Joseph Pestiau (1982) argued that people without state are people without history: to be against the state is to be against history and tradition is the best weapon against it. This is, in fact, a premise that is implicit in the anarchist anthropology of Pierre Clastres (2001): he asserts that "the Savages know very well that all alteration in the social life (all social innovation) can only be translated into the loss of liberty" (Clastres 2001: 214).

This is the other good reason why so many small-scale egalitarian communities reject history. All the practices of history that have triumphed in modernity are characterized by the emphasis they put on change: they all help to bear witness of a past Other. Many indigenous groups do not want a past Other, they want a past Same and reject change (Pestiau 1982; Hernando 2002). They dislike any reminders that the past might have been different or rather that they might have been different, because change is usually equated with trouble and inequality. This is the case with the Dats'in people of the Sudanese-Ethiopian borderland, with whom my colleagues and I have been working during the last three years. As for many other groups in the region, change is for the Dats'in the same as violence and external imposition. Their history, which unfolds as a homogeneous static space, is only disturbed by war, slavery and exile. With information provided by the Dats'in, we found dozens of archaeological sites (Figure 3.1). When I asked them about their relationship to the sites, they claimed to have none. The remains belong to the *Anäj*—often rendered Aneg or Anag in the literature (Newbold 1924, Chattaway 1930). *Anäj* is a term that means "indigenous" and the Dats'in emphatically assert that they are not indigenous: they come from Jebel Gule in the Sudan, over 200 km away. This is a difficult situation for the postcolonial archaeologist, which is made more difficult by another fact: the material culture that we find does prove that the so-called Anäj are indeed strongly related to the Dats'in. Their sherds are traces of the ancestors, after all, but the Dats'in do not want and do not need that history and there is little that we can offer them. This situation is the reverse of the one that characterizes mainstream indigenous archaeologies, where contemporary native communities consider the archaeological remains in their territories as related to their ancestors, often against the criteria of archaeologists (McGhee 2008).

A similar disinterest for history can be found among their neighbors, the Gumuz. We found a prehistoric site near a Gumuz village and conducted test pits with their permission. At the beginning, men and children were curious about us, rather than about what we were finding. After a while, they got bored and we were left alone (Figure 3.2). Interestingly, the women did not show even a minimal interest in our excavation. More recently, we were informed of a group of ancient burials next to a Gumuz village. We asked the people in the village if we could go to the place and they gave their authorization. However, when we were about to reach the burials, a man came running and shouting. He was clearly angry and prohibited us from going to the site. He took us to the village, the elders gathered again and they decided that we could not see the cemetery. I told him the very postcolonial truth: that I wanted to visit the site because I wanted to know about Gumuz history; I wanted to prove that the Gumuz had as much history as any other people in Ethiopia (including those that had traditionally marginalized and exploited them), and that the material remains of the past were a way of demonstrating this. They were not impressed. For them, "experts" such as myself mean trouble: in their view, there is not much difference between a historian, an agricultural engineer, or a geologist. They are all state agents and potentially dangerous. They explained to me that the last time a white man came to the area, 20 years ago, he took samples of soil, and some time later thousands of peasants from the Ethiopian Highlands were resettled in their valley. For them, the burial site has nothing to do with the past, nor with their own past for that matter, but is a place where spirits appear and sacrifices of goats and chickens are made on their behalf. Theirs is a practice of cultural amnesia with political implications: they refuse to transform a sacred place into a place of history and to read the land as antiquarians.

In the course of my investigations, I have found a phenomenon that could be at first sight considered proof of antiquarianism in a stateless society. It is the ritual house of the Sith Shwala, a minority group living in Western Ethiopia south of the Blue Nile. Elsewhere, I have considered the ritual house as an example of "wild museography" (González-Ruibal 2014: 310).

Figure 3.1. Fragments of an incense burner on the surface of an Anäj site (sixteenth to eighteenth century A.D.) pointed out to us by a Dats'in (author's photograph).

Figure 3.2. Test-pitting in a Gumuz village (author's photograph).

Inside this structure, the ritual specialists of the Sith Shwala preserve artifacts of the past: spears, shields, old beer pots, beehives, an elephant's ear, drums (Figure 3.3). To identify this wild museography as antiquarianism, however, would misinterpret its cultural and political logic. The ritual house does not intend to document history, but the opposite: to abolish it. It is a device to make the past ever present, to deny any difference between contemporary times and the remote history of the Sith Shwala. This is so because the artifacts that are displayed inside the hut are presented as proof of the never-changing nature of the Sith Shwala: they have always been people of the forest, hunters, beehive-keepers, and warriors that have fought for their autonomy. Unlike the cabinet of curiosities of the European antiquarian or the collection of fine bronzes of the Chinese connoisseur, the Sith Shwala are not interested in a past Other, but in a past Same. They are counter-antiquarians, because they deny the existence of antiquity itself.

Meaningfully, the neighbors of the Sith Shwala, and the former dominant group in the area, the Busase, do have a concept of history that is closer to us. When interviewing old Busase (Figure 3.4), they demonstrated an impressive cultural memory going back several centuries. Some of the events that they transmitted could be dated in the mid-sixteenth century. Even the less knowledgeable among them could trace their genealogies for seven generations. This was in stark contrast with the amnesia of the Sith Shwala and neighboring communities that hardly remember ancestors beyond their grandparents and whose history is both short and sketchy. The history of the Busase is a history of their occupation of the land, their ruling over the local subalterns, and their association with other powerful groups. While it is mostly oral history, it is anchored in landscape in a way that vaguely resembles the topographical sensibility of European antiquarianism (Shanks and Witmore 2010), but with the crucial difference that for the Busase reading the landscape is both a historical and a religious practice.

Strictly speaking, there are probably no antiquarian practices among the tribal societies of Ethiopia, Sudan, and most other regions of sub-Saharan Africa. If we are to find them somewhere, it is in dominant, state societies: we have something of an antiquarian spirit in the monasteries of the dominant Christian society, where sacred books and artifacts, at times many centuries old, attest to the prestige of the monastic foundation and to the antiquity of Christianity in the country, and where the revival of the ancient Axumite style in the Middle Ages demonstrates something of an antiquarian gaze among architects and religious authorities (Hirsch and Fauvelle-Aymar 2001; Phillipson 2012: 227–243). Do we have history? Yes: in the king's palace, whose chroniclers left records of royal deeds since the Middle Ages. Do we have archaeology and heritage? Of course, in the institutions of the modern nation-state.

Concluding Remarks

It is not my intention to deny that antiquarianism has existed in the past in a variety of societies. Looking for antiquarian cultures is an exciting project that can throw much light both on the way other societies deal with the past and on the nature of archaeology itself. What I have tried to defend here are two things. First, I have argued that before indiscriminately extending antiquarianism, archaeology, or heritage to other societies, we should critically scrutinize the political economies that lie behind these practices of history. Their absence should not be regarded as a problem but, perhaps, as an indication of a regime of historicity that rejects the traps of change, durability, and inequality. Admittedly, practices that look like antiquarianism are sometimes deployed in order to counteract hierarchization or external domination: the wild museography of the Sith Shwala mentioned here is a case in point. However, we should ponder whether antiquarianism is the best rubric for this practice. In my opinion, it is not, for two main reasons: on the one hand, Sith Shwala's antiquarianism is oriented towards the abolition of the past-present dichotomy, it does not emerge out of a curiosity for the past; on the other hand, antiquarianism proper sits uncomfortably with a purely mythical understanding of history. Although I do not want to categorically dismiss the existence of antiquarian practices among egalitarian, small-scale societies, my impression is that they are an oddity, rather than a common occurrence. Objects of the past can be mobilized to counteract dominant visions of the past, but this is hardly ever done in the guise of antiquarianism.

The second, and perhaps main point that I have tried to defend in this chapter is that we should be ready to respect radical Otherness and admit that other societies might have had a relationship with the past that is not translatable in the familiar terms of antiquarianism, heritage, archaeology, or historiography. Considering that peoples should fit in our regimes of historicity—no matter how flexibly defined—is a lenient form of epistemic imperialism. We should be willing to accept that some people are against history and they remain as human and intelligent as ourselves. And perhaps more critical with power.

Acknowledgements

I would like to thank Benjamin Anderson and Felipe Rojas for their invitation to participate in the workshop and for their thought-provoking

Figure 3.3. Inside the ritual house of Adam Yeme, a Sith Swala. Left of the ritual specialist there are several ancient artifacts on display, including a hippopotamus tail used as a drumstick (author's photograph).

Figure 3.4. Interviewing Itafa Fido, an old Busase with a deep knowledge of the history of his people (author's photograph).

comments on this paper, which have helped to improve it. The rest of the participants in the workshop are also thanked for an interesting discussion.

References

Alberti, Benjamin, Severin Fowles, Martin Holbraad, Yvonne Marshall, and Christopher Witmore

    2011   Worlds Otherwise. *Current Anthropology* 52: 896–912.

Anderson, Benjamin

    2015   "An Alternative Discourse": Local Interpreters of Antiquities in the Ottoman Empire. *Journal of Field Archaeology* 40: 450–460.

Assmann, Jan

    1992   *La memoria culturale: scrittura, ricordo e identità politica nelle grandi civiltà antiche.* Einaudi, Turin.

Atalay, Sonya

    2006   Indigenous Archaeology as Decolonizing Practice. *The American Indian Quarterly* 30: 280–310.

Bradley, Richard

    2002   *The Past in Prehistoric Societies.* Routledge, London.

Braidotti, Rosi

    2013   *The Posthuman.* Wiley, Oxford.

Byrne, Denis

    2014   *Counterheritage: Critical Perspectives on Heritage Conservation in Asia.* Routledge, London.

Chataway, J. D. P.

    1930   Archaeology in the Southern Sudan. I: Some Ancient Sites Near Roseires. *Sudan Notes and Records* 13: 259–267.

Clastres, Pierre

    2001   *Investigaciones en antropología política.* Gedisa, Barcelona.

Comaroff, John, and Jean Comaroff

    1992   *Ethnography and the Historical Imagination.* Westview, Boulder.

Descola, Philippe

    2005   *Par-delà nature et culture.* Gallimard, Paris.

Gnecco, Cristóbal

    2011   *Indigenous Peoples and Archaeology in Latin America.* Left Coast Press, Walnut Creek, California.

    2013   Digging Alternative Archaeologies. In *Reclaiming Archaeology: Beyond the Tropes of Modernity*, edited by Alfredo González-Ruibal, pp. 67–78. Routledge, London.

González-Ruibal, Alfredo

    2014   *An Archaeology of Resistance: Materiality and Time in an African Borderland.* Rowman & Littlefield, Lanham.

    2015   Malos nativos: una crítica de las arqueologías indígenas y poscoloniales. *Revista de Arqueología* 27: 47–63.

Goodrum, Matthew R.

2008   Questioning Thunderstones and Arrowheads: The Problem of Recognizing
                and Interpreting Stone Artifacts in the Seventeenth Century. *Early Science
                and Medicine* 13: 482–508.

Haber, Alejandro

2013   Evestigation, Nomethodology and Deictics. In *Reclaiming Archaeology:
                Beyond the Tropes of Modernity*, edited by Alfredo González-Ruibal, pp.
                79–88. Routledge, London.

Habu, Junko, Claire Fawcett, and John M. Matsunaga (editors)

2008   *Evaluating Multiple Narratives: Beyond Nationalist, Colonialist, Imperialist
                Archaeologies.* Springer, New York.

Hamilakis, Yannis

2008   Decolonizing Greek Archaeology: Indigenous Archaeologies, Modernist
                Archaeology and the Post-Colonial Critique. In *A Singular Antiquity:
                Archaeology and Hellenic Identity in Twentieth-Century Greece*, edited by
                Dimitris Damaskos and Dimitris Plantzos, pp. 273–284. Benaki Museum,
                Athens.

Hernando, Almudena

2002   *Arqueología de la Identitad.* Akal, Madrid.

Hirsch, B., and F. X. Fauvelle-Aymar

2001   Aksum après Aksum: royauté, archéologie et herméneutique chrétienne de
                Ménélik II (r. 1865–1913) à Zär'a Ya'qob (r. 1434–1468). *Annales d'Ethiopie*
                17: 59–109.

Holtorf, Cornelius

2005   *From Stonehenge to Las Vegas: Archaeology as Popular Culture.* Altamira,
                Lanham.

Lane, Paul

2011   Possibilities for a Postcolonial Archaeology in Sub-Saharan Africa:
                Indigenous and Usable Pasts. *World Archaeology* 43: 7–25.

Lévi-Strauss, Claude

1966   *The Savage Mind.* University of Chicago Press, Chicago.

Liebmann, Matthew, and Uzma Z. Rizvi (editors)

2008   *Archaeology and the Postcolonial Critique.* Altamira, Lanham.

Lucas, Gavin

2004   Modern Disturbances: On the Ambiguities of Archaeology. *Modernism/
                modernity* 11: 109–120.

McGhee, Robert

2008   Aboriginalism and the Problems of Indigenous Archaeology. *American
                Antiquity* 73: 579–597.

Newbold, D.

1924   Some Links with the Anag at Gebel Haraza. *Sudan Notes and Records* 7:
                126–131.

Pestieau, Joseph

1982   Peuples sans Etat et sans histoire: réflexions sur le conservatisme et sur
                Rousseau. *Dialogue* 21: 473–482.

Phillipson, David W.

2012   *Foundations of an African Civilisation: Aksum and the Northern Horn, 1000 BC–1300 AD*. James Currey, Woodbridge.

Quijano, Aníbal

2000   Coloniality of Power and Eurocentrism in Latin America. *International Sociology* 15: 215–232.

Rodríguez-Mayorgas, Ana

2010   Romulus, Aeneas and the Cultural Memory of the Roman Republic. *Athenaeum* 98: 89–109.

Rojas, Felipe, and Valeria Sergueenkova

2014   Traces of Tarhuntas: Greek, Roman, and Byzantine Interaction with Hittite Monuments. *Journal of Mediterranean Archaeology* 27: 135–160.

Sahlins, Marshall

1985   *Islands of History*. University of Chicago Press, Chicago.

Said, Edward

1978   *Orientalism*. Vintage, New York.

Santos-Granero, Fernando

1998   Writing History Into the Landscape: Space, Myth, and Ritual in Contemporary Amazonia. *American Ethnologist* 25: 128–148.

Schnapp, Alain

1997[1993] *The Discovery of the Past*. Harry N. Abrams, New York.

Schnapp, Alain (editor)

2013   *World Antiquarianism: Comparative Perspectives*. The Getty Research Institute, Los Angeles.

Scott, James C.

2009   *The Art of Not Being Governed: An Anarchist History of Upland Southeast Asia*. Yale University Press, New Haven.

Shanks, Michael, and Christopher Witmore

2010   Echoes Across the Past: Chorography and Topography in Antiquarian Engagements with Place. *Performance Research* 15: 97–106.

Sklenar, K.

1983   *Archaeology in Central Europe: The First 500 Years*. Leicester University Press, Leicester.

Smith, Laurajane

2006   *Uses of Heritage*. Routledge, London.

Smith, Claire, and H. Martin Wobst (editors)

2004   *Indigenous Archaeologies: Decolonising Theory and Practice*. Routledge, London.

Straight, Bilinda, Paul J. Lane, Charles E. Hilton, and Musa Letua

2015   "It Was *Maendeleo* That Removed Them": Disturbing Burials and Reciprocal Knowledge Production in a Context of Collaborative Archaeology. *Journal of the Royal Anthropological Institute* 21: 391–418.

Suzman, James

2004   Hunting for History: Rethinking Historicity in the Western Kalahari. In *Hunter-Gatherers in History, Archaeology, and Anthropology*, edited by Alan Barnard, pp. 201–216. Berg, Oxford.

Thomas, Julian
    2004   *Archaeology and Modernity*. Routledge, London.
Trigger, Bruce G.
    1984   Alternative Archaeologies: Nationalist, Colonialist, Imperialist. *Man* 19:
                    355–370.
    1992   *Historia del pensamiento arqueológico*. Crítica, Barcelona.
Viveiros de Castro, Eduardo
    1998   Cosmological Deixis and Amerindian Perspectivism. *Journal of the Royal
                    Anthropological Institute* 4: 469–488.
Wolf, Eric
    1982   *Europe and the People Without History*. University of California Press,
                    Berkeley.

Las Relaciones Mediterratlánticas: Comparative Antiquarianism and Everyday Archaeologies in Castile and Spanish America, 1575–1586

Byron Ellsworth Hamann

A recurring motif in histories of Renaissance Europe is what Jakob Burckhardt called "The Revival of Antiquity": a renewed engagement with the detritus of the ancient world quite distinct from earlier, medieval fascinations—such as the Carolingian revivals, or the Renaissance of the twelfth century. Fifteenth-century Italian innovations inspired similar engagements in other lands north of the Mediterranean: surveys of ancient monuments, compilations of ancient inscriptions, collections of ancient stones. This was an antiquarianism of educated men, often humanists or clerics, and their names and publications dominate our current histories: Petrus Apianus, Aldus Manutius, Bartolomeo Marliano, Jacopo Mazzocchi, Ambrosio de Morales, Onofrio Panvinio, Conrad Peutinger, Valerio Probo, Carlo Sigonio.[1]

At the same time, however, this elite and scholarly antiquarianism coexisted with a more mundane, everyday antiquarianism: the archaeological awareness of farmers and villagers who were accustomed to living in a landscape sedimented with the remains of earlier occupations. Plowing the soil turned up strange potsherds, iridescent glass, unfamiliar coins. The ruined stonework of ancient buildings was scattered across the countryside, and was visibly incorporated into the architecture of early modern towns.

European immigrants—whether illiterate conquistadors or university-educated missionaries and bureaucrats—brought these everyday and elite antiquarian sensibilities with them to the Americas. As a result, they were often attentive to the ruins and ancient remains they saw there. But they did not simply stumble across antiquities. They discovered that indigenous people had already developed their own traditions of archaeological interpretation. In other words, Europeans in the Americas encountered not only ancient artifacts, but antiquarian interlocutors as well.

And yet in present-day scholarship, these coeval and connected traditions of archaeological interpretation have seldom been brought together.[2] The antiquarian ideas (both scholarly and everyday) developed by early modern Italians and Iberians were *contemporary* with the antiquarian ideas developed by early modern Aztecs and Incas. European expansion brought these independent antiquarian traditions into contact—and conversation. Present-day discussion of these early modern antiquarianisms is, in contrast, fragmented. On the one hand, we have a massive bibliography on Renaissance antiquarianism in Italy, complemented by a more modest list of publications about Spain, say, and the Germanies.[3] On the other, we have a much smaller literature devoted to indigenous archaeologies in the Americas.[4]

The disconnected treatment of Amerindian and European traditions is especially curious, because dialogues between these antiquarianisms were already taking place, and being recorded, in the sixteenth century. These dialogues can be accessed in the pages of two projects for imperial knowledge production usually studied separately: the *relaciones topográficas* town surveys of central Castile (1575–1581), and the *relaciones geográficas* town surveys of Spanish America (1577–1586). These surveys provide the archive for the following pages.

There are several reasons behind this scholarly divide in the study of early modern antiquarianisms. Most important is a pervasive denial of coevalness in academic worldviews, in which the fifteenth, sixteenth, and seventeenth centuries are "early modern" in Europe, but "colonial" in the Americas (Fabian 1983; Hamann 2015). Also relevant is the academic insistence on an aesthetics of misperception: that is, assuming that cultural frameworks brought by early modern Europeans to the Americas could only ever allow them to misperceive what they encountered. The cultural framing of perception is at issue in all times and places—including the present—and the early modern tendency to see the Americas through the framework of ancient Greece and Rome still persists (Hamann 2015; see also Boas 1889; Elliott 1970: 7, 8, 12–13, 18, 21–22; Greenblatt 1991; MacCormack 2007). But if the always-inevitable cultural framing of perception can cause some things to go unobserved, or be misunderstood, it can also focus attention on details that might otherwise go unnoticed.

In the case of antiquarianism, at least, European perspectives do not necessarily corrupt and debase the indigenous worlds they describe. Instead, European "biases" made accounts of prehispanic antiquities *possible*—and surprisingly detailed and rich. European modes of seeing enabled European antiquarians in the Americas to be *better chroniclers*. And it made them attentive to what indigenous antiquarians had to say. But we cannot appreciate how European attitudes enhanced archaeological descriptions in the Americas if we sever those New World accounts from accounts being produced at the very same time within Europe itself. Paying attention to coeval, "Mediterratlantic" frameworks of knowledge production allows us, as Michel-Rolph Trouillot would insist, to understand the process by which the antiquarian archive of early modernity was itself compiled.

I begin with a brief introduction to the two *relaciones* projects: their origins, their connections, their chronologies and contents and (especially important) the ways both of them allow us to see how top-down demands for information by the King of Spain, materialized in a set of standardized questionnaires, were themselves transformed "from below" when they were used to collect information in the field—which ranged from Toledo in Castile to Trujillos in both Peru and Venezuela. With this broad context in mind, the next sections of the chapter move back and forth across the Atlantic to consider a set of five themes shared by both of the *relaciones* projects: houses and abandoned towns, the aesthetics of masonry, manufactured gods, ancient writings, and archaeologies at war.

Local Knowledge and Imperial Interrogation

Between 1575 and 1586, two massive historical-geographical surveys were undertaken in the Spanish empire: the *relaciones topográficas* of central Castile (1575–1581) and the *relaciones geográficas* of Spanish America (1577–1586). Both were projects of epistolary knowledge. That is, each generated local responses to printed questionnaires: responses written down on paper, mailed across hundreds or thousands of miles, and then combined with other reports to form a composite whole.

The results of both surveys shared a sustained interest in archaeological documentation. Both described ruined cities and buildings; both included transcriptions of ancient texts written in alien scripts. Since the boundary between past and present is a fluid one, their accounts engaged with objects ranging in age from decades to centuries to millennia. Considered together, the *relaciones* projects raise productive questions about the relations between local knowledge and imperial interrogation.

The *relaciones geográficas* project for Spanish America is perhaps more famous. In 1577 and again in 1584, 50-item questionnaires were printed in Iberia and shipped across the Atlantic. Over the course of a decade, the replies slowly traveled back to Seville: 12 from Venezuela (1578–1579); 33 from Oaxaca and 54 from Yucatan (1579–1581); 33 from Mexico, 15 from Tlaxcala, and 17 from Michoacan (1579–1582); 13 from Guadalajara and two from Guatemala (1579–1585); seven from New Granada (1580–82); six from Quito and one from Puerto Rico (1582); and 15 from Peru (1583–1586).

In all, 208 responses survive today, divided between the Real Academia de la Historia in Madrid, the Archivo General de Indias in Seville, and the Benson Latin American Library in Austin (Cline 1972).

These 50-item questionnaires had a complicated backstory. They were based on a similar project of epistolary knowledge undertaken within Iberia: the *relaciones topográficas*. In 1575 and again in 1578, 57- and then 45-item questionnaires were printed and circulated throughout central Castile. Their responses were penned between 1575 and 1581, thus overlapping for four years the writing of similar responses in the Americas (1578–1581). Today, 721 of these Iberian *relaciones* survive, bound in eight stout volumes shelved in the palace library of El Escorial (Campos 1994).

These two projects were clearly connected. Although their lists of questions are not identical, they share basic thematic contours. In many cases the phrasing of the American surveys was copied word-for-word from the Iberian surveys. Both projects began their lists with questions about the town's name and its meaning, and about the town's conqueror-founder. Several questions further on, both ask for a textual description of the town's location relative to other towns. Starting with question 17, both interrogate the quality of the land, asking for information about local resources: nearby mountains, rivers, water sources, pastures, mines. Around question 30, both query the presence of fortresses, and request details about how local houses are built. Nearing their end, both ask about monasteries, hospitals, and abandoned towns (*despoblados*). Finally, both conclude with an open request for "all of the other notable things" which deserve to be recorded (Jiménez 1881: cxx).

These parallels are important to consider, because it is the differences between the two projects that are usually emphasized. The American project included more questions about local natural history; the Iberian project was more interested in the overlapping webs of local authorities and jurisdictions (nobles, military and religious orders, royal prerogatives, *fueros*). The questionnaires for the American project were also internally divided: items 1–10 were to be asked only of Spanish towns, and 11–15 of indigenous towns—although in practice these separations were not always followed. Most famously, in items 10 and 42 the American project asked for maps to be created (Mundy 1996).

But even here, in the best-known contrast between the two projects, any claims to simple Iberian-American binarisms break down. Almost all of the American maps were made in one region, in New Spain, and that was because the request for cartography was accidentally in keeping with prehispanic practices. Other American regions without prehispanic traditions of mapmaking ignored these cartographic requests: only one map, for example, was made for Peru (Mundy 2008). At the same time, although not officially requested, a handful of maps were created by respondents in Iberia.

This geographical complexity (American-Iberian binaries are unproductive; responses from the Americas have historically significant internal variations) points to a broader issue. We cannot treat the *relaciones* produced in Iberia and those produced in the Americas as two equal and opposing halves. Although far more *relaciones* survive from Iberia than the Americas (721 compared to 208), the vast majority of Iberian surveys were collected in central Castile (today's provinces of Madrid, Toledo, Ciudad Real, Guadalajara, and Cuenca), a region roughly the same size as Central Mexico (today's states of Mexico, Hidalgo, Morelos, and Puebla). Although there are of course many ways in which the *relaciones* from the Americas are similar, in contrast to those from Iberia (remember that the American responses were all generated by the same questionnaire), we should not reify a simple Iberian-American divide. Instead, we need to be attentive to the regional contrasts within this corpus as a whole—and be open to the possibility that (for example) accounts from central Castile may share commonalities with those from Central Mexico and Oaxaca not found in Peru or New Granada.

These projects of questionnaire-based epistolary knowledge are an imperial appropriation of what Michel Foucault identified as Catholic rituals of confession (Foucault 1976: 58). With the establishment of the sacrament of penance at the Fourth Lateran Council (1215), the Church created techniques by which sinners could unburden their souls and thus receive forgiveness. By the sixteenth century, these techniques had spread to other social contexts, and often involved formalized questionnaires: from the lists of queries published in confessional manuals for priests, to the itemized questions for witnesses prepared by prosecution and defense alike when gathering testimonies for legal investigations (Klor de Alva 1999).

But as Carlo Ginzburg (1983) pointed out for inquisitorial interrogations, although formalized questionnaires certainly shape witness testimonies, they do not constrain them completely. Witnesses may claim ignorance, or—and this is of great importance for my project here—they may respond to a question by talking about issues *they* find important, issues that may have nothing to do with the question supposedly being answered. In other words, the questionnaire—whether prepared by priests, inquisitors, or the state—certainly creates a charged and hierarchical framework for gathering information. But the information gathered may diverge (and sharply) from the information requested. In these divergences, we can often access ideas and desires quite different from those of the questioning power (see Hamann n.d.).

For example, one of the most striking differences between Iberian and American questionnaires and responses has to do with antiquarianism. Both in 1575 and 1578, *Iberian* respondents were asked to provide descriptions of ancient remains:

> 36. The notable buildings which the town had, and the remains of ancient buildings, epitaphs, and inscriptions, and antiquities about which there was information (1575; question 31 in the 1578 list).

Surprisingly, this was *not* one of the items carried over to the *relaciones geográficas* questionnaires printed for the New World. For whatever reason, America's material history before the Europeans arrived was not of interest to the bureaucrats who prepared the New World survey. But of course the landscape of the Americas, no less than the landscape of central Castile, was deeply sedimented with the physical remains of previous civilizations. This landscape was of great significance to indigenous people. It was also of interest to European settlers, in part because of their own "everyday" archaeological familiarity with sedimented landscapes in Iberia. As a result, although the imperial questionnaires prepared for the two sides of the Iberian Atlantic were different, the *answers* given to those questionnaires—at least where issues of antiquarianism are concerned—were surprisingly parallel.

And so when Europeans and Americans set out to respond to the New World *relaciones geográficas* (whose answers, even when written down by local European landlords or clerics, make clear the key role of indigenous interlocutors), they created commentaries filled with archaeological information that are in many ways parallel to the archaeological information provided for the *relaciones topográficas* in Iberia. Again, this parallel is striking, in that it is not a parallel ready-made in the questions themselves. In spite of what they ask, the *relaciones* projects reveal—and preserve for the future—a shared stratum of everyday archaeological awareness on both sides of the Iberian Atlantic.

To illustrate this, the following pages sketch out five fields of comparison that the two *relaciones* projects accidentally reveal. With the first four, the presence of a state-mandated questionnaire as the framework for gathering information seems incidental. But with the last—Archaeologies at War—we are reminded that relations between local knowledge and outsider interrogations, on both sides of the Atlantic, could be fraught with conflict. And so although the *relaciones* projects accidentally reveal the broadly parallel contours of everyday antiquarianism in Iberia and America, we should also be aware that both Iberian and American locals may have kept important features of their archaeological knowledge from entering the imperial archive. Or at least attempted to, as my final anecdote suggests.

The Foundations of Everyday Archaeology:
Houses and Abandoned Towns

One notable feature of archaeological replies in the *relaciones* from both sides of the Atlantic is their careful attention to questions of facture and materiality: that is, *how* objects and buildings have been made, and what they have been made *from*. As anthropological and art-historical studies over the past two decades have shown, these properties were very important from Native American perspectives (e.g., Klein and Nona 2009). But in order to understand how it was that Iberian surveyors (rural priests, local officials, or landlords) were attentive to these details in the New World—in spite of the absence of a specific item on antiquarian remains in the *relaciones geográficas* questionnaires—we need to consider two foundations for everyday antiquarianism: techniques of house construction, and the omnipresence of abandoned towns.

Tellingly, a question about how local houses were built, and where construction supplies came from, was included in the printed lists for both sides of the Atlantic:

> 35. The kinds of houses and buildings that are used in the town, and of what materials they are constructed, and if those materials are available locally or if they are brought from elsewhere (*relaciones topográficas* 1575; see item 30 in the 1578 version).

> 31. The form and construction of the houses, and the materials which exist for building them, in the said towns, or in other parts, from where they are brought (*relaciones geográficas* 1577).

Throughout the early modern world, the houses of ordinary people were dependent on whatever construction materials were available nearby. Iberian answers to this question make clear the extreme poverty of rural Castile. Many towns had no local building supplies, and so were dependent on imports from elsewhere:[5]

> The buildings are three *tapias* [about 2.5 meters] in height, of earth, and some are roofed with broom and straw, and these materials are acquired beyond the town limits, and there are other houses of tile and pine wood, and for all of this one goes outside of the town and [also] for the tile …
> —Miguel Esteban, Toledo, 5 December 1575 (Viñas y Mey and Paz 1963: 113).

> The buildings of this town are made of earth, as is their foundation, and [they are] low buildings of middling quality for fieldworkers, and there is no plaster or lime, which are brought from two and three leagues distant from this town …
> —Cozar, Ciudad Real, 16 December 1575 (Viñas y Mey and Paz 1971: 214).

In contrast, this problem of building materials is seldom if ever recorded for the Americas. Instead, material abundance is usually stressed:

> The houses are made of wood and roofed in straw, in the style and shape of haystacks; of the said wood and straw there is a great amount ...
> —Tenerife, New Granada, circa 1580 (Patiño 1983: 149).

> The forms of the houses are like those in the other cities, and the materials are stones and adobes and plaster and lime, which they have in their towns and do not go outside to acquire ...
> —Trujillo de Cotaguaci, Peru, 30 January 1586 (Jiménez 1885: 16).

As a whole, these answers reveal close attention to the material spaces of daily life, and an awareness of how difficult it could be to build even simple houses. Yet the result of such efforts could be extremely ephemeral. Another transatlantically-shared pair of questions highlights how fragile early modern urban existence was. These questions asked about abandoned towns:

> 56. The locations of depopulated towns and places found in the land, and the name which they had, and the reason they were abandoned (*relaciones topográficas* 1575; see item 43 in the 1578 version).

> 48. And in general the locations of depopulated Spanish towns, and when they were settled, and abandoned, and that which can be known of the reasons for their abandonment (*relaciones geográficas* 1577).

The Iberian answers to this question are often attentive to sedimented time. They reveal that the landscape of central Castile was filled with broken buildings and depopulated settlements. In many cases, respondents had no idea when, or why, these places were abandoned. But other accounts of these *despoblados* were able to connect them to histories that were decades or even centuries old. For example, it was often remembered that recently-abandoned towns had been depopulated by plague:

> They have notice of another depopulated place which they say is called Alcubillete ... and it has its church and baptismal font, and from the said church it seems to have been a large settlement, and it has another old church, ruined, without a roof, and a very old structure, and they have heard that it was abandoned because of plague ...
> —Burujón, Toledo, 1 January 1576 (Viñas y Mey and Paz 1951: 166).

> A place which is called Santas Gracias, which is next to this town on the other side of the Henares River which they say was abandoned because of plague, and these witnesses report adobe walls in the said place, and foundations ...
> —Espinosa de Henares, Guadalajara, 13 December 1580 (Ortiz García 2000).

In other cases, unusual features of architecture or artifacts led locals to attribute the ruins to more ancient inhabitants:

> In some parts of the boundary of this place such as in El Hontanar and the pasture of Corralejo are found some old buildings and stone foundations, which are assumed to be Moorish houses because they are so old ...
> —Cazalegas, Toledo, 2 April 1576 (Viñas y Mey and Paz 1951: 292).

> In front of this island is a small orchard, which is called San Pablo, whose buildings are ruined, and from the "anatomy" it appears that its "bones" say that here was an ancient house of the Templars ...
> —Toledo, Toledo, 1576 (Viñas y Mey and Paz 1963: 50).

The recognized fragility of town life in central Castile is one reason why the *relaciones geográficas* also asked about the "locations of abandoned *Spanish* towns" in the Americas. At the same time, town depopulation had important political ramifications on both sides of the Atlantic. As Helen Nader (1990) makes clear, the glory of the Spanish monarch was intimately tied to the number of towns over which he ruled, and so the abandonment of towns was at the same time a diminution of royal prestige. But it is striking that no direct question about the depopulation of *indigenous* towns appears in the *relaciones geográficas*. Plague depopulation in the sixteenth-century Americas was even more dramatic than it was in sixteenth-century Europe, and although depopulation was raised in Question 5 ("whether there are many or few Indians; whether there have been more or fewer in former times, and any reasons for this that may be known; whether or not they are presently settled in regular and permanent towns"), references to abandoned towns are far less common in the American responses than in those from central Castile.

Indigenous *despoblados* were sometimes, as in Iberia, linked to the effects of plague:

> It is seen by experience in this town of Itztepexic, that it has few Indians; although, formerly, it was a large town of 10 or 12 thousand inhabitants, as is apparent from the houses and old houses where they were settled. And, when the Spaniards came and conquered it, it began to depopulate and, after, with two or three plagues which have come upon this said town (and others of the region), many Indians died ...
> —Itztepexic, Oaxaca, 26 August 1579 (Paso y Troncoso 1905: 13).

> The other depopulated town which was to the west was called Xahualtepec: asking what had expelled the said Indians from the said town, they responded that all were dead because 6 years ago, more or less, they died of some sicknesses ...
> —Citlaltomáua, Mexico, 12 January 1580 (Paso y Troncoso 1979: 156).

Occasionally, abandoned towns in the Americas were, as in Iberia, offered as evidence of a long-occupied landscape:

> This land appears to have been well-populated, because everywhere in it there is not a handful of earth which has not been worked and populated with large and medium-sized buildings of stone, and domed houses very well constructed …
> —Cansahcab, Yucatan, 20 February 1579 (Garza 1983: 96).

> This town has a high mountain range two leagues away, towards the northeast … at the summit are great peaks, where they once sacrificed: to one side of its summit, towards the northeast, there appear old buildings. This reveals that this region had been well-populated …
> —Nexapa, Oaxaca, 12 September 1579 (Paso y Troncoso 1905: 352).

Finally, some Peruvian responses linked abandoned indigenous towns to Spanish policies of forced resettlement:

> This said *repartimiento* is reduced in seven towns, which I, the said corregidor, reduced and completed in that which exists today … building beautiful churches and hospitals and tearing down (*asolando*) all the old towns and bringing the Indians to live in the said *reducción* …
> —Yauyos, Peru, 15 January 1586 (Jiménez 1881: 70;
> see also Hamann 2016: 267–270).

House construction techniques, and abandoned towns: in the printed *relaciones* questionnaires, these two issues are kept separate. But in lived experience, these seemingly-distinct topics provided a practical foundation for everyday archaeology.

The Aesthetics of Masonry

Many of the men responding to the *relaciones* combined themes of construction and abandonment when they described the unusual masonry and materials of abandoned or repurposed buildings. In other words, an awareness of how much effort it took to erect houses in the present was used to turn a critical eye towards construction methods preserved in ancient ruins.

In many cases, this architectural-antiquarian vision had a very practical motivation: old buildings and building materials could be put to new uses:

> Within this town there is a chapel to Mary Magdalene which was once a Moorish mosque, which is clearly manifested by its structure …
> —Almedina, Ciudad Real, 15 December 1575
> (Viñas y Mey and Paz 1971: 61).

In a mosque built by the Moors, which is today in a courtyard of the hospital which they call the Misericorida, there are some Arabic letters on a pillar, and when the Moorish King of Vélez passed through this town they were read by his secretary, and he said that they read "In this place is it forbidden not only to speak ill, but even to think bad thoughts" ...
—Talavera de la Reina, Toledo, 1 April 1576 (Viñas y Mey and Paz 1963: 454).

But in other examples, the description of ancient construction details seems to have been undertaken for its own sake, in a sheer appreciation of labor that had endured the ravages of time:

There is only a tower which has already been described, which is very old and it is owned by the said Comendador of Sigura as comendador, who is also from this town, and there are collected the tithes of bread and wine (as has been described in the chapters above), and the fabric which the said tower has is of plaster and stone, and inside it has a brick dome very well made ...
—Albaladejo, Ciudad Real, 10 December 1575 (Viñas y Mey and Paz 1971: 7).

In the jurisdiction of this town, two leagues away, is a hermitage which is called Our Lady of Melque, which is a very ancient building and apparently one of the most notable to exist in Spain, because all of its stones, from the foundation to the dome above are worked very curiously, and fit one to the other so well that it does not use mortar or any other material, beyond locking some [stones] to others, and it is very strong, and he heard his father say that in ancient times the entire hermitage was gilded, and that fire was put to it thinking that this was fine gold leaf, and so now it is blackened with smoke, and it is said that the Templars constructed it ...
—Puebla de Montalbán, Toledo, 10 February 1576
(Viñas y Mey and Paz 1963: 258).

In turn, these Castilian examples of everyday archaeological awareness illuminate the surprisingly detailed descriptions of ruined monumental architecture recorded for the Americas. The stonework in the palaces of Mitla (A.D. 1300–1500) or the courtyards of Tiwanaku (A.D. 400–1000) is truly stunning, even today. But when reading Spanish accounts of these places in the *relaciones geográficas*, we should remember that these descriptions were made possible because an aesthetics of ancient masonry was already part of how early modern Iberians viewed the world. The description of American stonework at Tiwanaku and Mitla has a surprising kinship with the description of Iberian stonework from Puebla de Montalbán; the Mitla account even makes Old World/New World parallels explicit, with a comparison to ancient Roman masonry:

It consists of some ancient buildings and huacas [Quechua *wak'a*; see Ch. 5 below], and it is a thing of admiration to see the art and style of massive stones

from which they began to build the said buildings, and for this reason this town of Tiwanaku was very memorable, having constructed in it a building so sumptuous and large, which could be counted as one of the wonders of the world, for being made of very large stones, and in the working and laying of them there is found no mixture of mortar, nor sand, nor clay, and they are so fitted and well-laid, that one cannot even insert in their joins the point of a knife …
—Provincia de los Pacaxes, Peru, 1586 (Jiménez 1885: 55–56).

And in addition to this there are in this town of Mitla two buildings of the greatest grandeur and renown to be found in this New Spain: they are situated one harquebus shot in length from the location of the town itself [about 200 meters], towards the north and on level ground: these buildings are of worked white stone, and all are one story, rising to a height of thirty feet … the walls of these halls are strangely worked in the Roman style: they are all worked of white stone four fingers in size, some a bit larger, the joins and fitting of these stones is of one stone on another, without any mix of mortar or any other substance, which is something to admire …
—Mitla, Oaxaca, 23 August 1580 (Paso y Troncoso 1905: 151).

Iberian precedents also help explain why preconquest architecture in the Americas was put to new uses or incorporated into new constructions. But this was a prehispanic practice as well, and so the political implications of architectural appropriation would have been understood by both indigenous people and Europeans—something made clear by the description of multilayered spolia at Vilcas Guaman, a case study in early modern comparative antiquarianism:

There was in this said town of San Pedro de Mama a famous temple before the conquest of this kingdom, which the Indians adored as the wife of the idol—or devil, more accurately—Pachacama, which was the greatest idol and temple of this kingdom; and the blindness of this people was so great, that there was no idol to whom they did not give a wife and children; and since the aforementioned two rivers joined near the said town of Mama, a bit below, they said these were the breasts of the goddess, wife of Pachacama, and from her breasts flowed the said two rivers; and so the name means "mother's breast." I, the said corregidor, managed to tear it down, and in the said *reducción* [a European-imposed resettlement of indigenous communities] I installed the house of the corregidor and hospital and jail inside the said temple, since it had good walls, once the embankments were cleared …
—Yauyos, Peru, 15 January 1586 (Jiménez 1881: 75).

After the Inca Tupac Inca Yupanqui conquered these kingdoms and pacified the land, he founded in this place of Vilcas Guaman a city and frontier with a garrison of 30,000 Indians, and he began, after founding the city, to build forts and buildings in it, and today some of them and their foundations can be seen, and all was of worked masonry; and for this he ordered the bringing of stones from Quito and Cuzco and other places, to demonstrate his valor and greatness; and likewise he formed and built in the said settlement a temple conforming to their gentility, all of worked masonry, where he had a sun of worked gold; and in another house, next to the temple, he had a great moon of silver, which they had for gods, and they adored them and ordered that all the Indians who were conquered should adore these gods, destroying the huacas of stone which they had had. This temple or house where the sun was, is at present standing and serves as a church, where the mass is now said to the people of the Venta Real which is founded here …

—Vilcas Guaman, Peru, 17 March 1586 (Jiménez 1881:166–167).

These descriptions of prehispanic ruins are interesting not only because of how much they echo the materially-detailed descriptions of ruined buildings in central Castile. Over and over again, these New World reports make clear that accounts of ruins in the Americas were informed by indigenous knowledge about what those ruins *meant*, and what they had been used for in the past. In many cases the names of indigenous experts are included at the beginning or end of a town's *relación*. In other words, because daily life in Iberia produced an everyday archaeological sensitivity in many people (a sensitivity not limited to antiquarian scholars), when European observers arrived in the Americas, they were often receptive to hearing, and recording, *indigenous* archaeological knowledge:

They had in the said town a very tall pyramid [the Pyramid of the Sun at Teotihuacan, A.D. 150], which had three levels for climbing to the top; at its summit was an idol of stone which they called Tonacateuctli, which was of a rough and very hard stone, all of a single piece: it was 3 large *brazas* [over 5 meters] in height and another in width and another in depth: it was turned to the west, and in a flat area which was in front of the said pyramid was another much smaller pyramid three *estados* [five meters] high, on which was another idol a bit smaller than the first called Mictlanteuctli, which means "Lord of Hell" …

—San Juan Teotihuacan, Mexico, 1 March 1580
(Paso y Troncoso 1979: 222, 224).

Next to the town of La Vera Cruz de Cauana is a ruined town [the Warí site of Jincamocco, A.D. 600–1000], which appears to be extremely ancient. It has walls of worked stone, although the masonry is rough; some of the doors of the houses are somewhat higher than two *varas* [just under two meters], and the lintels made from very large stones; and there are signs of streets. The old Indians say that according to what they have heard from their ancestors, in very ancient times, before the Incas ruled over them, there came to this land another people whom they call Viracochas, although not many, and that the Indians followed them, coming after them to hear their speech, and the Indians now say that they must have been saints. For them they built roads, which can be seen today, as wide as a street, and low walls at each side, and to sleep they built them houses which are still remembered today, and for these people they say that they built this said town; and some Indians remember having seen in this ancient town some burials with bones, made of rectangular stone slabs and brightened from within with white earth, and at present one cannot find of these bone nor skull …

—La Concepción de Huayllapampa de Aparca, Peru,
27 January 1586 (Jiménez 1881: 210).

Manufactured Gods

Descriptions of abandoned settlements and curiously-constructed buildings are not the only points of antiquarian comparison between the *relaciones topográficas* and *relaciones geográficas*. Another parallel theme is provided by accounts of sacred images that stress the details of their materiality. Again and again, writers filling out these questionnaires took time to describe local images of divine beings, and their accounts reveal a sustained fascination with what these images were made from. This attentiveness is, in part, an extension of the similarly materialist everyday archaeological sensibilities explored in the previous two sections.

But there is another reason for this attentiveness as well—especially by the 1570s, when Protestant critiques of Catholic image-worship as "idolatry" had been going on for half a century. Although the *relaciones topográficas* from central Castile are an amazing source of information about "local religion"— as William Christian made clear in two classic studies (1981a, 1981b)—they are in general surprisingly vague about the appearance and form of the sacred images worshipped in rural communities. We learn the names of patron saints, and the reasons for their then-current prestige (a plague ended, a swarm of locusts diverted), but very little about what their divine effigies looked like. Perhaps discomfort with the base materiality of sacred Catholic images caused *relación*-respondents to shy away from detailed descriptions.

In contrast, no such reservations were needed when accounting for pagan images, whose status as idols was intimately connected to their human-made forms. As with accounts of ancient architecture, accounts of Roman and pre-Roman statues in central Castile can be quite evocative:

They say that in this town there are a few antiquities, which include two hogs carved from granite, very powerful, and some granite stones which are sunk into the earth with many burials and antiquities and also there is a basin by a well which has an inscription, which says "Here lies Vera sacrificed to the gods, that they should provide us Hell" and the *-era* is erased; and also near this town there are many small hamlets and burials which seem to be a thing of Muslims or gentiles …

—Torrecilla, Toledo, 1 April 1576 (Viñas y Mey and Paz 1963: 612).

There have been found bronze idols, badly formed, so that it is impossible to interpret which gentile god they represent. I saw one many days ago of Hercules of admirable facture, small, standing and very well gilded; it was of copper; there have been found many Roman coins and walls and they tell me that there have been found clay coins …
　　—Bolaños, Ciudad Real, 6 December 1578 (Viñas y Mey and Paz 1971: 133).

This materialist tendency is also found in accounts of indigenous god-images from the Americas. The dismissal of non-Catholic divinities as nothing more than crude matter is well-illustrated by the stereotyped description of such images (from Central Mexico to Oaxaca to New Granada to Peru) as "idols of stones and sticks" (Paso y Troncoso 1979: 3, 21, 29, 36, 180, 196, 297; Jiménez 1885: 208, 209; Patiño 1983: 189). Acquired prejudice may also explain why indigenous witnesses from Central Mexico to Yucatan to Peru claimed that the "idolatrous" practices so hated by the Spaniards were recent innovations, imposed on local populations by foreign invaders: the Aztecs in Central Mexico, the Mexicans in Yucatan, and the Incas in Peru (Garza 1983: 411; Paso y Troncoso 1979: 54).

　　But the rejection of sacred materiality is only part of the story told by these *relaciones*. In some instances, it is clear that European reporters are describing vanished prehispanic images *that they had never actually seen*. In these cases, information on the appearance of ancient sculptures must have been provided by Native American interlocutors—people for whom those images had once been sacred, the physical properties of which were important features of their power. In other words, physical descriptions that for Europeans provided proof of pagan powerlessness were, for the indigenous people providing those accounts, evidence of intrinsic value. And here we can see how even when the details of European and Native American antiquarianism were at cross-purposes, their overall contours were remarkably compatible:

They had many idols made in the form of a boy without head or arms, some idols smaller than others, and they had one which was for maize, and another for tubers, another for pregnant women, another for war, and thus for all of the things which were in the land they had an idol for each thing. They were made of cotton string, and some beads of bone which they call *quitero* …
　　—Trujillo, Venezuela, 20 December 1578 (Arellano Moreno 1964: 167).

They adored and sacrificed to, as a god, a black knife, more than two *codos* [almost a meter] long, without any figure, other than the rich green feathers they added to it. And they carried it to high hills and pyramids for their sacrifices, and to battles …
　　—Itztepexic, Oaxaca, 26 August 1579 (Acuña 1984: 255–256).

They adored high hills, those which fell in the local territory of each one, having in these hills their huacas and temples, and there were some [sculptures] like the sheep of this land [llamas] made of stone, and other little sheep made of clay …
—La Concepción de Huayllapampa de Aparca, Peru,
27 January 1586 (Jiménez 1881: 206–7).

Escrituras antiguas, pinturas antiguas

Another point of comparison in our Mediterratlantic archive of *relaciones* has to do with textual materiality. Both in Iberia and the Americas, physical documents provided important repositories for historical knowledge. Many of the *relaciones* from central Castile make reference to, and even quote from, "ancient writings" about a town's past. As was common throughout medieval and early modern Europe, the material properties of these texts were important guarantees of their authenticity, and so these details were duly noted by *relación*-respondents (see also Clanchy 1979):

And they know that it is its own independent town by a grant and privilege conceded to it by the Lord King don Alfonso the Tenth of glorious memory in the year of 1310, as is shown by his privilege, written on parchment, rolled and lead-sealed …
—Ves, Murcia, December 18, 1575 (Cebrián Abellán and Cano Valero 1992: 308).

This village says it was won from the Moors 500 years ago, more or less, for this reason: the charter which this town has was given by the Lord King don Alfonso, of glorious memory, this town being already settled; at the beginning and head of the said charter is written in large capitals, red and on parchment these letters …
—Sigura de la Sierra, Ciudad Real, 1575? (Viñas y Mey and Paz 1971: 475).

At the same time, respondents were also interested in more ancient texts, especially stone inscriptions from the Muslim or Roman past. As with our previous discussion of ruined buildings and physical gods, these accounts are often attentive to material details, and even to the style of the letters themselves. In some cases, copies of ancient inscriptions were included in the *relación* (even written in all-capital letters to mimic the ancient Roman forms):

And in addition there have been found stones with inscriptions, of which stones there is a granite stone, with good texture, squared and well-carved, which is today placed in a corner of the house of Gaspar de Arevalo, curate of Casarrubios, and its dependencies, which is next to the church of this place, on which there is an inscription which says in gothic letters
L. AESYMACHO
QVIRINA ANNO
RVM. LXXXX. S. T.

T. L. AELIAE. PON.
PEI VCSORI
AR. XXX
—Villamanta, Toledo, 3 February 1576 (Viñas y Mey and
Paz 1963: 694–695).

> And in another part of this jurisdiction, in the place called Fountain of the Moor, it seems that in past times there was a large settlement, at which is a tall crag, carved with eight letters, and it is not known if they are in Greek or another language, and no one understands or has understood the signification or meaning of them …
> —Castillo de Bayuela, Toledo, 4 October 1578
> (Viñas y Mey and Paz 1951: 279).

Moving from central Castile to the Spanish Americas, the first thing that becomes clear is why so many writers of the *relaciones geográficas* were interested in the town foundation histories recorded in indigenous texts: town foundation charters, written in *escrituras antiguas*, were of great importance in early modern Iberia as well. The *relación* of Coatepec (Mexico, 16 November 1579) repeatedly mentions the use of ancient paintings, and the *relación*'s Spanish author retells the painting-recorded actions (and names) of the town's three founders. Similar foundation-history texts are mentioned in Oaxaca and Yucatan:

> And according to what the Indians say, and as it appears in their histories, the natives descend from those who made the said buildings, and there is in the land a lineage of them who descend in a direct line from the said ancient ones …
> —Cansahcab, Yucatan, 20 February 1579 (Garza 1983).

> That which one could know and find out according to the account that these old people give of their antiquity is that it could have been nine or ten ages or eras, counting for an age a hundred or more years, which means it could have been 900 years ago, a little more or less, that three lords departed from the town of Yoloxonequila, which is in the province of Chinantla … the said *relación* is certain and true according to that which they know and understand and have known and have understood from their fathers and grandfathers and other older ancestors, who told and declared this (it is said) by means of their paintings for the remembrance of those to come …
> —Itztepexic, Oaxaca, 26 August 1579 (Paso y Troncoso 1905: 14, 22).

Perhaps because early modern Iberians knew that the validity of their own town foundation documents often depended on their unusual materials (parchment, colored letters, pendant seals), they also recorded the physical properties of textual documentation in the New World:

> They had letters with which they wrote and were understood, which were certain characters, each representing a word-fragment, and by this they were understood,

as with our own letters, and these were only taught to noble persons, and because of this all of the priests, who were the most dedicated to them, were noble persons ...

—Mérida, Yucatan, 18 February 1579 (Garza 1983: 73).

And for all the time which the ruler of the Incas lasted in this land, the Indians of this *repartimiento* lived without being able to do anything or hear anything but the words of the Inca, and to achieve this, there was in this *repartimiento* a relative of the Inca, a principal lord, to whom were directed the quipus which the Inca dispatched, which were some knotted cords by which they understood and commanded, and he had to obey ...

—La Concepción de Huayllapampa de Aparca, Peru, 27 January 1586 (Jiménez 1881: 207).

As in central Castile, engagement with ancient records could even extend to entering copies of them in the texts of the *relación*. Don Gabriel de Chávez includes a schematic time-space calendar on the opening page of his *relación* for Meztitlan: although this at first appears fully Europeanized, details of layout and iconography reveal that he is copying an indigenous manuscript (Mundy 1996: 92–93). Actual indigenous images could also be joined to the *relación*-reports. The most famous examples of this are the many pictographic maps included in the reports from Mexico and Oaxaca. Some were created specifically for the survey project, but others seem to have been copied from already-existing documents (Mundy 1996: 113, 132).

Of course, European interests are not the only factor here—and they also have their limits. The most detailed accounts of indigenous writing systems in the *relaciones geográficas* were clearly dependent on the input from indigenous people. Gaspar Antonio Chi, a Maya nobleman, signed his name as co-author of the above-quoted *relación* for Mérida, which discusses hieroglyphs. No less than nine indigenous Andean elites are named as advisors at the beginning of the *relación* of La Concepción de Huayllapampa de Aparca, which discusses quipus.

***

Our Mediterratlantic survey of the *relaciones* projects from 1575 to 1586 has ranged from houses and abandoned towns, to notable architectural forms, to forcefully material images of the gods, to a textual archive manifested in parchment, seals, stones, and alien scripts. I have argued that everyday archaeology in Iberia made it possible for Europeans in the Americas to literally see, and want to describe, indigenous antiquities with some care—as well as to be interested in learning and recording what these antiquities meant to native peoples. And this despite the absence of a specific item about ancient things in the *relaciones geográficas* questionnaire.

But the past is rarely ever dead and buried and tranquil. The meaning of the past—and its implications for the present—can be a source of conflict. This is especially true in confrontations between locals and outsiders. In conclusion, let us consider archaeologies at war in the early modern Mediterratlantic.

Archaeologies at War

In Iberia, for local guardians of antiquities, the interests of outsiders—such as those manifested in the questionnaires of the *relaciones topográficas*—could be viewed with caution. A response from Maqueda, Toledo, copies a Roman inscription, and then notes that the stone had been moved to safety inside the local hermitage, out of fear that outsiders would take it (Viñas y Mey and Paz 1963: 52–53).

This is not to say that ancient remains were valued equally by all of the inhabitants of any given village in central Castile. At least one *relación*-writer answers Question 36 by complaining about a lack of local interest in the town's material heritage:

> Great buildings can be found, and ancient burials, and there have been found epitaphs in Arabic, and royal decrees, and because the villagers are farm workers, they have not valued these, and have not protected them …
> —Caracuel, Ciudad Real, 15 December 1575
> (Viñas y Mey and Paz 1971: 181).

Varied local attitudes towards the remains of the past, and the potential rapaciousness of outsiders, are perhaps best illustrated in the *relación geográfica* of Quiotepec, Oaxaca. In the Americas, the main danger to local relics was not theft by collectors, but destruction by Catholics:

> And, when the Franciscan Fathers had just arrived, wanting to sow the faith, they determined to bring out and find the idols in order to burn them and to break them. And having collected all that there were, some Indians, truly converted, who did not wish anything to be hidden, revealed to the said Fathers that they had hidden a book, which they held for a god, which they had held in great veneration because a white man, elderly, had written the whole thing and, leaving, he left it behind, either forgotten, or so that they should guard it. The Franciscan Father ordered that it be brought out and, not understanding the writing nor knowing how to read it, he burned it with the idols. It was of white paper, and of this size [that is, the same size as the paper on which the *relación*-respondent was writing], bound and tied with some ribbons, and in it they worshipped their gods (Acuña 1984: 236).

At first, the friars believed that they had "collected all [the sacred images] that there were." But if false compliance was the original strategy of Quiotepec traditionalists, those traditionalists were betrayed. For "some Indians, truly converted" felt that the tendered images were not a sufficient offering, and so surrendered to destruction a sacred book which some of their neighbors had tried to save.

Notes

1. See Elliot van Liere 2007; Morales 1576: 11r, 24v, 63r; Morán 2010: 90; Sánchez Madrid 2002; Wood 2001; additional references can be found in note 3.
2. For example, MacCormack (2007) focuses on how European antiquarian models of ancient Rome were brought to the Andes and used to interpret the Andean past. Surprisingly absent is a discussion of how those imported models interacted with Andean antiquarianisms, even when records of such indigenous interpretations were brought together in books which also pursued Roman analogies, such as the Inca ideas about Tiwanaku recorded in Juan de Betanzos' 1557 *History of the Inca Empire* and Bernabé Cobo's 1653 *History of the New World*.
3. On Italy, see Seznec 1953; Christian 2010; Cole 2009; on Italy and the Germanies, see Wood 2001; on Spain, see Lleó Cañal 1995; Sánchez Madrid 2002; Elliot van Liere 2007; Morán 2010.
4. See references in Hamann 2002; 2008.
5. For brevity, I will include only two examples of each theme, although many more could be provided.

References

Acuña, René (editor)
  1984   *Relaciones geográficas del siglo XVI: Antequera.* Universidad Nacional Autónoma de México, México.
Arellano Moreno, Antonio (editor)
  1964   *Relaciones geográficas de Venezuela.* Academia Nacional de la Historia, Caracas.
Boas, Franz
  1889   On Alternating Sounds. *American Anthropologist* 2: 47–53.
Burckhardt, Jakob
  1961[1860]   *The Civilization of the Renaissance in Italy.* Phaidon Press, London.
Campos y Fernández de Sevilla, Francisco Javier
  2003   Las Relaciones Topográficas de Felipe II: índices, fuentes, y bibliografía. *Anuario jurídico y económico escurialense* 36: 439–574.
Cebrián Abellán, Aurelio, and José Cano Valero (editors)
  1992   *Relaciones topográficas de los pueblos del reino de Murcia, 1575–1579.* Editum, Murcia.
Christian Jr., William A.
  1981a   *Local Religion in Sixteenth-Century Spain.* Princeton University Press, Princeton.
  1981b   *Apparitions in Late Medieval and Renaissance Spain.* Princeton University Press, Princeton.

Christian, Kathleen Wren
  2010   *Empire Without End: Antiquities Collections in Renaissance Rome, c. 1350–1527*. Yale University Press, New Haven.

Clanchy, Michael T.
  1979   *From Memory to the Written Record: England 1066–1307*. Cambridge University Press, Cambridge.

Cline, Howard F.
  1971   The Relaciones Geográficas of the Spanish Indies, 1577–1648. In *Handbook of Middle American Indians, Volume 12. Guide to Ethnohistorical Sources, Part 1*, edited by Howard F. Cline, pp. 183–242. University of Texas Press, Austin.

Cole, Michael W.
  2009   Perpetual Exorcism in Sistine Rome. In *The Idol in the Age of Art: Objects, Devotions and the Early Modern World*, edited by Michael W. Cole and Rebecca E. Zorach, pp. 57–75. Ashgate, Burlington.

Elliott, John Huxtable
  1970   *The Old World and the New: 1492–1650*. Cambridge University Press, Cambridge.

Elliott van Liere, Katherine
  2007   "Shared Studies Foster Friendship": Humanism and History in Spain. In *The Renaissance World*, edited by John Jeffries Martin, pp. 242–261. Routledge, London.

Fabian, Johannes
  1983   *Time and the Other: How Anthropology Makes its Object*. Columbia University Press, New York.

Foucault, Michel
  1976   *The History of Sexuality, Volume 1: An Introduction*. Pantheon Books, New York.

Garza, Mercedes de la (editor)
  1983   *Relaciones histórico-geográficas de la gobernación de Yucatán: Mérida, Valladolid y Tabasco*. Universidad Nacional Autónoma de México, México City.

Ginzburg, Carlo
  1983   *The Night Battles: Witchcraft and Agrarian Cults in the Sixteenth and Seventeenth Centuries*. Routledge and Keegan Paul, London.

Greenblatt, Stephen
  1991   *Marvelous Possessions: The Wonder of the New World*. University of Chicago Press, Chicago.

Hamann, Byron Ellsworth
  2002   The Social Life of Pre-Sunrise Things: Indigenous Mesoamerican Archaeology. *Current Anthropology* 43: 351–382.
  2008   Chronological Pollution: Potsherds, Mosques, and Broken Gods Before and After the Conquest of Mexico. *Current Anthropology* 49: 803–836.
  2015   *The Translations of Nebrija: Language, Culture, and Circulation in the Early Modern World*. University of Massachusetts Press, Amherst.
  2016   How to Chronologize with a Hammer, or, the Myth of Homogeneous, Empty Time. *Hau: Journal of Ethnographic Theory* 6: 261–292.

n.d.   Bad Christians, New Spains: Muslims, Catholics, and Native Americans in a Mediterratlantic World. Unpublished manuscript.

Jiménez de la Espada, Marcos (editor)
1881   *Relaciones Geográficas de Indias. Publícalas el Ministerio de Fomento. Perú. Tomo I.* Tipografía de Manuel G. Hernández, Madrid.
1885   *Relaciones Geográficas de Indias. Publícalas el Ministerio de Fomento. Perú. Tomo II.* Tipografía de Manuel G. Hernández, Madrid.

Klein, Ceceila F., and Naoli Victoria Lona
2009   Sex in the City: A Comparison of Aztec Ceramic Figurines to Copal Figurines from the Templo Mayor. In *Mesoamerican Figurines: Small-Scale Indices of Large-Scale Social Phenomena*, edited by Christina T. Halperin, Katherine A. Faust, Rhonda Taubet, and Aurore Giguet, pp. 327–377. University Press of Florida, Gainesville.

Klor de Alva, J. Jorge
1999   "Telling Lives": Confessional Autobiography and the Reconstruction of the Nahua Self. In *Spiritual Encounters: Interactions between Christianity and Native Religions in Colonial America*, edited by Nicholas Griffiths and Fernando Cervantes, pp. 136–162. University of Birmingham Press, Birmingham.

Lleó Cañal, Vicente
1995   Origen y función de las primeras colecciones renacentistas de antigüedades en Andalucía. In *La antigüedad como argumento II: historiografía de arqueología e historia antigua en Andalucía*, edited by Fernando Gascó la Calle and José Luis Beltrán, pp. 57–74. Scriptorium, Seville.

MacCormack, Sabine
2007   *On the Wings of Time: Rome, the Incas, Spain, and Peru.* Princeton University Press, Princeton.

Morales, Ambrosio de
1577   *Las antigüedades de las ciudades de España.* Juan Iñiguez de Lequeríca, Alcalá.

Morán Turina, José Miguel
2010   *La memoria de las piedras: anticuarios, arqueólogos y coleccionistas de antigüedades en la España de los Austrias.* Centro de Estudios Europa Hispánica, Madrid.

Mundy, Barbara E.
1996   *The Mapping of New Spain: Indigenous Cartography and the Maps of the Relaciones Geográficas.* University of Chicago Press, Chicago.
2008   Relaciones Geográficas. In *Guide to Documentary Sources for Andean Studies, 1530–1900*, edited by Joanne Pillsbury, vol. 1, pp. 144–159. University of Oklahoma Press, Norman.

Nader, Helen
1990   *Liberty in Absolutist Spain: The Habsburg Sale of Towns, 1516–1700.* Johns Hopkins University Press, Baltimore.

Ortiz García, Antonio (editor)
2000   *Relaciones topográficas de la provincia de Guadalajara.* CD-ROM. Diputación Provincial, Guadalajara.

Paso y Troncoso, Francisco del (editor)

1905   *Relaciones geográficas de la Diócesis de Oaxaca.* Sucesores de Rivadeneyra, Madrid.

1979   *Relaciones geográficas de la Diócesis de México.* Editorial Cosmos, México.

Patiño, Victor M. (editor)

1983   *Relaciones geográficas de la Nueva Granada, siglos XVI a XIX.* Imprenta Departamental, Calí.

Portuondo, María

2009   *Secret Science: Spanish Cosmography and the New World.* University of Chicago Press, Chicago.

Sánchez Madrid, Sebastián

2002   *Arqueología y humanismo: Ambrosio de Morales.* Universidad de Córdoba, Córdoba.

Seznec, Jean

1953   *The Survival of the Pagan Gods.* Harper, New York.

Trouillot, Michel-Rolph

1995   *Silencing the Past: Power and the Production of History.* Beacon, Boston.

Viñas y Mey, Carmelo, and Ramón Paz (editors)

1951   *Relaciones histórico-geográfico-estadísticas de los pueblos de España hechas por iniciativa de Felipe II: Reino de Toledo.* CSIC, Madrid.

1963   *Relaciones histórico-geográfico-estadísticas de los pueblos de España hechas por iniciativa de Felipe II: Reino de Toledo-Yuncos.* CSIC, Madrid.

1971   *Relaciones histórico-geográfico-estadísticas de los pueblos de España hechas por iniciativa de Felipe II: Ciudad Real.* CSIC, Madrid.

Wood, Christopher S.

2001   Notation of Visual Information in the Earliest Archaeological Scholarship. *Word and Image* 17: 94–118.

Ancient Artifice: The Production of Antiquity and the Social Roles of Ruins in the Heartland of the Inca Empire

Steve Kosiba

The mighty shall lie in ruins. This is the lesson of Percy Bysshe Shelley's famous poem, in which a weary traveler comes across the crumbling stone legs of Ozymandias and reflects on how the hubris of power is in part buried beneath and in part revealed by the shifting desert sands. The ruin of Ozymandias urges this traveler to see the fate of empires in the broken statue of a despot (cf. Vine 2010: 150–151). Contrast this poetic representation with another Ozymandias, an immense concrete pair of legs in the desert plain next to Highway 27 in Amarillo, Texas (Figures 5.1 and 5.2). The legs, completed in 1996 by artist Lightnin' McDuff, are part nod to Shelley and part American roadside attraction. This constructed ruin not only tells of the fragility of monuments, but also offers a medium for social expression. Since its installation, it has repeatedly changed face as local people and informal artists have painted stockings, etched initials, or spray-painted community team names onto its surface. These two versions of Ozymandias suggest different kinds of ruin: one in which the past is distant and represented by the decayed remnants of an ancient king; and another in which past intentions and creations become material for contemporary social action. Both reveal that ruins, and the pasts they invoke, only matter as they are considered in the present (cf. de Certeau 1988: 23; Trouillot 1995: 14).

Ruins are not simply "facts on the ground" (Abu El Haj 2001). Rather, they are created and defined through discourses and acts, which work to alter surfaces, affix meanings, and anchor memories (Stoler 2013). Frequently the definition of ruins, whether in verse or concrete, manifests a claim about a particular kind of past that might be called *antiquity*—that is, a claim that specific events, people, or places constitute the foundation for present social

Figure 5.1–5.2. Two views of the Ozymandias in the Texas desert, a ruin that artists and travelers alike have repeatedly painted and decorated (often with socks) since the monument's installation. Figure 5.1 (top): 2009 (AMBOO213/FLICKR [CREATIVE COMMONS]); Figure 5.2 (bottom): 2011 (NICHOLAS HENDERSON/FLICKR [CREATIVE COMMONS]).

life. To stake such a claim is to emphasize some events, stories, and places, while silencing or obscuring others (Cohen 1994; Trouillot 1995: 25). Several scholars have demonstrated that these claims are part of a political process by which actions on the ground are fitted into narratives that address present concerns (e.g., Assmann 1997; Chartier 1997; Chase 2015; de Certeau 1988; Guha 1983; Marx 1994 [1852]; Schaff 1976; Todorov 1995). But few have studied how material things participate in this process—that is, how artifacts present obstacles to claims about antiquity, how the destruction of places heralds historical changes, and how select ruins become hallowed grounds while others are forgotten (e.g., Barkan 1999; Dean 2010; Grazia Lolla 2003; Stoler 2013). To inquire into antiquity is to study the cultural confrontations and political struggles through which places and things come to be ruins and artifacts that speak of the past in the present.

In this chapter, I examine the production of antiquity and the social roles of ruins within the early colonial Americas (ca. 1532–1650 A.D.), focusing on the Andean region, where Inca ruins brought about new ideologies and understandings of the past during Spanish rule. The Incas lacked a written history, but during the process of Spanish colonization the physical remains of recently ruined buildings were invoked—in historiographies, courtrooms, and public ceremonies—to exemplify or stand for a bygone Inca past. Building on recent theories of historical production (Todorov 1995; Trouillot 1995), I seek to understand the courtroom arguments and ruination practices through which these Andean things and places became models of a past that held meaning and political value for both colonizers and the colonized, Christian and Inca. In reviewing archaeological and historical evidence pertaining to these ruins, I complement studies of Spanish colonization in the Andes that concentrate on official written histories and their authors (prose about the past akin to Shelley's "Ozymandias"), by identifying the practices through which Spanish and Andeans sought to produce ruins that lay outside of the centers of politics and learning (vernacular practices of transformation akin to the changes effected on McDuff's Ozymandias). With these practices, actors of diverse cultural background sought to fix materials and memories of the past, creatively drawing on indigenous American and European idioms of historical production to both direct and make sense of the colonial encounter (Chase 2015; Gose 2008; Lamana 2007; Urton 1990; Yannakakis 2008). Taking this approach, I complement studies that focus on how colonial regimes attempted to impose visions of past and present social orders through historiography and aesthetic representation (e.g., Dean 2010; MacCormack 2007; Niranjana 1992), but concentrate more on how places and things in the countryside became what I term "sites of articulation"—that is, sites that incite conflict and demand cooperation precisely because they held value for both local people and colonial authorities (cf. Amin 1995).

Ruining the Andes

When the Spaniards began to ascend the Peruvian Andes in 1532, they entered a landscape that, in many areas, had only been recently reduced to ruin. Cristóbal de Mena, one of the conquistadors who first entered the Inca realm, noted that he saw once vibrant towns depopulated and demolished (Mena 1930[1534]: 224–226). The ruins were the result of a vicious civil war between aspiring Inca emperors, the consequences of which were especially dire for the towns that had taken the losing side (see Hemming 1970). This process of ruination continued during the early decades of Spanish colonization, as disease and warfare ravaged the empire. The astute Spaniard Pedro Cieza de León noted that he frequently encountered ruins of the Incas as he journeyed throughout the Inca domain only a few years after the Spanish invasion. Cieza's writings contain multiple lamentations that, like Shelley, recall classical antiquarian tropes about how crumbling temples and abandoned plazas reveal both the prowess and ephemerality of empire (e.g., Cieza 1946[1553]: 371, 386, 407, 450). Ruins from the recent past often existed alongside still functioning Inca structures[1] (Cobo 1964[1653]: 130) in a landscape that at once bespoke both social cataclysm and continuity. The Inca Empire was falling to the Spanish invaders, and as this occurred its buildings were becoming ruins—things of a distant and defunct era.

Many of these ruins were not only materially produced due to violent conflict with the Spaniards, but also discursively constructed through the writing of Inca history. The Incas lacked a written history, and for various reasons the Spaniards were keen to record details about the Inca realm. Cieza's account is an example of what are often called the chronicles of the Incas, a series of sixteenth- and seventeenth-century Spanish writings about Inca society, religion, and history. These writings widely vary in their interpretations of the Inca realm but, whether penned by Spanish or indigenous authors, they all employ Iberian historiographic tropes to represent Inca history. Hence, as Frank Salomon remarks, the chronicles are not a unified historical corpus—they are "works of recall or comment on [Inca] civilization's rupture … addressed to emerging colonial concerns" (2015: 23; see also Salomon 1999). In contrast to writings about antiquity in Europe, which derived authority through their references to classic texts, these chronicles became widely accepted as valid accounts because of their authors' personal observations and experiences of the Inca realm and its ruins (von Ostenfeld-Suske 2012b: 563). On one hand these observations and experiences drew on Spanish cultural understandings of the past. On the other hand, they often provided a medium for Incas and former Inca subjects to express their particular social memories or to opportunistically invent histories, and this resulted in inconsistent chronologies and incongruent pasts (Covey 2006; Urton 1990).

The chroniclers often sought to create coherence from inconsistent accounts by constructing a linear and epochal historical sequence grounded in their empirical observations of ruins. Most commonly, the monumental pre-Inca city known as Tiahuanaco[2] appears in early chronicles as the place of creation for humanity after a global flood or a primordial state of darkness (Betanzos 1968[1551]: 9; Cieza 1967[1553]: 3, 8; Cieza 1946[1553]: 445; Molina 1947[1573]: 19, 22; Sarmiento 1965[1572]: 207). Though details vary, these stories agree that a creator deity shaped humans at Tiahuanaco (Betanzos 1968[1551]: 9; Cieza 1967[1553]: 8; Molina 1947[1573]: 19–22, 28; Sarmiento 1965[1572]: 208–209). Many state that this creation was necessary because the original humans had sinned, so the creator turned them into the monolithic statues that are still visible at Tiahuanaco (Figure 5.3) (Molina 1947[1573]: 22, 25; Sarmiento 1965[1572]: 207; also Garcilaso 1976[1609]: 124; Calancha 1974–1981[1638]:76).Translated into Spanish writing, these stories imply that there is evidence at Tiahuanaco for the flood[3] of Christian myth, an historiographical move to cast Andean legend in knowable and familiar terms (MacCormack 2007: 49–50).[4]

The ruins of Tiahuanaco were important to the process by which Spaniards translated Andean myths into a global epochal history. The Spaniards often wrote that flood myths were beyond the memory of Andean people (e.g., Betanzos 1968[1551]: 9; Cieza 1967[1553]: 3), but could be empirically verified at Tiahuanaco. In absence of texts, the Spaniards relied on observations about the grandeur of the structures at Tiahuanaco, the measurements of the stones, and the spatial layout of the site (Acosta 1954[1590]: 193–194; Cieza 1946[1553]: 456; later sources: Cobo 1964[1653]: 52–57, 195–198; Garcilaso 1976[1609]: 124). Similar to antiquarian trends in Europe, the buildings and the past that they invoked were beyond familiar and classifiable historical knowledge, based on textual and literary sources, so they had to be converted into objects of knowledge via conventions of measurement and observation (Vine 2010: 112, 166).

In highlighting Tiahuanaco and its grandeur, these Spanish sources emphasize a story of universal creation while obscuring other Andean Spanish voices or perspectives. The stories of Tiahuanaco authorize one way of representing the deep past via the actions of a creator at a single place of foundation. It is clear that, among Andean people, Tiahuanaco played a prominent role in one narrative of the past—it was one past among many.

Figure 5.3. The Ponce monolith provides an example of the stone figures of Tiahuanaco. In the early colonial era, some authors mixed indigenous and Spanish tropes of origins to tell of an original species of humans whom the creator deity had turned to stone because of their sins (photograph by John Janusek, used with permission).

Given the claim to universal origins of the Tiahuanaco myth, it was likely a narrative of the past tied to Inca imperialism, with its paternalistic claim to manage a vast Andean family (e.g., Kolata 2013). But early chroniclers recorded multiple other myths of origin (Molina 1947[1573]: 31–33), and noted a variety of impressive and inexplicable ancient ruins throughout the Andes, such as Huamachuco (Cieza 1946[1553]: 401–403) or Aconcagua (Cieza 1967[1553]: 97). Local Andean people, such as the Checa kin group of Huarochirí, Peru, told of their origins in terms of the combined actions of deities, animals, and people, rather than a universal creation at one place, suggesting competing narratives of the past in the Andean world (Salomon and Urioste 1991). Instead of the Tiahuanaco myths' emphasis on the universal beginning of time, many Andean myths are more focused on spatial relationships, stating that different communities, comprised of humans made from distinct materials, emerged at disparate locations (Betanzos 1968[1551]: 9–10; Cieza 1946[1553]: 445; Cobo 1964[1653]: 150–151; Sarmiento 1965[1572]: 209). Each of these communities established and named a *wak'a*—a personified place, whether a built structure or a natural feature of the landscape such as a rock outcrop or a spring—to mark and memorialize the very location where they said they had emerged (*pacarina*) (Cobo 1964[1653]: 152–153; Molina 1947[1573]: 21–22). Hence, for Andean people, these myths demonstrated more than simply the existence of a creator and a flood: they indicated that distinctions between communities were natural and rooted in geography.[5] *Wak'as* not only anchored the identities of communities, but also proved that they had been in place since time immemorial. The Spaniards sought to reconcile these tales of geographic difference by placing them in a Western and Christian temporal framework, and they did so by making Tiahuanaco the place that stood for the epoch of the flood.

These stories suggest that it was important for both Spanish and indigenous Andean actors to refer to specific places to make claims about the past, but for different reasons. The authors and informants of the chronicles emphasized details important to their own cultural schemas—semiotic conventions and knowledge categories (*sensu* Sewell 1992)—through which they understood history (see also Sahlins 1981, 1985). Though not all of these actors would have possessed full knowledge of these cultural schemas (Obeyesekere 1992), their repeated emphasis on places and processes of foundation suggests cultural rules for constructing history. This is not to say that Andeans and Spaniards subscribed to absolutely irreconcilable renderings of history. Indeed, we shall see that Andeans and Spaniards drew from both kinds of schema during the colonial era. A brief description of these schemas is necessary before we inquire into how different actors creatively transposed them throughout the colonial encounter (compare with Hutson 2009: 34; Sewell 1992: 17).

Noah and the *Wak'a*

Many of the Spanish writers sought to construct history in terms of lineages, by tracing ethnic and royal groups to classical or biblical times. This schema was invented slightly before the conquest of the Americas, when European monarchs began to sponsor a new genre of tightly controlled "official histories" to regulate knowledge of the past, typically by recounting their heroism and linking it to classical myths (Burke 1969; Linehan 1993; von Ostenfeld-Suske 2012a).[6] That which was old demanded authority in early modern Europe, and accordingly these monarchs claimed ancient pedigrees for their courts—the Tudors declared they rose from Arthur; the Habsburgs from Jason and Noah; the French from the Trojans; and the Spaniards from Heracles or Noah's grandson (Burke 2012: 263; MacCormack 2007; von Ostenfeld-Suske 2012a: 433). Moreover, these monarchs sought to ground these claims to classical lineages in ruins. For instance, in 1533 Henry VIII commissioned John Leland, the first official *antiquarius* on record, who asserted the importance of ruins to the authentication of royal genealogy (Vine 2010: 24–28). In similar ways, other ruling regimes hastened to identify *any* classical ruins and artifacts that might support their claim to ancient lineage, while they simultaneously quashed counter-claims by divesting rival nobles or monasteries of the materials that proved the antiquity of their authority (Vine 2010).

In Spain, the official histories introduced a linear reckoning of history by underscoring a causal sequence from classical to current times. The histories legitimated the union of Castile and Aragon (1492), which at the time was a controversial and contested move, by casting the newly consolidated kingdom as a process that began in classical times (Linehan 1993). Historians claimed Carthaginian and Roman roots for the monarchy, and sought the most ancient ruins and sources to argue that a unified Spanish Crown and ethnicity had existed in antiquity. Writers such as Joan Margarit, who published his *Paralipomenon Hispaniae* in 1483, presaged this trend by using classical sources (such as Strabo) to locate Iberian ruins that, he argued, denoted ancient Spanish ethnicity (von Ostenfeld-Suske 2012a: 432–433). Similarly, Fernando del Pulgar's *Crónica de los Reyes Católicos* (1493) borrowed Livy's Roman literary style to emphasize the divine favor whereby the monarchs of Castile and Aragon vanquished their Moorish foes and conquered new lands (von Ostenfeld-Suske 2012a: 430–433). These histories served the Crown's political aims by presenting the monarchy as a return to a classical state, instead of a divestiture of power from local communities (*behetrías*).

Given these European schemas, it is no wonder that many chronicles of the Incas repeatedly described history in terms of lineages and origins (MacCormack 2007: 49–50; cf. Julien 2000, 2012). But the chronicles did not only contain European schemas. They also suggest Inca and Andean understandings of the past that, similar to the more vernacular traditions of Europe, emphasized the social roles of material things—personified places and ancestral artifacts—in the present (Ramírez 2005). As Alfredo González-Ruibal (2014) has recently suggested, it is naïve to expect that non-Western schemas of the past accorded with European linear narratives that derived social meaning from lineages and causal sequences. Reflecting on the discussion above, it would be inaccurate to presuppose an Inca or Amerindian concept of "antiquity" that resembles the schemas of lineage and ruins that emerged when European monarchies first traced genealogy and ethnicity to Noah or other mythical sources.[7]

Among the Incas, the past was not a kind of text that could be read from inert ruins or connected to authoritative texts. Rather, things from the past acted and spoke to people in the present. The Incas used a system of knotted cords (*khipu*) to record historical information and to monitor the tribute obligations of subjects (Quilter and Urton 2002; Salomon 2004, 2015; Urton 1998, 2003). But frequently, Incas and their subjects engaged with things from the past in an effort to resolve social problems of the present or to actively experience the past, rather than to shed light on historical events or causes. Indeed, the Inca rendering inverts the causes and events of many Western notions of the past. For the Europeans, events (e.g., Julius Caesar crossing the Rubicon to take Rome) were the causes of history; for the Incas, very often, timeless forces and persons from the past acted in the present in order to make events occur (e.g., the Incas told of how boulders in Cusco helped them to defeat an invading enemy).

Several researchers have suggested that the Incas were embedded in a landscape of superhuman actors and voices who played political roles—in particular, personified places (*wak'as*) and mummies (*malquis*) (Figure 5.4) (e.g., Classen 1993; Curatola 2008: 16–18; Gose 1996; Salomon 1995). In the highland Andes, *wak'as* could be of any material or size, but they were often features of the landscape that appeared striking or odd (e.g., Acosta 1954[1590]: 144; see also Bray 2015; Chase 2015; Kosiba 2015a; van de Guchte 1999). Given these material attributes, many early Spanish sources mistranslated *wak'a* as temple or idol (e.g., Cieza 1946[1553]: 336; Pizarro 1978[1571]: 83), missing that a *wak'a* in essence was a place or a thing that denoted kinship affiliation between people, soils, and natural forces

Figure 5.4. Photographs of Inca *wak'as*, which could be modified environmental features such as rock outcrops or water sources (pictured here, major Inca origins *wak'as* at Lake Titicaca [left] and the volcanic rock of Puma Urco in Cusco [right], author's photographs), or unaltered things such as trees or corn cobs (*mamazara*) (not pictured).

(Mannheim and Salas 2015; Kosiba 2015a). This relationship was always material. It could be manifested in features in the landscape such as fields or caves, anthropogenic structures such as carved stones or architectural complexes, or human artifacts such as mummies or bones. But more specifically, it was perpetuated through material acts of feeding whereby people[8] engaged with the *wak'a* (Mannheim and Salas 2015).

There are multiple ethnohistorical and ethnographic examples of how these Inca *wak'as*, which were often things from the past, grounded collective history and identity. Inca *wak'as* operated as *lieux de mémoire* (*sensu* Nora 1989) that invoked and instantiated social memory. Combined archaeological and historical research has demonstrated that the Incas orchestrated massive state ceremonies, during which songs and dances both created and solidified memories of Cusco's foundations by naming the *wak'as* and reenacting their deeds (Kosiba 2015b). Recognizing the potency of these celebrations and their material constituents, the Spanish regime sought to ban singing and dancing (Arriaga 1968[1621]: 275), and destroy Inca tunics and artifacts (Albornoz 1989[1582]: 19; see also Cummins 2015: 183).

But the *wak'as* and the *malquis* also spoke to the present. Hence, many of the Spanish authors referred to *wak'as* and *malquis* as things through which the devil (*el demonio*) could speak (Arriaga 1968[1621]: 205; Pizarro 1978[1571]: 48, 205). A striking example of this form of speech comes from the early days of the Spanish invasion, when a young Inca captain pleaded to the *conquistador* Pedro Pizarro to help him gain an Inca nobleman's permission to marry his daughter. Pizarro agreed to the task, and later wrote:

> I, who believed that I was going to speak to some living Indian, was taken to a bundle, [like] those of these dead folk, which was seated in a litter, which held him, and on one side was the Indian spokesman who spoke for him, and on the other was the Indian woman, both sitting close to the dead man. Then, when we arrived before the dead one, the interpreter gave the message, and being thus for a short while in suspense and silence, the Indian man looked at the Indian woman (as I understand it, to find out her wish). Then, after having been thus as I relate it for some time, both the Indians replied to me that it was the will of the Lord the dead one that she go, and so the captain already mentioned carried off the Indian woman, since the Apoo [*wak'a, malqui*] … wished it [Pizarro 1921(1521): 204–205; translation from Bauer 2004: 165].

Another, more recent example comes from the work of Frank Salomon (2004) in the highland village of Tupicocha, Peru. Here, villagers used ancient *khipus* to verify narratives of the past and authorize ideas for community organization. If the *khipu* was present when a person spoke of the way things were or the way they should be, then it validated this speech in the same way as a human witness or expert. These two examples, and many others,[9] illustrate a fundamental difference between Spanish official history text, which was only a vehicle for the written word, and Inca *wak'a* or *malqui*, which was a concrete, personified thing from the past. Indeed, for the Spaniard the text was an object *in the present* through which the past was known, but for the Inca the *wak'a* and the *malqui* were entities *from the past* through which present social aims were authorized. The difference outlined here—between written texts about the past and materials from the past—influenced countless social conflicts in the early colonial era, and has undergirded longstanding academic disagreements about the nature of Inca history.[10]

Articulating Inca History

In attending to the colonial encounter in the Andes, scholars often stress an ontological distinction between Spanish writing and Inca oral performance, and this distinction has long shaped our understanding of the Andes. For instance, Cieza lamented that the absence of writing was a barrier to knowledge of the Andean past (MacCormack 2007: 39), and the anonymous source for the myths of Huarochirí, Peru bemoaned that so many Andean traditions had been lost due to the absence of writing (Ávila 1987[1598]: 41). Given this distinction between written and oral history, many scholars have concentrated on the *imposition* of Spanish history onto Andean prehistory, in particular by examining how Roman literature provided Europeans with the tropes necessary to understand the Inca Empire (MacCormack 2007),[11] or how Andean historical "narratives" may lurk between the lines of Spanish historical writing (Julien 2000, 2012; cf. Covey 2006). These scholars suggest an irreconcilable difference between Spanish and Inca modes of recounting the past. But they concentrate on the writing of history in the centers of colonial rule. Inevitably, they often cast only the Spaniards in active roles, as actors who can impose and define colonial terms, and in so doing, they suggest the Andeans were passive or conservative actors largely concerned with maintaining cultural tradition. They also neglect to inquire into other practices through which antiquity was produced.

Recognizing the limitations of such a top-down approach to historical production, other scholars have more sharply focused on the practices through which Spanish and indigenous actors alike improvised a new kind of colonial landscape and carved new historical categories from preexisting schemas (e.g., Chase 2015; Lamana 2007). Some ethnohistorians have concentrated on the indigenous ripostes and responses to colonial legal institutions and Christian doctrine (e.g., Spalding 1984; Stern 1993). Still others such as Gonzalo Lamana (2007) have sought to attribute a somewhat equivalent degree of agency to both Spaniard and Andean by examining what Gloria Anzaldúa and Walter Mignolo have called "border thinking"— the concepts and practices that actors forged through the recombination of different forms of knowledge at the borders of colonial power (e.g., Anzaldúa 1999; Mignolo 2000; Mignolo and Tlostanova 2006: 206). Lamana (2007) suggests a semiotic struggle in which both Andeans and Spaniards attempted to redefine the essential signs of one another's cultural schemas in an effort to both understand and redirect the colonial predicament. Though this approach provides needed attention to political maneuvering within the colonial encounter, it largely focuses on the agency of Andean and Spanish actors, depicting how they creatively manipulated the cultural schemas and signs of their adversaries. We are left to wonder how preexisting cultural materials, precisely because of their materiality, influenced these actors as they endeavored to define the Andean past and shape the colonial present. In other words, we might build on and complement Lamana's work to ask: how did the stones and *wak'as* of the Incas, which persisted as visible and salient reminders of a recent (and recently deposed) Inca social order, affect colonial discourses about antiquity?

I suggest we shift our examination from an inquiry into cultural imposition and semiotic improvisation, to a study of the materials and sites that drew both Andeans and Spaniards into contests over the things that could stand for history. For instance, the archaeologist Steven Wernke (2013) contends that "community" became a particularly contested social concept during Spanish colonization: simultaneously a claim to local indigenous identity, a category for colonial administration, and a target of colonial power. Community, materialized in Andean towns and field boundaries, thus served as a site of articulation for local and colonial, commoner and elite, lay and ecclesiastical agendas, all of which focused on bounding a physical entity and space (whether Andean village or Spanish parish) that would represent the historical and traditional foundation of social life. Similarly, specific places and materials came to articulate different visions of history. For instance, Carolyn Dean (1998, 2010: Ch. 4) examined how the Spaniards in Cusco built the foundations of their cathedral and their palatial homes by tearing apart the Inca fortress and temple of Saqsaywaman. Though the Spaniards sought to materialize the domination of Cusco by transposing these materials, many of the immense stones of the principal façade of Saqsaywaman could not be moved. These stones, and their implicit invocation of Inca power, remained. Over time the immovable stones came to articulate multiple imaginaries of the past, whether Pan-Andean identity, Peruvian nationalism, or tourist expectations of ancient grandeur (Dean 2010: 147–161).

In these instances, the material things of the Andean landscape, whether Inca monuments or indigenous land divisions, presented obstacles to a nascent colonial order bent on organizing space according to European values and models. These things became what I term *sites of articulation*: materials that because of their enduring materiality or location resisted redefinition and came to be important to Spanish, Inca, and other Andean conceptions of the past. *Wak'as* in particular were sites of articulation essential to both Spanish and indigenous claims about the past.

Case One: The *Wak'a* as Mute Object

Many Andean *wak'as* and *malquis* lost their voices during the Inca social crisis that began with the civil war between Inca emperors and ended with Spanish colonization. This is because Spaniards often used their own schemas to categorize the *wak'as* as representations of the past, rather than things from the past. In other words, it would be wrong to assume that Spaniards at this time simply subscribed to a modern Christian or Cartesian ontology in which material things such as rocks, rivers, and relics were inanimate objects. In contrast, the Spaniards distinguished things that could speak, recognizing that some things, if pregnant with the Christian "holy spirit," could act and affect social life in positive ways, while others (in this case, Andean things through which the devil spoke), could not. Hence, these latter things needed to be converted into mute objects. As history came to be manifested in written words, places dedicated to *wak'as* were reduced to ruin and mummies were burned. But the *wak'as* did not die: rather, they became sites through which different actors staked claims to the past.

Early litigation documents from the Cusco region are throwing new light on claims to the past during the colonization of the Andes. Such documents reveal the court procedures and practices through which both indigenous and Spanish petitioners employed, mixed, and invented cultural schemas to delimit land and claim resources. The documents considered here are from early seventeenth-century land disputes and inspections (*visitas*) regarding the Inca urban complex of Ollantaytambo, which comprised an extensive archipelago of settlements and fields (see Kosiba 2015a; Archivo Regional de Cusco [ARC]. 1557–1729. Fondo: Beneficencia Pública, Sección: Colegio de Ciencias, legajo 46:fol. 11v-12; Archivo General de la Nación [AGN]. 1576. Fondo: Real Audiencia "Causas Civiles," legajo 15, cuaderno 77) (Figure 5.5). At Ollantaytambo, Inca monuments and *wak'as* adjoined striking environmental features, such as caves and springs, making it appear as though Inca power arose from the earth itself (see also Dean 2010). The

Figure 5.5. Ollantaytambo, an extensive Inca urban landscape and agricultural system (author's photograph).

boulders and features, many of which were *wak'as*, materialized an Inca claim that their social order was as old as the bedrock.

These constructions were relatively new at the time of the Spanish invasion. Ollantaytambo was established at the apex of Inca rule, during the mid-fifteenth century when the Incas ordered laborers to channelize the Vilcanota and Patacancha rivers, which intersected where the city's center would be built (Kosiba 2015a: 174–175; Protzen 1993). The laborers built streets and terraced fields in areas that would have been inundated when the rivers rose during annual wet seasons. Situated in Inca lands far from their kin, these laborers built and recognized *wak'as* in the new environment (Kosiba 2015a; for comparable cases, see Chase 2015; Makowski 2002, 2015). The establishment of these *wak'as* would have framed agricultural labor on Inca land in terms of an Andean idiom of kin affiliations to the soil.

These *wak'as* were short lived, and quickly reduced to ruins. Shortly after the Spanish invasion, the Inca ruler Manco converted Ollantaytambo's temples into a fortress where he scored a victory against the Spaniards. He then retreated, and the Inca administrator (*kuraka*) in the city answered to the new Spanish authority (*encomendero*), Hernán Pizarro. The labor population drastically decreased throughout the sixteenth century, as many indigenous Andeans died from Spanish diseases or fled to avoid tribute obligations (Glave and Remy 1983). Lands were left fallow, Inca buildings were reduced to ruin, and canals were rendered dysfunctional (Biblioteca Nacional del Perú [BNP]. 1629. Fondo: Manuscritos, Documento B-1030:fol. 89–158). Enterprising Spanish monasteries sought to claim many of Ollantaytambo's fields and canals, using the pretense that these resources had previously been harvested for the Inca cult of the Sun, and did not have a rightful owner (Burns 1999; BNP 1629:fol. 89–158). The city's laborers and *kurakas* argued against these claims, at times referring to the *wak'as* to suggest that they had cared for these lands since time immemorial.

Thus the *wak'as* became ruins as they became material evidence in colonial courtroom dramas. A comprehensive set of land partition (*repartimiento*) documents details the process by which laborers, *kurakas*, and monasteries sought to claim these lands (ARC 1557–1729; ARC 1568–1722. Fondo: Educandas, legajo 2; BNP 1629:fol. 89–158; see also Burns 1999; Kosiba 2015a). In particular, one of the documents contains a curious description of a *wak'a* named *Hatun Kancha Raqay*, a ceremonial complex and boulder next to the village of Pachar at the eastern entrance to Ollantaytambo (ARC 1557–1729) (Figure 5.6). The document reveals that, during Inca times, the *wak'a* personified Mama Ocllo, an Inca queen (*coya*), cited in the document as the mother of the emperor Huayna Capac who lived a generation before the conquest (ARC 1557–1729:fol. 181, 181v, 182). The *wak'a* and its adjoining

Figure 5.6. The boulder of Hatun Kancha at Pachar personified the Inca ruler Mama Ocllo. Large Inca buildings and walls adjoined the boulder, demarcating the space of the *wak'a* (author's photographs).

lands were dedicated to the Inca nobility and the cult of the Sun, and they were the responsibility of sequestered female workers (*mamakuna*) whom the Incas had transplanted from the nearby town of Maras (ARC 1557–1729:fol. 181v). My 2006 archaeological survey clarified that the *wak'a* was established when the laborers constructed Ollantaytambo and its fields—the boulder partially supported a canal that brought water from a nearby spring to the newly constructed Inca fields along the river banks. Furthermore, recent excavations substantiate this point, suggesting that the *wak'a* complex was constructed in the later, imperial phase of the Inca Empire (Solís Diaz and Olazábal 1998).

In the documents, petitioners categorized the *wak'a* as a ruin from the bygone Inca era. In a petition from 1574, a Spanish administrator in Cusco named Hernando Bachicao stated that he had inspected fields near Ollantaytambo to record land parcels and identify uncultivated lands (ARC 1557–1729:fol. 181). He described Hatun Kancha Raqay, stating that this was a place where the Inca used to conduct sacrifices, associating the *wak'a* with olden times (ARC 1557–1729:fol. 181). Bachicao portrayed Pachar in ruins, lending evidentiary support to his claims by stating that people who lived nearby told him in their language, which he could understand (*el qual dixo en su lengua e yo lo entendi como hombre que entiende y sabe su lengua*), that this town and its *wak'a* had been abandoned for as long as anyone could remember. The petition drew on specific witnesses, such as Francisco Manya Ura the mayor of Ollantaytambo, as well as Don Sancho Usca Paucar from the town of Maras, both of whom added that nobody had revered or used the *wak'a* since the Incas' departure and defeat. These statements not only describe an Inca ruin, but also solidify an emerging definition of an "Inca period," facts about which could only be known through ruins and memories.[12]

By gathering evidence that this *wak'a* was a ruin, Bachicao manipulated an Andean framing of relationships between people and places, which saw the *wak'a* as a founding ancestor who spoke for its people. The *wak'a*, abandoned and redefined as ruins, became a mute evidentiary object—that is, a token of a type and an artifact that stood for a period.

When these *wak'as* and their fields became objects of knowledge in the courtroom, they were classified according to a Spanish logic of value that ranked things and spaces depending on their use and chronological position, rather than their social roles (see also Chase 2015; Ramírez 2005). In 1629 the Spanish administrator Luis Enríquez arbitrated a hearing about agricultural lands and their use in Ollantaytambo, a hearing that was regrettably necessary because so many of the town's inhabitants had died since the last land apportionment (*repartimiento*) by Alonso Maldonado de Torres in 1591 (BNP 1629:fols. 68v, 159, 163; see also Glave and Remy 1983). The majority of depositions in the hearing concerned whether land was vacant (e.g., BNP 1629:fols. 186, 188, 209), a definition of value that pivoted on public memory of who had cared for the land, and public agreement on whether the land had been neglected and was not productive. For instance, in arguing for the right to plant wheat in the fields of Tambobamba and Colcabamba of Ollantaytambo, the Mercederian convent in Cusco stated that it is clear these lands had been deserted (BNP 1629; see detailed synopsis in Burns 1999). As in Pachar, these depositions contain multiple references to ruins (ancient towns from Inca times, or *pueblos antiguos de tiempo de ynga*) and suggest a defunct social order of *wak'as* and fields for the Sun, a period relegated to history (ARC 1568–1722:fols. 402, 435v).

At the same time, Andean people began to stake claims to land by referring to Inca ruins. Such depositions use the ruins as evidence that an indigenous ethnic group cared for the lands in question for as long as anyone can remember. They reveal that Andeans learned and manipulated European schemas of the past, which ground history in empirical evidence and material representations, rather than social relationships with things and land. Indeed, references to an Inca time beyond memory, or time immemorial (*tiempo ynmemorial*), are common statements within 1576 hearings pertaining to Amaybamba, an Inca estate near Ollantaytambo (AGN 1576). Archaeological research confirms information from the documentary record, showing that the Incas transplanted workers from distant provinces to build and care for this estate (Wilkinson 2013). In 1568 hearings, the former *kuraka* Don Juan Yanqui Yupanqui staked a claim to lands by citing grants from the Inca emperor (*Ynga Yupanqui*), structures (*casas de camayos*), and boundary markers (*mojones*) (AGN 1576:fols. 71–75). In this case, then, the *kuraka* refers to the historical establishment of an Inca estate to, somewhat ironically, claim that specific lands had been the responsibility of his people since time immemorial. As with the Spanish claims about abandoned Inca lands, these court proceedings converted Inca sites into mute objects of history, and defined the "Inca period" (*tiempo de los yngas*) as a bygone era.

Case Two: The Death of a *Wak'a*

The Ollantaytambo example illustrates how *wak'as* were divested of their personhood as they came to be used as evidence of antiquity, an Inca period, or a time beyond memory. It shows how this occurred, in part, through legal proceedings. But the process by which *wak'as* were converted to representations of the past was also a material process that happened on the ground. In many cases, the Spaniards and their indigenous allies physically ruined places that obstructed their claims about the nature of the Andean past and the character of colonial society.

The colonial era destruction often focused on *wak'as* (e.g., Griffiths 1996; Mills 2012), and was in part aimed at negating the claims to the past that the Incas had previously established. In building the landscape of Cusco, the Incas dedicated several ritual complexes and *wak'as* to events or beings that were said to have occurred or existed in the past (see Kosiba 2015b). This landscape centered on *wak'as* that embodied the Inca ancestors, and foremost among them was the *wak'a* Huanacauri (Figure 5.7), embedded in the rock of a mountain that bore the same name. My excavations at the small ceremonial complex on this mountaintop demonstrate that the Incas constructed the temple of their most ancient deity during their period of imperial expansion, in the early fifteenth century. The construction of Huanacauri was essential to an Inca effort to consolidate the identity of a Cusco elite by establishing a *wak'a*—a place that was a founding ancestor (Kosiba 2015b). How did this place, designed to *embody* the living past within the present, come to *represent* the past as a bygone era?

Huanacauri was one of most important *wak'as* in the Inca Empire. According to legend, one of the first Incas joined his flesh to the stone of this 4,120 m peak, becoming a deity who materialized Inca sovereignty. Huanacauri exemplified the Incas' claim that they were unique beings who

Figure 5.7. View from the mountaintop of Huanacauri toward the city of Cusco. The Incas recognized this place as a sacred and ancient site where their ancestors first saw, appropriated, and then founded their capital (author's photograph).

alone held the capacity to ally with superhuman telluric forces in their effort to cultivate order throughout an unruly Andean landscape. Such claims were declared through the retelling of myths during performances and processions, such as the Capac Raymi ceremony. In these ceremonies, initiates to the Inca elite personally engaged with and perceived the powerful *wak'as* whose heroic deeds had solidified the foundations of Inca rule. The initiates became Incas as they traversed a mythic landscape of mummies, *wak'as*, and personified mountains (*apus*). Places such as Huanacauri—perceived to be ancient entities—were essential to the constitution of this landscape and its authority. Hence, to support this claim to antiquity, the Incas built the ceremonial complex of Huanacauri on a remote mountaintop, away from centers of population. What is more, they planned the ritual procession road to Huanacauri so that it passed the abodes of mummified Inca rulers and crossed many of the Cusco Basin's largest and most visible pre-Inca ruins (Kosiba 2015b). In brief, things from the past were essential to how Incas experienced Huanacauri.

Early in the process of colonization, the Spaniards aimed to reduce this *wak'a* to ruin, an effort to strip its authority and consign it to the past. Two colonial testimonies tell of how the Spaniards attacked the Inca ceremonial complex in 1536, shortly after some of the Incas mounted a massive offensive against the Spaniards in Cusco. The historian Gonzalo Lamana (2007: 133–137) offers a compelling interpretation of these testimonies, highlighting how the Spanish attack was more a symbolic move derived from Andean precepts of warfare than it was a strategic charge undertaken because of military necessity. In this interpretation, the Spaniards appear to draw on an Andean cultural schema in which conflict required actions to weaken the enemy's *wak'a* (e.g., Acosta 1954[1590]: 160; Murúa 1962–1964[1590]: 105; Polo 1916[1571]: 38). The intention of the Spaniards is perhaps reflected in the date of Huanacauri's ruination, which coincided with Corpus Christi, the Spanish celebration of victory over non-Christian foes. The ruination also occurred soon after a major Inca ceremony: the austral Winter solstice, which honored the older persona of the Sun (Lamana 2007).

Lamana (2007) argues that to destroy Huanacauri on this date signaled a fundamental change in the Inca social order. Although compelling, this interpretation suggests that the Spaniards orchestrated the attack by drawing on their knowledge of Andean belief systems in an effort to redefine or erase this place. Though their knowledge certainly informed their actions to some degree, my excavations in the ceremonial complex of Huanacauri reveal that there was more to this story. The excavations revealed that the invading party burnt and toppled the walls of at least three of the seven buildings in the Inca complex (Figure 5.8). In particular, a building that the Incas had

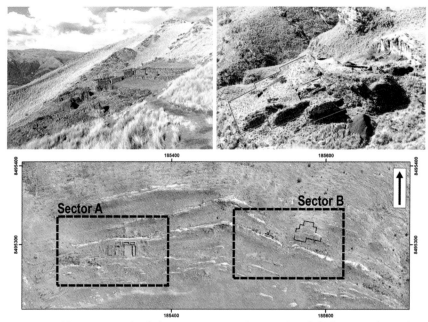

Figure 5.8. Huanacauri is divided into two sectors. Sector A (top left) features a large plaza and was likely used for theatrical feasting and beer (*chicha*) drinking ceremonies. Sector B features a jagged boulder *wak'a* enclosed within a zig-zag wall (author's photographs).

Figure 5.9. Our 2014 excavations (which are ongoing) in Sector A revealed a dense layer of *chicha* service and fermentation vessels broken *in situ* and covered with ash from the burnt roof, as well as a thin layer of red clay (author's photograph).

previously used for processing and fermenting beer (*chicha*) was the site of violent demolition. Broken vessels, ashes, and maize kernels lay *in situ* on the clay floor of this structure, indicating that its destruction was quick and complete (Figure 5.9). The excavations uncovered a layer of burnt wood and grass (*paja*), suggesting that the attackers torched the roof of the structure, which collapsed onto its floor. The walls of this structure fell inward, either from the heat of the burning roof or removal of their stones.

It appears as though the attackers destroyed Huanacauri according to Andean practices of decommissioning, or they worked with Andean people to destroy the complex.[13] That is, they not only attacked it close to a date significant for the Incas, but they also razed it by employing some of the same techniques that the Incas themselves used to annul the power of rival *wak'as* or potent sites. Indeed, the evidence suggests careful practices of burial and decommissioning, rather than wanton acts of destruction. At Huanacauri, the attacking party placed large *chicha* vessels (*aríbalas*) containing burnt organic matter or offerings of animals in the doorways of buildings. They laid cut andesite stones atop these vessels, forming false thresholds that blocked the doorways (Figure 5.10). Then, they spread red clay above these stones and vessels—in particular, clay gathered from the same (distant) source that was used to build Huanacauri. In other instances, they smashed large vessels directly in front of the doorways, signaling that they had annulled the social role of these buildings. What is more, in the ashes of the collapsed roofs, they placed offerings or sacrifices of particular animals, such as vicuña and predatory birds, known to hold value for the Incas. These materials suggest a conscious effort to not only destroy, but to inter the site. These data are strikingly similar to the destruction sequences recorded at sites that the Incas appropriated or rebuilt, such as Wat'a and Matagua, where excavations uncovered layered deposits of ash, broken vessels, and clay, indicating a ritual process of site interment (Catalán and Mantúfar 2007; Kosiba 2012, 2015b).

The destruction of Huanacauri signaled the end of the Inca, a signal that allowed for the emergence of discourses about a bygone Inca period (*tiempos de los yngas*). Though it is likely that few people participated in the destruction of Huanacauri, many witnessed it. Our excavations uncovered 190 square meters of terrain on the mountaintop, including areas both within and beyond the ceremonial complexes. Almost all of these units revealed a thin (5–7 cm) ash layer above the occupation levels. This layer contained pieces of evenly distributed charcoal, tiny bits of charred animal bone, and concentrations of burnt organic material, suggesting that a conflagration covered the entire summit. Huanacauri's lofty peak is covered in dry grass, and the invading party attacked at the height of the Andean dry season. Hence it is probable that when they torched the buildings they

Figure 5.10. Excavations at Huanacauri revealed the practices by which Spaniards put this *wak'a* to death in 1536. In the building pictured here, test excavations revealed a sequence of decommissioning, including: a false threshold (a line of rocks that closed off the doorway) (top); a smashed *chicha* storage vessel with a burnt guinea pig (*cuy*) offering (middle); and the original, burnt threshold of the door (bottom). The excavations found evidence for similar sequences in three other buildings of the site, revealing that Andean people participated in or directed the destruction of the Inca *wak'a* (author's photographs).

inadvertently (or intentionally) lit a fire that burned the mountaintop. The death of Huanacauri would have been an event visible to people in Cusco, who would have perceived a sign of the end of Inca times as their *wak'a* was buried and burned.

In destroying Huanacauri, the invading party converted this *wak'a* into a ruin. More particularly, they sought to convert it into a dead ruin, and a mute object that could no longer speak to the present. By burning the mountain in this way, they transformed the very foundation of Cusco into a visible signal that the reign of the Inca was in the past. The process of interment suggests reverence for the site. In short, the attack on Huanacauri demonstrates how Spanish and Andean actors likely combined cultural schemas in a performance that transformed a living ancestor into an inert artifact. In these practices, we see an effort to redefine this place as a token of a type—an object from a bygone era and a representation of antiquity.

Ancient Artifice? Or the Politics of Antiquity

In early colonial Cusco, Andean and Spanish actors became embroiled in culturally and politically inflected struggles over the meaning and role of particular ruins. They often sought to convert these places from the Inca past into evidentiary artifacts that suited present concerns or representations of a past. Many Andean people used the courtroom to project their stories of olden times, attributing a deep past to the lands that their forbears had recently worked and maintained under the Incas. *Wak'as* became evidence for these claims. Emphasized in this way, these *wak'as* were no longer subjects from a particular past that actively spoke in the present; rather, they became mute objects that represented a general past to a public audience. Similarly, Spaniards and their allies produced ruins on the ground by physically converting *wak'as* and other Inca monuments to artifacts of Inca times—that is, things no longer in use. In both cases, the social roles of *wak'as* and Inca buildings had drastically changed. Reduced to ruins, they no longer held value through their own discourse, so they became discursive signifiers of antiquity.

In these practices, the Inca Empire was reduced to ruins. The ruination of the Inca Empire required the deployment of both Spanish and Andean schemas to redefine particular *wak'as* as knowable objects, whether proof of a flood, signs of abandonment, landmarks of deep antiquity, or memories of past land use. The process was selective, which raises a question of how some places come to stand for colonial processes and historical events, while others do not (Stoler 2013: 5). In courtrooms and on the ground, Andeans and Spaniards highlighted places that they deemed appropriate and acceptable for presenting a past while disregarding others (see Grazia Lolla 2003: 12). The *wak'as*, recognized as ancient sites by both Andean and Spaniard, became the basis for a developing colonial idiom that was mutually understandable to all parties. By pointing to *wak'as* and other Inca structures, Andean people could claim that their community existed since time immemorial, and consequently, they could secure their rights to land and resources. Similarly, in emphasizing particular *wak'as* that were no longer in use, Spaniards were able to justify their appropriation of land that had previously been dedicated to the Inca and to the Sun. But these were not simply strategic maneuvers in the courtroom. For the *wak'as*, which were ubiquitous sites in the landscape and embodiments of the Andean past, were impossible to ignore. Because of their enduring materiality, they had to be converted into legible objects of history if Spaniards and Andeans were to negotiate land claims within the new colonial terrain.

In consequence, the *wak'as* themselves were conceptually converted and physically destroyed. This process of conversion pivoted on what Mannheim (2015) (drawing on Quine) calls "radical translation," i.e., a situation in which there was no scaffolding, no manuals, no courses, and no competent interpreters. In such a dialogue, there is a strong probability of "transduction," when the source material, which is always bound to context and essential associations, was: "[re]contextualized in specific ways into configurations of semiosis of a sort substantially or completely different from those … started with." (Silverstein 2003: 91). This does not imply miscomprehension, *per se*. Rather, it suggests an effort to establish equivalence between an Andean sign (e.g., *wak'a*) and a European sign (e.g., ancient ruin), both of which manifest and invoke the past but in markedly different ways. This effort entailed a process of transduction by which some if not all of the meaning of the original term "*wak'a*" was lost because its particular associations were erased as it was translated from animate matter to mute artifact. In the cases discussed above, practices in the courtroom and on the ground detached *wak'as* from their *particular* semiotic associations that had long defined them—local assemblages of soils, stones, people, practices, and animals—and instead emphasized how they embodied a *general* past. These practices worked in subtle ways. With these petitions and depositions, both Andean people and Spaniards drew on their own and one another's cultural schemas to define *wak'as* as ruins, making political statements that the Inca Empire was a thing of the past.

The cases presented here provide glimpses of a broader regional phenomenon that occurred throughout the colonial Andes, and the Americas more generally. Ollantaytambo and Huanacauri only provide particular analytical points of entry to understand this phenomenon, adding to a growing body of scholarship concerned less with the opposition of Spanish and Andean cultural frameworks, and more with the variety of social dialogues and contests through which Andeans and Spaniards negotiated and shaped the colonial predicament. For instance, Alan Covey and Donato Amado's (2008) recent archival research on the Yucay Valley near Cusco reveals a series of litigation procedures by which the Spanish courts recognized an Inca royal mummy cult's claims to rich agricultural land. In this case, the Inca noblewoman Beatriz Clara Coya, who descended from the emperor Huayna Capac, argued that a 1571 Spanish land allotment and census wrongly divested her and her husband of 250 laborers who had, under the Incas, arrived with the mummy of her great-grandfather, Huayna Capac, to care for his resources (Covey and Amado 2008: 28–29, 183–184). In short, Beatriz Coya implicitly argued in Spanish court that she was the rightful manager of these laborers because of their enduring obligation to the lands of the mummy, an actor from the Inca past that, objectified in testimonies, became evidence. And she won. Moreover, at Huarochirí, Peru, Zach Chase (2015) has emphasized how some Andean kin groups such as the Checa claimed the deep past of both their central town and their essential social standing during the early colonial era. The Checa established claims to antiquity through the performance, retelling, and recording of tales that narrated the deeds of their principal *wak'as*. In particular, the myths that they recounted suggest that, similar to the cases above, their ancestors occupied the region since time immemorial, though archaeological data suggests that they likely built these places during the later Inca period (Chase 2015). As Chase cogently reminds us, these tales are political claims to the past, rather than evidence of actions and ancestry.

Such studies are shedding light on the artifice and artifacts that contribute to the politics of antiquity. In particular, they suggest that, if there is anything universal about claims to antiquity, it is that they always entail a degree of artifice—that is, a political attempt to emphasize specific objects at the expense of others and to highlight one version of the past in present terms. The cases presented here suggest that a new set of discourses and practices about antiquity began to take shape during the Andean colonial encounter. This is not to say that there were no coherent beliefs about the past during the Inca reign. However, during the colonial era beliefs about the past became a discursive complex—a conversation about the past held in particular settings, using specific schemas—that did not previously exist. This conversation pivoted on claims that certain things were evidence of the past, artifacts that contained facts. To study these claims is to inquire into the effects of discourses that seek to establish facts or truths (Foucault 1980: 94). Such a study shifts our analysis from a positivistic concern with "what really happened," as well as a constructivist concern with "how people fomented ideas about what happened." It reorients our analytical vision toward an examination of the "effects of truth claims about what happened." Because of their enduring materiality, ruins are often key constituents of these claims to antiquity.

The Inca case expands our knowledge of the historical processes during which ruins come to play social roles. The colonial encounter in the Americas was not a confrontation between coherent "cultures," each of them with a fixed ontological definition of the past that they struggled to impose on inert ruins. Prior to the invasion both the Incas and Europeans were at war with themselves, and these wars often pivoted on definitions of history. New Inca rulers were engaged in a civil war, and they were rewriting history by killing rival mummy cults and demolishing *wak'as* whose prognostications did not fit imperial designs (e.g., Topic 2015). New European monarchs were silencing local histories and razing monasteries to construct a universal history rooted in biblical and classical times. These actors ruined some valued places, while simultaneously placing value on other ruins. They elevated the importance of ruins in a political conversation that came to rely on material, measurements, and markers to make sense of the past.

The ruins that lay at the heart of claims to antiquity are not inert or passive vestiges of ancient people and practices. Rather, in situated practices and discourses they are continually called to act as witnesses, to embody a version of history, or to stand in the shadows as mute objects of an intentionally forgotten past. Like the legs of Ozymandias in the opening vignette, ruins are never "over" (Stoler 2013: 26). Ruination is a social process whereby materials from the past continually and differentially impinge on, affect, and create obstacles for the present. And not all ruins are created equal. Human agency, historical contingency, and natural processes affect how some sites are called "ruins" and seen as valued places from the past, while others are not. Ruins, as both materials in the landscape and as claims to antiquity, will preserve, decay, and hence enter into social affairs in different ways because of their matter—their material state of being—and because of the degree to which they matter to communities in the present.

Acknowledgments

I dedicate this paper to the memory of my mentor and professor, the late Michel-Rolph Trouillot, without whom few of these academic arguments would have taken shape. I thank Ben Anderson and Felipe Rojas for inviting me to submit this paper. I presented an earlier version at Brown University, and I am grateful to Parker VanValkenburgh, Stephen Silliman, Robert

Preucel, and Peter Miller for their helpful and productive comments. The current paper emerged from several conversations with esteemed scholars of the Andes, Donato Amado, Marco Curatola, and Bruce Mannheim. I am extremely grateful to these scholars for their insights, many of which are the backbone of this study. In this regard, I acknowledge the scholarship of Zach Chase and Gonzalo Lamana, whose innovative interpretations of the Colonial Andes have greatly influenced this study. I am also indebted to Jesús Galiano Blanco, with whom I worked to interpret the archival documents employed in this study. I am grateful to Rebecca Bria, Zach Chase, and Felipe Rojas, who offered invaluable comments on an earlier draft of this paper. Finally, I thank the National Geographic Society, the Brennan Foundation, and the University of Alabama, who provided funding for the archaeological and archival analyses that informed my study. All errors in this paper are my own.

Notes

1. A century after Cieza, the Jesuit priest Bernabé Cobo wrote that many of the Inca administrative stations (*tambos*) were intact and still in use.

2. I use the sixteenth- and seventeenth-century orthography for Tiahuanaco to signal that I am writing of the ruin as an object of early historiography, rather than the subject of archaeological investigation. In terms of archaeology, we know that Tiahuanaco antedated the Incas by eight centuries, and it was the center of a regional polity (Janusek 2008).

3. Writing in early seventeenth-century Spain, the mestizo chronicler "El Inca" Garcilaso de la Vega (1976[1609]: 44) notes the obvious, stating that many European readers will see these Andean stories of floods as nothing more than the imposition of Christian values and beliefs. He states that he cannot verify the credibility of Andean beliefs about a global flood, but he can testify that the people with whom he grew up in Cusco used to tell these stories.

4. There is evidence that at least some Incas or Andeans also saw Tiahuanaco as place that represented a prior epoch, or an earlier stage of humanity. The point here is that the Spaniards translated this myth into evidence for their version of a universal global history.

5. In fact, the chronicler Cristóbal de Molina (del Cusco) (1947[1573]: 28) adds that at Tiahuanaco the creator established all kinds of ontological differences, for example between species of animal, sexes of all beings, and the defining characteristics of things.

6. I thank Mariusz Ziółkowski for this observation. Indeed, in sixteenth-century Europe, despite Christian condemnations of idolatry, many local and vernacular myths persisted about the agency of ancient beings in material things, forests, or uninhabited places. The point here, though, is that the official histories in Europe establish a dominant way of seeing the past that affects how the histories of the Andes are written. Hence, we do not see references to European beliefs about animate material or anthropomorphic non-humans in *any* of the Spanish writings about the Andes.

7. There are, in fact, few archaeological data to suggest that the Incas explicitly recognized or elevated the importance of earlier Andean civilizations, such as Tiahuanaco or Chavín. There is some evidence that the Incas constructed new temples on islands in Lake Titicaca where Tiahuanaco had earlier religious spaces (Bauer and Stanish 2001); the Incas established an administrative site at Tiahuanaco (Sarmiento 1965[1572]: 257); and people near Tiahuanaco held rituals at the site during the early colonial era (Arriaga 1968[1621]: 227). But, in general terms, besides an architectural style that resembles the megalithic aesthetic of Tiahuanaco, there is very little evidence that the Incas curated earlier artifacts, moved earlier monuments, embellished earlier ruins, or staged ceremonies at ancient places. In this sense, though the Incas undoubtedly recognized the antiquity of places such as Tiahuanaco, they did so in ways that were different than their European counterparts.

8. Several authors state that ritual specialists called *Huacapvillac* heard and interpreted the *waka's* speech (Arriaga 1968[1621]: 205; Cobo 1964[1653]: 147–149; Molina 1947[1573]: 41–47; Santillán 1968[1563]: 112), but little is known about the practices through which they performed their ability to speak to the *waka's*, or whether a single *Huacapvillac* could speak to multiple *waka's*, or only one.

9. Another example comes from the meeting of the Spaniards and the Inca ruler Atahualpa in Cajamarca. In this fateful event, the Spanish priest Valverde presented a copy of Christian written word (*breviario*) to the Inca (Pizarro 1978[1571]: 37). The Inca held it, perhaps expecting it to speak because it was a sacred thing. He hurled it to the ground, and some scholars have stated that he did so because he was frustrated with this voiceless object (see interpretations in Lamana 2007; Ziółkowski 2015). Another example can be found in the myths recorded in Huarochirí, Peru, in which the creator meets the Inca ruler Huayna Capac and tells him that they must go to Lake Titicaca, where he can tell Huayna Capac of his (the creator's) existence (Avila 1987[1598]: 243). The passage indicates that the lake (a *waka*) must be present to speak of such things.

10. This is not to say that the *waka's* held absolute power. Indeed, specialists could perform rites to diminish the power of rival *waka's* (Acosta 1954[1590]: 160; Polo 1916[1571]: 38). Inca rulers sought to exterminate *waka's* such as Catequil, who spoke of a present that countered their imperial objectives (Arriaga 1968[1621]: 203; Topic 2015).

11. In a detailed study of Roman historical forms in the chronicles, MacCormack (2007: xvi) argues that classical texts were "… more than instruments of description and analysis. Rather they also became constituents of collective consciousness and identity." In other words, by dressing the Andean past in the robes of Roman antiquity, Spanish authors constituted a familiar version of history while creating a vision of themselves as rightful conquerors repeating the actions of their heroic forbears.

12. Such statements are significant because of their timing. Indeed, the Spaniards had only recently defeated the last stronghold of the Incas, in 1572.

13. Huanacauri is situated far from the center of the Inca capital, and the Spaniards would have required indigenous knowledge and guidance to ascend the mountain and identify this complex among other Inca sites (e.g., the site of Inca Raqay [Inca ruin] on another side of the mountain).

References

Abu El Haj, Nadia
    2001   *Facts on the Ground: Archaeological Practice and Territorial Self-Fashioning in Israeli Society.* University of Chicago Press, Chicago.

Acosta, José de
    1954[1590]   Historia natural y moral de las Indias. In *Biblioteca de Autores Españoles*, no. 73. Ediciones Atlas, Madrid.

Amin, Shahid
    1995   *Event, Metaphor, Memory: Chauri Chaura 1922–1992.* University of California Press, Berkeley.

Anzaldúa, Gloria
    1999   *Borderlands/La Frontera: The New Mestiza.* Aunt Lute Books, San Francisco.

Arriaga, Pablo José de
    1968[1621]   Extirpacion de la idolatria del Piru. In *Biblioteca de Autores Españoles*, no. 209 (Crónicas Peruanas de Interés Indigena), pp. 191–277. Ediciones Atlas, Madrid.

Assmann, Jan
    1997   *Moses the Egyptian: The Memory of Egypt in Western Monotheism.* Harvard University Press, Cambridge.

Ávila, Francisco de
    1987[1598]   *Ritos y tradiciones de Huarochirí del siglo XVII*, edited by G. Taylor. Instituto de Estudios Peruanos, Instituto Frances de Estudios Andinos, Lima.

Barkan, Leonard
    1999   *Unearthing the Past: Archaeology and Aesthetics in the Making of Rennaissance Culture.* Yale University Press, New Haven.

Bauer, Brian
    1998   *The Sacred Landscape of the Inca: The Cusco Ceque System.* University of Texas Press, Austin.
    2004   *Ancient Cuzco: Heartland of the Inca.* University of Texas Press, Austin.

Bauer, Brian, and Charles Stanish
    2001   *Ritual and Pilgrimage in the Ancient Andes: The Islands of the Sun and Moon.* University of Texas Press, Austin.

Betanzos, Juan de
    1968[1551]   Suma y narración de los Incas. In *Biblioteca de Autores Españoles* no. 209 (Crónicas Peruanas de Interés Indigena), pp. 1–56. Ediciones Atlas, Madrid.

Bray, Tamara (editor)
    2015   *The Archaeology of Wak'as: Explorations of the Sacred in the Pre-Columbian Andes.* University Press of Colorado, Boulder.

Burke, Peter
    1969   *The Renaissance Sense of the Past.* Edward Arnold, New York.
    2012   History, Myth, and Fiction: Facts and Debates. In *The Oxford History of Historical Writing, Volume 3: 1400–1800*, edited by José Rabasa, Masayuki Sato, Edoardo Tortarolo, and Daniel Woolf, pp. 261–281. Oxford University Press, Oxford.

Burns, Karen
1999   *Colonial Habits: Convents and the Spiritual Economy of Cuzco, Peru*. Duke
                 University Press, Durham.

Calancha, Antonio de la
1974–81[1638]   *Cronica moralizada del Orden de San Agustin en el Peru, con sucesos
                 egenplares en esta monarquia, tomos 1–6*. Ignacio Prado Pastor, Lima.

Catalán Santos, Elizabeth, and Oscar Mantúfar Latorre
2007   *Informe Final Investigación Arqueológica en el Tramo Suriwaylla-Taukaray,
                 Wanakauri, Cusco*. Report presented to the Ministerio de Cultura, Cusco, Perú.

Chartier, Roger
1997   *On the Edge of the Cliff: History, Language, and Practices*. Johns Hopkins
                 University Press, Baltimore.

Chase, Zachary
2015   What is a Wak'a? When is a Wak'a? In *The Archaeology of Wak'as:
                 Explorations of the Sacred in the Pre-Columbian Andes*, edited by Tamara
                 Bray, pp. 75–126. University Press of Colorado, Boulder.

Cieza de León, Pedro de
1946[1553]   La crónica del Perú (Primera Parte). In *Crónica de la conquista del Perú*,
                 revised and annotated by J. J. Le Riverend Brusone, pp. 127–497.
                 Editorial Nueva Espana, Mexico.
1967[1553]   El señorio de los Incas. In *La Crónica del Perú* (Segunda Parte). Instituto
                 de Estudios Peruanos, Lima.

Classen, Constance
1993   *Worlds of Sense: Exploring the Senses in History and Across Cultures*. Routledge,
                 London.

Cohen, David
1994   *The Combing of History*. University of Chicago Press, Chicago.

Covey, Alan
2006   Chronology, Succession, and Sovereignty: The Politics of Inka Historiography
                 and its Modern Interpretation. *Comparative Studies in Society and History*
                 48: 169–199.

Covey, Alan, and Donato Amado González
2008   *Imperial Transformations in Sixteenth-Century Yucay, Peru*. Memoirs of the
                 Museum of Anthropology 44. University of Michigan Press, Ann Arbor.

Cummins, Thomas
2015   Inka Art. In *The Inka Empire: A Multidisciplinary Approach*, edited by
                 Izumi Shimada, pp. 165–196. University of Texas Press, Austin.

Curatola Petrocchi, Marco
2008   La función de los oráculos en el imperio Inca. In *Adivinación y oráculos
                 en el mundo andino antiguo*, edited by Marco Curatola Petrocchi and
                 Mariusz Ziólkowski, pp. 15–69. Instituto Francés de Estudios Andinos
                 and Pontificia Universidad Católica del Perú, Lima.

de Certeau, Michel
1988   *The Writing of History*. Translated and introduced by Tom Conley.
                 Columbia University Press, New York.

Dean, Carolyn
  1998   Creating a Ruin in Colonial Cusco: Sacsahuaman and What Was Made
                  of It. *Andean Past* 5: 161–83.
  2010   *A Culture of Stone: Inka Perspectives on Rock.* Duke University Press,
                  Durham.
Garcilaso de la Vega, "El Inca"
  1965[1605]   Los Comentarios Reales de los Incas, in *Biblioteca de Autores Españoles*, nos.
                  132–135, edited by Carmelo Sáez de Santa María. Ediciones Atlas, Madrid.
Glave Testino, Luis M., and Marisa I. Remy
  1983   *Estructura agraria y vida rural en una región andina: Ollantaytambo entre
                  los siglos XVI–XIX.* Centro de Estudios Rurales Andinos Bartolomé de las
                  Casas, Cusco.
González-Ruibal, Alfredo
  2014   *An Archaeology of Resistance: Materiality and Time in an African Borderland.*
                  Rowman and Littlefield, Lanham.
Gose, Peter
  1996   Oracles, Divine Kingship and Political Representation in the Inca State.
                  Ethnohistory 43: 1–33.
  2008   *Invaders as Ancestors: On the Intercultural Making and Unmaking of Spanish
                  Colonialism in the Andes.* University of Toronto Press, Toronto.
Grazia Lolla, M.
  2003   Monuments and Texts: Antiquarianism and the Beauty of Antiquity. In
                  Tracing Architecture: The Aesthetics of Antiquarianism, edited by Dana
                  Arnold and Stephen Bending, pp. 11–30. Blackwell Publishing, Malden.
Griffiths, Nicholas
  1996   *The Cross and the Serpent: Religious Repression and Resurgence in Colonial
                  Peru.* University of Oklahoma Press, Norman.
Guha, Ranajit
  1983   The Prose of Counter-Insurgency. In *Subaltern Studies II: Writings on South
                  Asia History and Society*, edited by R. Guha, pp. 45–86. Oxford University
                  Press, Delhi.
Hemming, John
  1970   *The Conquest of the Incas.* MacMillan, London.
Hutson, Scott
  2010   *Dwelling, Identity, and the Maya: Relational Archaeology at Chunchucmil.*
                  Altamira Press, Lanham.
Janusek, John
  2008   *Ancient Tiwanaku.* Cambridge University Press, Cambridge.
Julien, Catherine
  2000   *Reading Inca History.* University of Iowa Press, Iowa City.
  2012   Inca Historical Forms. In *The Oxford History of Historical Writing, Volume
                  3: 1400–1800*, edited by José Rabasa, Masayuki Sato, Edoardo Tortarolo,
                  and Daniel Woolf, pp. 619–639. Oxford University Press, Oxford.
Kolata, Alan L.
  2013   *Ancient Inca.* Cambridge University Press, Cambridge.

Kosiba, Steve

2012	Emplacing Value, Cultivating Order: Places of Conversion and Practices of Subordination throughout Early Inka State Formation (Cusco, Perú). In *The Construction of Value in the Ancient World*, edited by John K. Papadopoulos and Gary Urton, pp. 97–127. Cotsen Institute of Archaeology, Los Angeles.

2015a	Of Blood and Soil: Tombs, Wak'as, and the Naturalization of Social Difference in the Inka Heartland. In *The Archaeology of Wak'as: Explorations of the Sacred in the PreColumbian Andes*, edited by Tamara Bray, pp. 167–212. University Press of Colorado, Boulder.

2015b	Tracing the Inca Past: Ritual Movement and Social Memory in the Inca Imperial Capital. In *Perspectives on the Inca*, edited by Monica Barnes, Inés de Castro, Javier Flores Espinoza, Doris Kurella, and Karoline Noack, pp. 178–205. Linden-Museum, Stuttgart.

Lamana, Gonzalo

2007	*Domination without Dominance: Inca-Spanish Encounters in Early Colonial Peru*. Duke University Press, Durham.

Linehan, Peter

1993	*History and Historians of Medieval Spain*. Clarendon Press, Oxford.

Lizarraga, Reginaldo de

1968[1605]	Descripción breve de toda la tierra del Perú, Tucumán, Rió de La Plata y Chile. In *Biblioteca de Autores Españoles*, no. 216, pp. 1–213. Ediciones Atlas, Madrid.

Maas, Michael

1992	*John Lydus and the Roman Past: Antiquarianism and Politics in the Age of Justinian*. Routledge, London.

MacCormack, Sabine

2007	*On the Wings of Time: Rome, the Incas, Spain, and Peru*. Princeton University Press, Princeton.

Makowski, Krzysztof

2002	Arquitectura, estilo e identidad en el horizonte tardío: el sitio de Pueblo Viejo-Pucará, Valle de Lurín. *Boletín de Arqueología PUCP* 6: 137–170.

2015	Pachacamac—Old Wak'a or Inka Syncretic Deity? Imperial Transformation of the Sacred Landscape in the Lower Ychsma (Lurín) Valley. In *Archaeology of Wak'as: Explorations of the Sacred in the Pre-Columbian Andes*, edited by Tamara Bray, pp. 127–166. University Press of Colorado, Boulder.

Mannheim, Bruce

2015	All Translation is Radical Translation. In *Translating Worlds: The Epistemological Space of Translation*, edited by Carlo Severi and William F. Hanks, pp. 199–220. Hau Books, Chicago.

Mannheim, Bruce, and Guillermo Salas Carreño

2015	Wak'a: Entifications of the Andean Sacred. In *The Archaeology of Wak'as: Explorations of the Sacred in the PreColumbian Andes*, edited by Tamara Bray, pp. 47–74. University Press of Colorado, Boulder.

Marx, Karl

1994[1852]	*The Eighteenth Brumaire of Louis Bonaparte*. International Publishers, New York.

Mena, Cristóbal de
  1930[1534]   La conquista del Perú, llamada la Nueva Castilla. In *The Anonymous La
                  Conquista del Perú (Seville, April 1534) and the Libro Vitimo del Summario
                  delle Indie Occidentali (Venica, October 1534)*, edited by Alexander Pogo, pp.
                  218–281. Proceedings of the American Academy of Arts and Sciences, Boston.

Mignolo, Walter
  2000   *Local Histories/Global Designs: Coloniality, Subaltern Knowledges, and Border
                  Thinking.* Princeton University Press, Princeton.

Mignolo, Walter, and Madina Tlostanova
  2006   Theorizing from the Borders: Shifting to Geo- and Body-Politics of
                  Knowledge. *European Journal of Social Theory* 9: 205–221.

Mills, Kenneth
  1997   *Idolatry and Its Enemies: Colonial Andean Religion and Extirpation, 1640–
                  1750.* Princeton University Press, Princeton.

Molina, Cristóbal de (del Cuzco)
  1947[1573]   *Ritos y fábulas de los incas.* Colección Eurindia 14. Editorial Futuro, Buenos Aires.

Niranjana, Tejaswini
  1992   *Siting Translation: History, Post-Structuralism, and the Colonial Context.*
                  University of California Press, Berkeley.

Nora, Pierre
  1989   Between Memory and History: Les lieux de mémoire. *Representations* 26:
                  7–24.

Obeyesekere, Gananath
  1992   *The Apotheosis of Captain Cook.* Princeton University Press, Princeton.

Pizarro, Pedro
  1921[1571]   *Relation of the Discovery and Conquest of the Kingdoms of Peru*, translated
                  and annotated by P. Means. New York Cortes Society, New York.
  1965[1571]   Relación del descubrimiento y conquista de los reinos del Perú. In *Biblioteca
                  de Autores Españoles,* no. 168, pp. 162–242. Ediciones Atlas, Madrid.

Polo de Ondegardo, Juan de
  1917[1571]   Informaciónes acerca de la religión y gobierno de los incas (Segunda parte).
                  Colección de Libros y Documentos Referentes a la Historia del Perú, serie
                  1, tomo 4, pp. 3–204. Imprenta y Libreria Sanmarti y Ca, Lima.

Protzen, Jean-Pierre
  1993   *Inca Architecture and Construction at Ollantaytambo.* Oxford University Press,
                  Oxford.

Quilter, Jeffrey, and Gary Urton
  2002   *Narrative Threads: Acounting and Recounting in Andean Khipu.* University
                  of Texas Press, Austin.

Ramírez, Susan
  2005   *To Feed and Be Fed: The Cosmological Bases of Authority and Identity in the
                  Andes.* Stanford University Press, Stanford.

Sahlins, Marshall
  1981   *Historical Metaphors and Mythical Realities.* University of Michigan Press, Ann Arbor.
  1985   *Islands of History.* University of Chicago Press, Chicago.

Salomon, Frank

1995   "The Beautiful Grandparents": Andean Ancestor Shrines and Mortuary
                Ritual as Seen through Colonial Records. In *Tombs for the Living: Andean
                Mortuary Practices*, edited by Tom D. Dillehay, pp. 315–353. Dumbarton
                Oaks, Washington, DC.

1999   Testimonies: The Making and Reading of Native South American
                Historical Sources. In *The Cambridge History of Native Peoples of the
                Americas, Volume III, South America*, edited by Frank Salomon and Stuart
                B. Schwartz, pp. 19–95. Cambridge University Press, Cambridge.

2004   *The Cord-Keepers*. Duke University Press, Durham, NC.

2015   Inkas through Texts: The Primary Sources. In *The Inka Empire: A
                Multidisciplinary Approach*, edited by Izumi Shimada, pp. 23–28. University
                of Texas Press, Austin.

Salomon, Frank, and George Urioste (editors)

1991   *The Huarochirí Manuscript: A Testament of Ancient and Colonial Andean
                Religion*. University of Texas Press, Austin.

Santillán, Hernando de

1968[1563]   Relación del orígen, descendencia, política y gobierno de los incas. In
                Biblioteca de Autores Españoles, no. 209, pp. 97–149. Ediciones Atlas,
                Madrid.

Sarmiento de Gamboa, Pedro

1965[1572]   Historia de los Incas. In *Biblioteca de Autores Españoles*, no. 135, pp. 193–
                279. Ediciones Atlas, Madrid.

Schaff, Adam

1976   *History and Truth*. Pergamon Press, Oxford.

Sewell, William

1992   *Logics of History: Social Theory and Social Transformation*. University of
                Chicago Press, Chicago.

Silverstein, Michael

2003   Translation, Transduction, Transformation: Skating "Glossando" on
                Thin Semiotic Ice. In *Translating Cultures: Perspectives on Translation and
                Anthropology*, edited by Paula G. Rubel and Abraham Rosman, pp. 75–108.
                Berg, Oxford.

Solís Diaz, Francisco, and Nancy Olazábal

1998   Arqueología de Pachar: una introducción a su pasado. Unpublished
                Licenciatura thesis in Archaeology. Facultad de Ciencias Sociales,
                Universidad Nacional de San Antonio Abad del Cusco (UNSAAC), Cusco,
                Peru.

Stern, Steven

1993[1982]   *Peru's Indian Peoples and the Challenge of Spanish Conquest: Huamanga to
                1640*. University of Wisconsin Press, Madison.

Stoler, Ann (editor)

2013   *Imperial Debris: On Ruins and Ruination*. Duke University Press, Durham.

Todorov, Tzevetan

1995   *The Morals of History*. University of Minnesota Press, Minneapolis.

Topic, John
    2015   Final Reflections: Catequil as One Wak'a among Many. In *The Archaeology
                    of Wak'as: Explorations of the Sacred in the PreColumbian Andes*, edited by
                    Tamara Bray, pp. 369–396. University Press of Colorado, Boulder.
Trouillot, Michel-Rolph
    1995   *Silencing the Past: Power and the Production of History.* Beacon Press,
                    Boston.
Urton, Gary
    1990   *The History of a Myth: Pacariqtambo and the Origin of the Inkas.* University
                    of Texas Press, Austin.
    1998   From Knots to Narratives: Reconstructing the Art of Historical Record
                    Keeping in the Andes from Spanish Transcriptions of Inka Khipus.
                    Ethnohistory 45: 409–438.
    2003   *Signs of the Inka Khipu: Binary Coding in the Andean Knotted-String Records.*
                    University of Texas Press, Austin.
van de Guchte, Maarten
    1999   The Inca Cognition of Landscape: Archaeology, Ethnohistory, and
                    the Aesthetic of Alterity. In *Archaeologies of Landscape: Contemporary
                    Perspectives*, edited by Wendy Ashmore and A. Bernard Knapp, pp.
                    149–168. Blackwell, Malden.
Vine, Angus
    2010   *In Defiance of Time: Antiquarian Writing in Early Modern England.* Oxford
                    University Press, Oxford.
Von Ostenfeld-Suske, Kira
    2012a   Writing Official History in Spain: History and Politics, c. 1474–1600. In
                    The Oxford History of Historical Writing, Volume 3: 1400–1800, edited by
                    José Rabasa, Masayuki Sato, Edoardo Tortarolo, and Daniel Woolf, pp.
                    428–448. Oxford University Press, Oxford.
    2012b   A New History for a "New World": The First One Hundred Years
                    of Hispanic New World Historical Writing. In *The Oxford History
                    of Historical Writing, Volume 3: 1400–1800*, edited by José Rabasa,
                    Masayuki Sato, Edoardo Tortarolo, and Daniel Woolf, pp. 556–574.
                    Oxford University Press, Oxford.
Wernke, Steven
    2013   *Negotiated Settlements: Andean Communities and Landscapes under Inka and
                    Spanish Colonialism.* University Press of Florida, Gainesville.
Wilkinson, Darryl
    2013   Politics, Infrastructure and Non-Human Subjects: The Inka Occupation
                    of the Amaybamba Cloud Forests. Unpublished PhD dissertation,
                    Department of Anthropology, Columbia University, New York.
Wilmer, Franke
    1993   *The Indigenous Voice in World Politics: Since Time Immemorial.* Sage
                    Publications, London.
Yannakakis, Yanna
    2008   *The Art of Being In-Between: Native Intermediaries, Indian Identity, and
                    Local Rule in Colonial Oaxaca.* Duke University Press, Durham.

Unpublished Colonial Documents

Archivo General de la Nación (AGN). 1559–60. Fondo: Derecho Indígena, legajo 31, cuaderno 614.

Archivo General de la Nación (AGN). 1576. Fondo: Real Audiencia "Causas Civiles," legajo 15, cuaderno 77.

Archivo Regional de Cusco (ARC). 1557–1729. Fondo: Beneficencia Pública, Sección: Colegio de Ciencias, legajo 46 (previously labeled as 26B).

Archivo Regional de Cusco (ARC). 1568–1722. Fondo: Educandas, legajo 2.

Biblioteca Nacional del Perú (BNP). 1629. Fondo: Manuscritos, Documento B-1030.

Inventing the Antiquities of New Spain: Motolinía and the Mexican Antiquarian Traditions

Giuseppe Marcocci

Antiquarian Convergences across the Atlantic

Arnaldo Momigliano (1950) associates the origins of antiquarianism with the Renaissance. What emerged in Europe between the fifteenth and seventeenth centuries, however, was just an early modern variant of a more widespread attitude towards the past, which had precedents in many cultures and societies across time and around the globe (Miller 2012; Schnapp et al. 2014). It was the antiquarian practices of Central Mexico under the Aztec Empire (1428–1521) that the still fledgling European antiquarian approaches initially encountered when they crossed the Atlantic in the early sixteenth century. The first Spaniards who wrote about pre-Hispanic Mexico showed increasing sensitivity to its remains and developed a clear interest in architectonic ruins, stone images, votive objects, and other relics. But how did they deploy their European antiquarian attitudes to the analysis of the material reality of Central Mexico? What was the effect of their interactions with native interpreters of local antiquities?

This article aims to explore mutual exchanges and reactions that contributed to the birth of colonial antiquarianism in the Americas. Although this hypothesis entails the idea of cultural commensurability, post-conquest Mexico did not see any harmonious mélange of antiquarianisms. This was in part because European and American antiquarian traditions were built on different notions of time and the past, but also because, during contact, the persistent attachment of Aztecs to their votive objects and relics at times went alongside forms of resistance to the Spaniards, while the latter's curiosity in pre-Hispanic remains formed part of a project to establish a new political and religious order.

My main focus is on the writings of the Franciscan friar Toribio de Motolinía, the author of the earliest surviving treatise on what he called the "antiquities of the Indians of New Spain." The first part of the chapter provides a preliminary discussion of the place things from the past occupied in both pre-Hispanic Mexico and Renaissance Europe on the eve of the conquest, as well as of the importance of material culture in colonial encounters more generally. I discuss the understanding of historical time by the Franciscans, who were the first to arrive as missionaries in Mexico and to classify its pre-Hispanic monuments and relics as "antiquities." The rest of the chapter considers the writings of one of these friars, Motolinía, as a key to penetrating not only the early elaboration of a Spanish representation of Mexico's complex past, but also the persistence and transformation of still surviving indigenous antiquarian practices. The advantage of concentrating on Motolinía derives from the fact that he started putting together his writings by the late 1520s, when the conquest was still ongoing, the indigenous memory of the pre-Hispanic period alive, and the colonial construction of the "history of New Spain" was in its early stages. To anticipate my argument, Motolinía's "invention" of the antiquities of New Spain follows two general lines. He carefully observes and comments on material evidence that he connects to three migratory waves to Central Mexico (by the Chichimecs, the Colhua and the Mexica, respectively). Motolinía uses these three waves to structure the pre-Hispanic history of the region. This tripartite schema, allegedly originating from a pictorial codex, allows Motolinía to make analogies between the Mexica (that is, the Aztecs) and the ancient Romans, as well as to record material interactions among Spaniards and "Indians."

The final part of the chapter deals with an alternative indigenous narrative about local antiquity. The legend of the seven sons of Iztac Mixcoatl (eponymous ancestors and mythical founders of Mexican cities) seems to contradict directly the tripartite story. The legend of Iztac Mixcoatl's sons records a radically different genealogy of the first inhabitants of Central Mexico because it is a product of the reshaping of American materials according to European morphology. Motolinía claims to have collected this tale from the mouth of an old native informant, but it is patently based on the model of the Italian Dominican and infamous forger, Annius of Viterbo. After exploring the effect that this previously unrecognized influence had on Motolinía and the rising colonial antiquarian interest in New Spain, I conclude by stressing the importance of fakes in the encounters between Aztec and European antiquarian practices, and, more broadly, their role in promoting cross-cultural circulation of knowledge.

Mexican Antiquities and Their Multiple Ages

An intriguing request by an Italian humanist can introduce us to the subject matter of the first part of this chapter. In the late 1530s, Paolo Giovio

(1483–1552) began to organize a collection of portraits of illustrious men in his villa on Lake Como (Zimmermann 1995: 159–163). In 1542 he wrote to Giovanni Poggio, the papal nuncio in Spain, asking for "a bizarre piece of an idol of Temistitan [Tenochtitlan, modern Mexico City]," in order to place it alongside a painting of the *conquistador* Hernán Cortés, portrayed "with a gilded sword at his waist, a gold necklace round his neck, and wearing costly leather" (Giovio 1956: 280; 2006: 924).[1] Giovio's request is one of many examples of the heightened interest in objects from the New World, which were collected as wonders and curiosities in Renaissance Europe (Shelton 1997; Yaya 2008; Bleichmar and Mancall 2011). What matters here is Giovio's desire to own a piece of a broken statue from Tenochtitlan, the capital of the Aztec Empire destroyed by Cortés in 1521. Giovio had many sources of information about the lands the Spaniards conquered in America, and even a codex from Mexico containing "annals that preserved the memory of their kings through various drawings" (Giovio 1552: 252), which he had the opportunity of consulting in Rome in the 1530s. It is difficult, however, to understand what inspired him specifically to ask for a "piece of an idol" of this kind. Perhaps he wanted material evidence of the destruction of the Aztec Empire to be placed next to the painting of Cortés in order to stage a setting that exalted his conquest. Alternatively, Giovio may have felt a more general antiquarian attraction to pre-Hispanic relics. At any rate, by asking for a "piece of an idol," Giovio was extending the life of an object that had an altogether different meaning for the Aztecs, connected to their relationship with the things from their past. The "idol" may have been a result of the practice of destroying all household goods every fifty-two years on the occasion of the New Fire ceremony, when the cycles of the Aztec solar calendar and ritual calendar started again (Figure 6.1).

This ritual, practiced extensively across Central Mexico, was associated with the belief that, on the convergence of the two calendars, the sun could cease to rise and the present age would come to an end, followed by a new conflagration that the gods would initiate through a fire lighted in the cosmic hearth. The symbolic reenactment aimed to ward off a cosmological catastrophe by ritually destroying and casting out clothes, pots, domestic votive statues and other objects connected to the sacred; it also required all household fires to be extinguished and a new fire lit by priests in the darkness of the land, which recreated the predawn before the beginning of a new age. As various scholars have argued recently, after such a cleansing, the things that had been discarded lost their original vitality (Elson and Smith 2001) and became *tlazolli*, a notion that was related to the sphere of pollution. More precisely, according to anthropologist Byron Hamann (2008: 805–812), the potsherds created in the context of the New Fire ceremony became "matter out of time", but they were

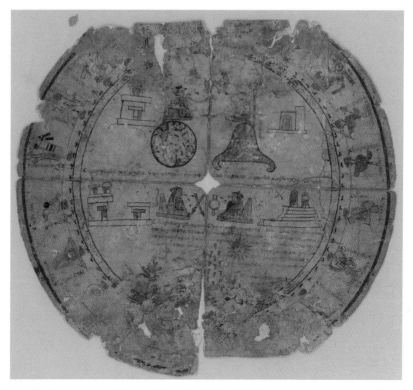

Figure 6.1. Boban Aztec Calendar Wheel (c. 1545–1546). Ink and colors on amatl fiber (35 cm × 38.1 cm). Codex Ind 42, The John Carter Brown Library, Providence, RI (Courtesy of the John Carter Brown Library at Brown University).

not considered mere "trash" or "waste," since they acquired a new, dangerous power and were thus manipulated. In the specific case of the afterlives of broken statues of gods, for example, there were two possible reuses: they could be left broken and employed to build up the external walls of temples, with spiritual effects due to their dangerous fragmentary power, or alternatively they could be repaired and returned to their original places.

Giovio's shattered "idol" might well have come from the wall of a temple abandoned after the arrival of the Spaniards, or from one of the many "middens" made by the deposition of *tlazolli* after New Fire house cleanings, which were scattered around Central Mexico. In any case, elements from different ages coexisted in the pre-Hispanic society's material landscape. This becomes still more evident if we consider that the relationship with *tlazolli* was part of a more complex attitude towards things from the past, which derived from a vision of historical time based on the belief in a succession of solar ages. This cyclical notion was at the heart of indigenous antiquarian practices, mainly based on the Aztec reuse of objects and artifacts from the four previous solar ages of creation. I use here the adjective "antiquarian" to describe a number of practices of collecting ancient stones and materials, which were seemingly regarded as particularly valuable for their antiquity and rarity, but also because they came from places connected with deities or powerful, admired groups, in the context of the solar chronologies. Our knowledge of Aztec antiquarianism is fragmentary and mainly based on the description of post-conquest written reports and archaeological excavations. Those carried out in the area of the Great Temple in what is now Mexico City during the last decades have shown how the sphere of sacred life encouraged possible antiquarian attitudes. For instance, artifacts from throughout the Aztec Empire, including things from the past, were incorporated into the Great Temple's structure. This is confirmed by the burial of votive objects from periods as remote as the Middle Preclassic (1200–400 B.C.), pertaining to the cultures of the Olmecs and their contemporaries (López Luján 2005). A special concern for ancient materials also emerges in relation to Teotihuacan, a city whose ruined sacred center had collapsed during the second half of the first millennium A.D. The whole city served as a kind of "antiquity." The Aztecs regularly organized processions to bring artifacts and ceramics from Teotihuacan to the Great Temple in Mexico City. Things from Teotihuacan were imagined to be "pre-sunrise things" because they came from the site where the sun of the fifth and current age of creation first rose. Not only did the Aztecs collect these relics and imagine a connection between them and the gods who had made their world possible, but they also fabricated their own Teotihuacan-style stone images, replicas of the past (Hamann 2002: 354–357). This last aspect casts light on the artistic side of the reuse or archaizing imitations of material remains, artworks and deity images, which provided the only direct link of the Aztecs with earlier societies, including that of Teotihuacan (Umberger 1987).

To sum up, then, when the Europeans started to collect Mexican antiquities, a substantial interest in things from the past had characterized the Aztecs for centuries. Their understanding of old stones and objects, however, relied on a cyclical vision of historical time, which seems to have shaped significantly the meaning they attributed to these materials and their reuse.

Disharmonious Chronologies in New Spain and the Franciscan Need to Understand the Past

What role did antiquities play in the colonial encounter? One of the oldest indigenous chronicles of the conquest contained in the so-called *Annals of*

Tlatelolco records the speed with which Cortés adapted to the new universe he penetrated once he had landed on the Mexican coast. The *Annals* record that the Aztec Emperor Moctezuma II (r. 1502–1520) sent his emissaries to meet Cortés in the coastal town of Tecpantlayacac, where he accepted their invitation to wear "suns of precious metal, one yellow [gold] and one white [silver], and a mirror for the back, and a golden helmet, and a golden shell headcover, and a head fan of plumes, and a shell shield" (Lockhart 1993: 257). What broke the precarious balance of this act of submission was not Cortés's understanding of the possible meaning the natives gave to his disguise, but his reaction to the sight of a vessel in the form of an eagle (*cuauhxicalli*) overflowing with human blood. That object was enough to disconcert Cortés's moral and aesthetic values, provoking fear, rage, and violence. Cortés' move from camouflage—by dressing up according to the natives' request— to rejection of the Mexican material world has much in common with the first Spaniards traversing Central Mexico in the aftermath of the fall of the Aztec Empire. They found themselves exploring a landscape that was still marked by great remains of the pre-Hispanic society, including the ruins of buildings and temples, which they described as Egyptian pyramids or Islamic mosques, as well as by the persistence of sacred ceremonies and practices they understood as idolatry or the worship of Satan, which was one false religion with many different faces around the world (Bernand and Gruzinski 1988). The first impulse of the Spaniards was to destroy the symbols of the former power and the stones that kept its memory alive across the many cities inhabited by tens of thousands of natives in Central Mexico. They launched themselves into a systematic attempt, which in the end remained incomplete (Gruzinski 1993), to eradicate any trace of complex local cultures.

The resilience of the "Indians" soon led the Spanish to realize that, in order to understand and eradicate the essence of the Aztecs' vision of the world, it was necessary to learn about the Aztecs' own understanding of time before the arrival of the Spaniards. This encouraged an extraordinary effort to collect and cross-check information and evidence about the Aztec Empire and other pre-Hispanic indigenous cultures, learn local languages, interpret pictograms and date material vestiges. This direct contact with Mexican remains stimulated archaeological and antiquarian attitudes in an intriguing parallel to those of humanists and other learned people in Renaissance Europe, who were contributing to the slow consolidation of archaeology and antiquarianism as forms of knowledge mostly by exploring relics and ruins from the Greek and Roman past (Momigliano 1950: 289–291; Schnapp 1996: 121–220).

A major difference was that humanists and antiquarians in Europe saw themselves and their own culture as successors of a remote past that they considered superior to the present and to which they could partly gain access through a body of ancient written texts. By contrast, in Mexico the Spaniards had the opportunity to interact physically with the natives and to question local informants who, especially in the first decades after the conquest, had first-hand memories of the last days of the pre-Hispanic period. Moreover, in Europe the complex process of retrieving classical culture led to the elaboration of an idea of the "Middle Ages," which marked an irreparable break with the Greco-Roman world. According to the Italian humanists, who were rediscovering that culture in order to rescue its greatness and aesthetic values, the "Middle Ages" that separated them from Classical Antiquity had been inaugurated by what they first regarded as "barbarian" invasions (Weiss 1969). In one sense, the emergence of colonial antiquarian interest in New Spain was also intimately connected to the idea of an irreparable break with the pre-Hispanic ages. Unlike the humanists in Europe, however, those who collected and studied Mexican remains were, paradoxically, the same people who had turned them into ruins. Moreover, the chronological tripartite schema that Renaissance antiquarians adopted for European historical time collided with a binary distinction used in the case of New Spain: the lack of distance between pre-Hispanic and colonial times derived from the interpretation of the complex process of conquest as an instantaneous event. This was the reason for the absence of any notion of "Mexican Middle Ages" in the writings of the Franciscan friars who inaugurated antiquarian inquiries into the past of New Spain.

The Franciscans' millenarian enthusiasm, inspired by the traditional theory of the seven ages conflated with the Cistercian abbot Joachim of Fiore's (c. 1135–1202) apocalyptical prophecy (Phelan 1970), reinforced the disharmony of chronologies in the vision of historical time in Europe and Mexico. The Franciscans were convinced that they lived in the sixth age inaugurating the dominion of the Spirit, which was to be consummated in the final millennium. Thus, the friars who arrived to Mexico in 1524 with collective salvation on their minds interpreted their mission as the beginning of the last preaching of the gospel on the eve of the end of the world (Brading 1991: 102–127). It is no coincidence that the first group of friars were allegedly twelve in number, in imitation of the apostles. These missionaries firmly believed that they had to quickly replace the pre-Hispanic order with a Christian one. This is fundamental to understanding why they took part in the Spanish colonial project of canceling any trace of indigenous culture and social life. Their frustration with the difficulty of converting the Indians was at the origin of the "antiquarian turn" of their mission. Because it was hard to eradicate the indigenous culture, they sought to understand it. They had convinced themselves that only the study of the local past would disclose the secrets of the Indian souls.

In carrying out their inquiries, the Franciscans paid much more attention to material culture than scholars have noted. Descriptions of ruined buildings, monuments and artifacts fill the reports, memoirs, and chronicles because the sixteenth- and early-seventeenth-century Spaniards regarded them as symbols of the political, religious and cultural order of pre-Hispanic Mexico. Significantly enough, many of those writings did not get beyond the manuscript stage at the time (Baudot 1995).

Entangled Antiquarianisms in Colonial Mexico
The Franciscans and the Antiquities of New Spain

The materials produced by the Franciscans represented the first step in the making of a colonial antiquarianism in Mexico. In the second half of the seventeenth century these materials came to be at the center of sophisticated strategies for the self-fashioning of creoles as local élites (More 2012), before being rediscovered and relaunched as a source of knowledge from the late eighteenth century onward (Cañizares-Esguerra 2001). Did pre-Hispanic indigenous antiquarian practices have any place in this process? Or, to put it differently, what happened to Aztec antiquarian traditions immediately after the conquest? The question is related to the complex dynamics following the collapse of the Aztec Empire, as well as to the reaction of the natives to the destruction of their material landscape perpetrated by the Spaniards.

One possible way to understand if there was an entanglement of antiquarian traditions from the two sides of the Atlantic in the first decades after the conquest is to turn to one of the twelve Franciscan friars who landed in New Spain in 1524, Toribio de Benavente (c. 1490–1568), better known as Motolinía. Together with friar Andrés de Olmos (c. 1485–1571), he was the initiator of Franciscan scholarship on pre-Hispanic Mexico. The work produced in the milieu of these missionaries is a source of the greatest importance for answering the general questions raised above about the contribution of persistent indigenous antiquarian traditions to the emergence of a colonial antiquarianism in the New World. The writings of the Franciscans are usually called "chronicles," although they are a mixed genre in which travel accounts, historical-geographical description and reports about missionary achievements intertwine. The open structure of these texts confirms their multiple nature, as does the regular lack of a strictly chronological narrative, which is often replaced by a taxonomical organization, not unlike the antiquarian literature in Renaissance Europe (Momigliano 1950: 286). Encouraged by the Franciscan superiors, who aimed to survey the most significant religious attempts of its missionaries, those writings catalogued what were considered the traditional customs, rites and beliefs of the Indians, in accordance with the idea that this would help to extirpate idolatry. Thus, the Franciscan "chronicles" took an increasing interest in the origin of the peoples of New Spain, their alleged genealogical lineages, the foundations of cities, the ruins of buildings and monuments, as well as in votive objects, artworks, and pictorial codices, which in Europe were prized as objects for collections of curiosities, rather than as historical sources (on their surprising effects in cross-cultural exchanges, see Mason 2001: 101–130).

All this was made possible only by the application of the classical notion of "antiquities," originating from Varro (116–27 B.C.), which the Europeans were reshaping for the Greco-Roman material evidence, to the remains of pre-Hispanic Mexico. Such understanding of Mexican traces and rituals, which was first advanced by Motolinía and Olmos, was not inevitable and produced relevant effects such as collecting and describing these tangible and intangible relics from the past. Interestingly, both friars referred to their writings as "books of antiquities" (*antiguallas*, *antigüedades*). These works are now lost or survive only fragmentarily (Baudot 1995: 163–245, 335–398), without entirely reliable critical editions. Starting from the late 1520s or the early 1530s, Motolinía and Olmos reinterpreted fragments of the different ages of pre-Hispanic Mexico, describing and organizing non-literary materials within largely European schemas. In effect, they were "inventing the antiquities of the Indians of New Spain." This is not to belittle the effort of missionaries to learn Nahuatl and other Mexican languages, nor their interaction with the natives and the decisive role of local informants in their texts, but rather to underline the striking ambiguity that pervades their work. In the case of Motolinía, the first point we need to make is that the various drafts that are available of his work—a fragment presumably written in 1528, the hastily concluded version of his *History of the Indians of the New Spain* (1541) that had to be sent to the Count of Benavente, and its later stratifications, which were to produce a different work known as *Memorials or Book of the Things of the New Spain and its Natives*—reveal a development in the description of Mexican antiquities, as well as of local antiquarian traditions.

Before looking at these sources, a preliminary clarification is required, to better understand Motolinía's perception of Mexican antiquarian practices. On the one hand, in the first complete version of Motolinía's work, the *History*, there is no explicit mention of the five solar ages, which make their appearance only in a later chapter, written in 1542 (Motolinía 1971: 387–390). Consequently, the short reference to the New Fire ceremony (Motolinía 1985: 145–146) is not related to the indigenous understanding of the past, nor does it contain allusions to the cleansing and destruction of household goods. On the other hand, although Motolinía was exposed to a humanistic education in Spain, in Mexico he was, first and foremost, a friar who shared the fervent Franciscan millenarianism. In his writings, however, we do not find any attempt to connect the apocalyptic character of both the Franciscan theory of the six ages of the world and the Aztec vision of historical time. Indeed, Motolinía's construction of the idea of the "antiquities of the Indians of New Spain" seems to be rather indifferent to this cyclical notion. Accordingly, Motolinía's antiquarian understanding frames the past of New Spain with an idea of linear development of chronology that also allows him to propose internal partitions.

To summarize, the Franciscans were mainly responsible for the emergence of an antiquarian approach to the past of New Spain. In doing so, they relied on local information about pre-Hispanic history and materials. Their reports, however, shape this colonial knowledge according to a limited understanding of Central Mexican societies and ceremonies. Moreover, they conformed only to the Franciscan vision of historical time and not to the indigenous one.

Motolinía, Ancient Mexico and Its Indigenous Antiquarian Traditions

Since the fragment of 1528, Motolinía had been faced with problems of periodization, particularly due to the lack of evidence for the Chichimecs having inhabited Central Mexico more than eight centuries before his own time (Baudot 1971: 31). "Chichimecs" was the Nahuatl name given by the Aztecs to what they considered rustic nomadic and semi-nomadic peoples living outside settled areas north of Central Mexico. Motolinía presents the Chichimecs as the first group to populate the region of Tenochtitlan and the Aztec Empire. In this draft and in the slightly different one that was included in the prefatory letter of his *History*, Motolinía attributes his relative lack of knowledge about the early period of the Chichimecs to the fact that they had not left "writings." By contrast, Motolinía found "writings" of the Aztecs in the pictorial codices, "books ... of figures and characters," which he admirably attempted to equate with the historiographical annals of European tradition. Although he explicitly asserts that the Aztecs "had no letters" (Motolinía 1985: 99), his description of the codices as "writings" and "books" proves that Europeans did not always see them just as curiosities (Boone 2010). In a slightly later version, however, Motolinía states that "there seem to be no writings or pictures of their [Chichimec] antiquities, *nor sculpted stones* earlier than eight hundred years ago, but from what we read in the books and antiquities they seem much more than eight hundred years old" (Motolinía 1971: 388; emphasis added).[2] The explicit effort to match the information allegedly collected from pictorial codices with material evidence is decisive, and is echoed in later works like the illustrated history of Mexico, attributed to the *mestizo* Jesuit Juan de Tovar (c. 1546–c. 1626), who several times discusses the origins and successions of ancient Mexican peoples on the basis of "traces and ruins" (Orozco y Berra 1979: 24) still visible on their migration routes.

The main source that Motolinía invokes to introduce the migratory waves of the various peoples who inhabited Mexico before the Spanish conquest is what he calls *Xiuhtonalamatl* (Baudot 1971: 31; on population migrations in Nahuatl sources, see Smith 1984), a pictorial calendrical codex. For Motolinía it was, above all, a relic, and he seems to rely on the interpretations that the old Indians gave of its content. On this basis, he writes that Central Mexico was populated by the "Colhua," a civilized agricultural Nahuatl-speaking people who arrived a few decades after the Chichimecs,[3] and finally by the "Mexicans," that is, the Mexica, or Aztecs. While any attempt of ours to find a consistent parallel between this tripartite schema and that of the Renaissance vision of historical time is destined to fail, Motolinía's attention to material evidence leads him to suggest specific analogies between Mexican and European histories. A case in point is that of the spectacular remains of Tenochtitlan's secular buildings, at which he exclaimed that the "Mexicans [Mexica] in this land were like the Romans in other times" (Motolinía 1985: 318). Motolinía's description, however, is much more detailed when he moves on to the temples, or *teocalme* (sg. *teocalli*). He is astonished by their size and number, and records them for "those who reach this land in future [...], as memory of them is now almost disappearing" (Motolinía 1985: 174).

Somehow, Motolinía's antiquarian interest in Mexican ruins seems to have grown as the temples and deity images were destroyed. For instance, there is no sign of it when he recalls that around 1525 in the city of Tlaxcala their remains "were used as cement for the churches; and since some were very large, they were the best cement of the world for such a great and holy work" (Motolinía 1985: 131), a possible case of unnoticed reuse of materials that had already been reused by natives in pre-Hispanic times. But when Motolinía describes another famous temple, the so-called pyramid of Cholula (Figure 6.2), which he assimilates to the Tower of Babel, there emerges a different interest in the monument. After stating the temple's measurements and recalling that the structure was "much higher than now appears," Motolinía concludes by observing that "this building really deserves to be seen even now," inhabited as it is by "rabbits and vipers" and its surface partly used for growing maize. An inspired description of these ruins follows, in which Motolinía notes that the local inhabitants had placed "a small, ancient *teocalli*," possibly considered of pre-sunrise origin, on the summit. The Spaniards involved in the campaign against idolatry were well aware of this eminent place when, in 1535, in Motolinía's presence, they destroyed it.

Figure 6.2. View of the Pyramid of Cholula, near Mexico. Ink on paper (21.6 cm × 12.5 cm). From Alexander von Humboldt, *Researches, Concerning the Institutions & Monuments of the Ancient Inhabitants of America* … (London: Longman, Hurst, Rees, Orme & Brown, J. Murray & H. Colburn, 1814), vol. 1, following p. 80. J814 H919r, The John Carter Brown Library, Providence, RI (Courtesy of the John Carter Brown Library at Brown University).

Then, excavating its foundations, they found "many idols" buried there (Motolinía 1985: 176–177).

It was precisely Motolinía's interest in "idols" that allowed him to sense the importance that most ancient "idols" had for the Mexican peoples. Scholars have already called attention to Motolinía's description of the ceremony in Tlaxcala in honor of Camaxtli, god of war (Umberger 1987: 72; López Luján 2014: 284–285). Camaxtli was represented by a great statue next to which was placed a "small, terrifying idol, which they said had come with those who had populated the land and province of Tlaxcala in the past … and they felt such reverence and fear they dared not look at it." The Tlaxcalans also placed over the statue of Camaxtli "a mask, which they said came with the small idol from a village called Tollan [Tula] and from another called Poyauhtlan, from which they said came the idol itself" (Motolinía 1985: 169). It seems the Tlaxcalans, who were Nahuatl-speakers but allies of the Spaniards at the time of the conquest, attributed to these ancient stones the power to forge bonds with their ancestors. This was so because the stones came from centers regarded as special for having been inhabited in previous solar ages or for being the alleged place of origin of the Tlaxcalans' ancestors.

Motolinía lived in Tlaxcala in the second half of the 1530s and was able to investigate local memories, traditions and customs in depth. And so he tells his readers that the Tlaxcalans also "kept as precious relics" two arrows brought by their ancestors from the lands of the north-east and that they used them "as the main sign for knowing if they would win a battle or if they should withdraw in time" (Motolinía 1985: 112). In the *Memorials* Motolinía makes his description of these arrows more effectively by a biblical comparison with "Joseph's cup, which the Egyptians thought contained the art of warfare" (Motolinía 1971: 13; see *Genesis* 44: 1–17). What we observe in the later drafts of Motolinía's writings is that he allows himself increasing space for reflection about indigenous antiquarian practices, a clear sign of interest and interaction.

Forging Antiquities and the Quest for the Authentic

Fake Images and a Genealogical Story

Motolinía's interest in the antiquities of New Spain was reinforced by his encounter with the Indians' antiquarian traditions. But it did not develop following the tripartite schema of the migratory waves in pre-Hispanic Mexico. The 1541 prefatory letter already presents an alternative genealogical explanation, which shows us the relevance and potentiality of the fakes in antiquarian entanglements. Before considering this second understanding of ancient Mexico, it might be worth recalling that forgery was not just a prerogative of the Europeans.

Let us first of all consider what Motolinía writes about the Spanish campaign against idolatry: when it erupted, the natives resisted, hiding underground deity images with their ceremonial accessories or entrusting them to a limited circle of guardians who protected them in secret. The result was that "if in a hundred years' time the ancient patios were dug up, many idols would be found." That was why, between 1539 and 1540, the missionaries started "digging up the land, disinterring the dead and rewarding the Indians who handed in their idols; and in some parts … they searched for all those that had been forgotten and had been ruined underground" (Motolinía 1971: 87). This is an unexpected point of convergence between the missionary and the modern archaeologist, following a dynamic like the one that Carlo Ginzburg (1989: 156–164) describes in his famous essays on the inquisitor as anthropologist. Motolinía, however, proves to be a superficial archaeologist, since he is content with explaining the deterioration of hidden "idols" by their being "forgotten" underground. He ignores the use of ritual burials among the Aztecs. Therefore, he does not allude to the possibility that those "idols" were "ruined" because they were more ancient than others (although we know from Hamann [2008: 809] that they could be repaired), and so were handed over last of all to the missionaries, as they were regarded as the most valuable. We can connect this aspect with another practice of some natives recorded by Motolinía in the same context: the copying of ruined deity images to hand over to the Spaniards. Alessandra Russo (2011) has recalled how the Mexican objects Cortés sent to Europe after the conquest, some of which ended up in antiquarian collections, did not belong to pre-Hispanic ages, but were produced by local artisans at the request of the Spaniards. This fact blurs the distinction between indigenous and colonial objects. If the Aztecs really made imitations of their ruined "idols" to be delivered to the Spaniards, such counterfeiting would not only be confirmation of the speed with which the natives adapted their manufacture to the demands of their new masters. This act would also make it possible to deceive the missionaries, protecting the most ancient, and valuable, "idols."

Forgery had an important role also in Motolinía's exposition of another explanation of the origins of the first inhabitants of Central Mexico. He presents this variant narrative in the prefatory letter of his *History* (but not in the fragment of 1528) after the theory of the three migratory waves of the Chichimecs, the Colhua, and the Mexica. It is the story of the common ancestor of the Indians of New Spain, identified in a later draft with Iztac Mixcoatl (Motolinía 1971: 10), who came from Chicomoztoc (Figure 6.3). The source is indicated as an old native informant, who told Motolinía that the common ancestor's first six sons were scattered across Mexico, founding cities and giving name to new peoples. In the three cases that give a name in the 1541 draft, an etymological connection is suggested: "From the second son Tenuch came Tenochca, who are the Mexicans, and so Mexico City is called Tenochtitlan"; "From the fifth son Mixtecatl came the Mixteca. Their land is now called Mixtecapan"; "The last son gave rise to the Otomi, so called from his name, Otomitl" (Motolinía 1985: 107–109). This technique is also associated with the seventh son, although in a different way. An "honest and moderate man," chaste and unmarried, his name was Quetzalcoatl and the common ancestor had him from a second wife. An Indian by name of Chichimecatl clamped Quetzalcoatl's shoulder (*acolli* in Nahuatl) with a belt, and for this reason he was also called "Acolhuatl, and it is said that the Colhua descended from him" (Motolinía 1985: 111). There are additions and complications to this legend in the later version (Motolinía 1971: 9–13).

Did Motolinía learn this genealogical story from the mouth of a native informant? Some doubts arise from the fact that Iztac Mixcoatl's divine nature goes unmentioned in the interest of emphasizing that from him "proceed great generations, almost as one reads of the sons of Noah" (Motolinía 1971: 10). The reference to the "generations" of the "sons of Noah" is a clue that would have immediately attracted a Renaissance European reader.

Figure 6.3. Chicomoztoc, or the seven caverns, with men and women (c. 1585). Painting on leaf (21 cm × 15.2 cm). Codex Ind 2, Juan de Tovar, *Historia de la benida de los yndios apoblar a Mexico de las partes remotas de Occidente* …, plate 1, The John Carter Brown Library, Providence, RI (Courtesy of the John Carter Brown Library at Brown University).

It echoed the technique of one of the most popular narratives about the population of the world: that which the Dominican friar Annius of Viterbo (1437–1502) had invented by twisting philology and antiquarianism into a collection of fakes (Grafton 1991: 76–103), significantly titled *Antiquities* (1498). Annius's purpose was to invent an alternative history of the world that preceded that of the Greeks and the Romans, in order to prove that cultured and refined societies had already existed before them, but also to fill in some gaps in the Bible narrative (Tigerstedt 1964).

Just like a humanist manuscript hunter, Annius claimed to have come across the lost manuscripts of many authors, which allowed him to rewrite ancient history. His extraordinary success in Renaissance Europe depended on the possibility of inventing traditions using these fake authors, particularly the *Antiquities* attributed to Berossos the Chaldean (third century B.C.), a priest of Bel Marduk and astronomer who wrote a history about Babylon in Greek, and whose work survives only in fragments (Haubold et al. 2013). An alleged translation of the original Greek work into Latin, Annius's Pseudo-Berossos asserts that Noah was a giant and the whole of humanity descended from his three sons, Shem, Ham and Japheth. Their offspring would have repopulated the world after the great flood, leaving unequivocal signs in the names of the lands they had inhabited and the peoples to whom they had given origin. One of Japheth's sons, the giant Tubal, father of Iber, the eponymous ancestor of the Iberian Peninsula and his inhabitants, was a case in point.

In establishing explanatory links between names of Mexican localities and their inhabitants on the one hand and their supposed founders on the other hand, exactly as happens in the *Antiquities* of Pseudo-Berossos, Motolinía, who equates Iztac Mixcoatl with the "sons of Noah," adheres to the same vortex of invented etymologies as that supporting Annius' incredible genealogies. Thus, he shapes a story, which is presented as indigenous, but is actually an attempt to channel fragments of an elusive past in an organic design that follows the European linear notion of time and can make sense of the ruins and relics of pre-Hispanic Mexico for his Spanish readers.

Annius of Viterbo and Mexico: Motolinía's Legacy

Being flexible and adaptable, Annius's model achieved great success in Renaissance Europe and countless authors reused it—sometimes implicitly, as Motolinía did—in order to legitimate narratives about the origins of a population, a city or a dynasty, as well as to provide consistent historical accounts. Partly thanks to the *Antiquities*' growing popularity in Spain, which may have been encouraged by the dedication of the first edition to the Catholic Kings, the encounter between Annius and the New World occurred early, essentially as soon as authors of the 1530s, like the chronicler Gonzalo Fernández de Oviedo and the Dominican friar Bartolomé de las Casas, debated the origins of the Indians and the Spanish right to rule over their lands, invoking Annius' *Antiquities* (i.e., his inventions). For Las Casas the account of the effort of Noah's progeny to repopulate the world provided by Annius's Pseudo-Berossos is "fully credible" (Las Casas 1958: 374). But he firmly rejects Oviedo's identification of the Antilles with the islands of the Hesperides mentioned by classical authors. Oviedo maintains it in order to claim that the Spanish crown had always had sovereignty over the Antilles (and America). The reason was that Hesperus—the twelfth king of Spain, according to Annius's list of its first twenty-four monarchs published in the appendix of the *Antiquities*—had ruled over them in ancient times, as their name proved (Gliozzi 1977: 16–19).

Motolinía, who met Las Casas in 1538, must have been fascinated by Annius when, three years later, he was preparing the draft of his *History* for the Count of Benavente. To present the subject of the antiquities of New Spain, which was obscure and slippery to Spanish readers, he recast it in a schema that was familiar to them, presuming to convey a stronger sense of authenticity to his report (Temple 2001, on Annius's fakes and the quest for the authentic). Thus colonial antiquarianism was animated from the start by the shadow of a forgery, Annius's *Antiquities*, which extended itself over Spanish and Nahuatl chronicles and other materials.

In the final part of this section I want to explore some possible effects of Motolinía's own invention, that is, the story of the founding of the cities by Iztac Mixcoatl's sons. The first and clearest example is the recovery and repetition of this genealogical legend about the origin of the ancient Mexican peoples in the extended variant explicitly giving the name of Iztac Mixcoatl, not only in other Franciscan missionaries' writings such as the *Indian Ecclesiastical History* (1611) by Jerónimo de Mendieta (1525–1604), but also in the *Conquest of Mexico* (1552) by Francisco López de Gómara (1511–1566), the private chaplain of Cortés after his return to Spain. Quotations are almost literal (see Mendieta 1945: 159–161; Gómara 1553: 120r) and show a direct influence of Motolinía's text. Things are less clear-cut in the case of Chimalpahin, an indigenous annalist from Chalco, who also made a revised translation of Gómara's chronicle into Nahuatl. The main question here is how to reconcile his literal translation of Gómara's passage about Iztac Mixcoatl (Schroeder et al. 2010: 443–445) with the fact that in the third of his *Original Relations*, concerning the history of ancient Mexico, Chimalpahin describes Iztac Mixcoatl as the Mexica at the head of the seven family lineages (*calpolli*) that left Aztlan (Chimalpahin Cuauhtlehuanitzin 1997: 3–7), a city often associated with Chicomoztoc, the place from where, according to Motolinía, Iztac Mixcoatl came.

A final example of Motolinía's legacy deals with the legend of the seven giant sons of Iztac Mixcoatl, which modern dictionaries of Mexican mythology record with the names provided in the *Memorials* (Robelo 1980). The shaping of this legend is unclear. It involves a complex, stratified tradition whose traces are difficult to identify. Motolinía never says that Iztac Micxoatl and his sons were giants (while Pseudo-Berossos does say that about Noah's sons and grandsons). Therefore, a possible connection can be made with the supposedly native traditions about giants that abound in post-conquest sources related to ancient Mexico. A case in point is the so-called Ríos Codex (Anders et al. 1996). Now in the Vatican Library, this pictorial codex with Italian annotations reproduces and extends an original produced in the mid-sixteenth century in the Tehuacan Valley by order of the Dominican friar Pedro de los Ríos, who recounts that the native artists drew local glyphs in it. More than half a century later, the Paduan priest and antiquarian Lorenzo Pignoria copied one image of a Mexican god from the Ríos Codex in the 1626 edition of the *Images of the Deities of the Ancients* (1556) by the humanist and antiquarian Vincenzo Cartari (c. 1531–*post* 1571), taken from marbles, bronzes and medals. The reprints of this work are considered among the precedents for an attitude that emerged definitively "towards the end of the seventeenth century," when "it became clear that the study of religion would increasingly have to reckon with the non-literary evidence collected by the antiquarians" (Momigliano 1950: 309). The 1626 edition appeared with a remarkable *Discourse on the Deities of the Eastern and Western Indies*, written by Pignoria. Referring to the theory that the biblical region Ophir (from which King Solomon is said in the Old Testament to have received a cargo of gold and other precious goods) was in America (Romm 2001), Pignoria conjectures that the religion of the ancient Mexicans derived from the Egyptians and, for this reason, "the peoples of this part of the world fashion their idols with images similar to the Egyptian deities" (Cartari 1626: 547). This passage has a source in common with the manipulation of the antiquities of New Spain that Motolinía inaugurated. The idea of an Egyptian origin for religions, which allowed comparison between the images of the deities of the different parts of the world, derived from Annius of Viterbo's *Antiquities*. Even before publishing them, Annius had already fabricated visual evidence, forging stones and inscriptions in support of his theory of a very distant foundation of his native city, Viterbo. These included the so-called Osirian Marble, a counterfeit agglomerate of medieval marble fragments that sought to prove that Viterbo had been founded by the Egyptian deity Osiris after defeating the giants (Nagel and Wood 2010: 247–250).

Interestingly, one of the earliest mentions of the existence of giants (*tzocuillixeque*) in ancient Mexico is precisely in the Ríos Codex (Anders et al. 1996: 58, 60) (Figure 6.4). At the time of its transcription, Olmos had already attributed to the Mexicans a belief in giants, which is also present in a later draft of Motolinía's writings (1971: 388) with reference to the second solar age. However, Olmos seems to have not mentioned the legend of the sons of Iztac Mixcoatl in his lost work. Olmos's reference to giants is explicitly recalled by the Franciscans Mendieta (1997: 41) and Juan de Torquemada (c. 1562–1624). One should not be surprised to find that in his work *Indian Monarchy* (1615) the latter cites explicitly the authority of the "Annian Berossos" as evidence that once there were giants "in the world, not in small, but abundant number" (Torquemada 1975: 51–55).

Concluding Remarks

As Paula Findlen (2012: 6) has argued, antiquarians were in a perfect position to know that "remaking the past produces new things or, put in a different way, a new use for old artifacts." This statement is also true of

Figure 6.4. Prehispanic giant, or *tzocuillixeque* (second half of the sixteenth century). Painting on leaf (46 cm × 29 cm). Detail from Codex Vaticanus Latinus 3738 (also known as Codex Vaticanus A, or Ríos Codex), fol. 4v, Vatican Library, Vatican City (Courtesy of the Vatican Library).

pictorial codices and much other material evidence produced in Mexico in the aftermath of the Spanish conquest (Boone 1998). We need to rethink the whole of Motolinía's contribution to the birth of a new antiquarianism in colonial Mexico in the light of his partial dependence on Annius of Viterbo. Only a detailed analysis of these sources will be able to demonstrate if, through Motolinía's writings and their circulation, Annius' inventions infected chroniclers like Gómara and Mendieta, and also complex, hybrid materials, such as the codices that natives and *mestizos* produced in collaboration with Spaniards in post-Conquest Mexico. For the moment, we can observe that deception and forgery were at the heart of the complex encounter between the Indigenous American and European antiquarian practices and traditions. Antiquarian practices and traditions influenced each other in multiple ways: the Aztecs replaced ancient deity images with copies, perhaps to preserve them from the violence of the Spanish destruction; at the same time, despite the campaign against idolatry, the Spaniards, particularly the Franciscans, developed an increasing interest in the material evidence of the time before the conquest, which they described as "antiquities." In doing so, they started to collect objects and fragments, measure buildings and monuments, and recognize and date styles and forms, eventually producing a structure to organize knowledge about the past of New Spain. This slow process involved constant, intense interaction with local cultures and the reshaping of the ideas and worldview of natives in accordance with a new sense of time and explanatory models of the past. These new notions derived from the impossibility of adapting the Aztec cyclical ideas of time to the European linear ones.

The appropriation of the antiquities of the Indians of New Spain was not only the result of inevitable mistakes and misunderstandings, but also of a deliberate invention that allowed missionaries like Motolinía to "package" this knowledge in a way that was understandable for their Spanish audience. It was especially true in the case of the accounts recorded by pictorial codices and the oral memory of native peoples, which remained ambiguous and elusive in the eyes of those who collected them. From this point of view, the acceptance of Motolinía's manipulation, based on the adaptation of indigenous materials to Annius' model, as legitimate knowledge points towards a more general epistemological problem. As scholars like Anthony Grafton (1990) have argued, fakes can have an important role in the production of knowledge, making it possible to give an order to what appear to be scattered and confusing traces. Although they did not pass down to us fully reliable information, they sometimes rescued authentic pieces of the past that otherwise would have been irretrievably lost. In post-conquest Mexico, colonial antiquarianism arose partly from fakes.

Acknowledgements

I owe a debt of gratitude to Serge Gruzinski for inviting me to present a part of this research at the École des Hautes Études en Sciences Sociales (Paris) in 2013. Thanks to a generous fellowship, I also had the opportunity to continue my investigation at the John Carter Brown Library in 2015. I wish to recall a night I spent in Providence, having a delightful conversation with Earle Havens and sharing our scholarly enthusiasm for Renaissance forgers. My final thanks are to the co-editors of the present volume, whose critical remarks helped me to make the final version of this article much better.

Notes

1. All translations are by the author unless otherwise indicated.
2. In fact, in the chapter on the solar ages, Motolinía (1971: 389) suggests a chronology for the fifth age that is consistent with this dating, but he does not modify the rest of his work accordingly.
3. The passage confuses the "Colhua" and the "Acolhua"—that is, the modern inhabitants of Texcoco. The two names are often interchangeable in early colonial sources. The overlapping is already in the 1528 fragment (Baudot 1971: 32–33), which was probably influenced by Motolinía's stay in Texcoco, so much so that he presents the "Colhua" as direct informants about their own origins. Commenting on Motolinía's three migrations, Mendieta (1945: 162) still writes: "Colhua, who are the Texcocans."

References

Anders, Ferdinand, Maarten Jansen, and Luis Reyes García (editors)
    1996   *Religión, costumbres e historia de los antiguos mexicans: libro explicativo del llamado Códice Vaticano A (Codex Vatic. Lat. 3787 de la Biblioteca Apostólica Vaticana)*. Fondo de Cultura Económica, Mexico D.F.

Baudot, Georges
    1971   Les premières enquêtes ethnographiques américaines. Fray Toribio Motolinía: quelques documents inédits et quelques remarques. *Cahiers du monde hispanique et luso-brésilien* 17: 7–35.

    1995   *Utopia and History in Mexico: The First Chroniclers of Mexican Civilization, 1520–1569*. Translated by B. R. Ortiz de Montellano and T. Ortiz de Montellano. University Press of Colorado, Niwot.

Bernand, Carmen, and Serge Gruzinski
    1988   *De l'idolâtrie: une archéologie des sciences religieuses*. Éditions du Seuil, Paris.

Bleichmar, Daniela, and Peter Mancall (editors)
    2011   *Collecting Across Cultures: Material Exchanges in the Early Modern Atlantic World*. University of Pennsylvania Press, Philadelphia.

Boone, Elizabeth Hill
    1998   Pictorial Documents and Visual Thinking in Postconquest Mexico. In *Native Traditions in the Postconquest World*, edited by Elizabeth Hill Boone

and Tom Cummins, pp. 149–199. Dumbarton Oaks Research Library and Collection, Washington D.C.

2010   *Stories in Red and Black: Pictorial Histories of the Aztecs and Mixtecs.* University of Texas Press, Austin.

Brading, David A.

1991   *The First America: The Spanish Monarchy, Creole Patriots, and the Liberal State, 1492–1867.* Cambridge University Press, Cambridge.

Cañizares-Esguerra, Jorge

2001   *How to Write the History of the New World: Histories, Epistemologies and Identities in the Eighteenth-Century Atlantic World.* Stanford University Press, Stanford.

Cartari, Vincenzo

1626   *Seconda novissima editione delle imagini de gli dei delli antichi* … Pietro Paolo Tozzi: Padua.

Chimalpahin Cuauhtlehuanitzin, Domingo Francisco de San Antón Muñón

1997   *Primer Amoxtli libro: 3a relación de las Différentes histoires originales*, edited by Víctor Castillo. Universidad Nacional Autónoma de México, México D.F.

Elson, Christina M., and Smith, Michael E.

2001   Archaeological Deposits from the Aztec New Fire Ceremony. *Ancient Mesoamerica* 12: 157–174.

Findlen, Paula

2012   Early Modern Things: Objects in Motion, 1500–1800. In *Early Modern Things: Objects and Their Histories, 1500–1800*, edited by Paula Findlen, pp. 3–27. Routledge, New York.

Ginzburg, Carlo

1989   *Clues, Myths, and the Historical Method.* Translated by J. Tedeschi and A. C. Tedeschi. Johns Hopkins University Press, Baltimore.

Giovio, Paolo

1552   *Historiarum sui temporis*, vol. II. Lorenzo Torrentino, Florence.

1956   *Lettere*, edited by Giuseppe Guido Ferrero, vol. I. Istituto Poligrafico dello Stato–Libreria dello Stato, Rome.

2006   *Elogi degli uomini illustri*, edited by Franco Miconzio. Giulio Einaudi, Turin.

Gliozzi, Giuliano

1977   *Adamo e il nuovo mondo. La nascita dell'antropologia come ideologia coloniale: dalle genealogie bibliche alle teorie razziali (1500–1700).* La Nuova Italia, Florence.

Grafton, Anthony

1990   *Forgers and Critics: Creativity and Duplicity in Western Scholarship.* Princeton University Press, Princeton.

1991   *Defenders of the Text: The Traditions of Scholarship in an Age of Science, 1450–1800.* Harvard University Press, Cambridge.

Gruzinski, Serge

1993   *The Conquest of Mexico: The Incorporation of Indian Societies into the Western World, 16th–18th Centuries.* Translated by E. Corrigan. Polity Press, Cambridge.

Hamann, Byron E.

2002   The Social Life of Pre-Sunrise Things: Indigenous Mesoamerican Archaeology. *Current Anthropology* 43: 351–382.

2008   Chronological Pollution: Potsherds, Mosques, and Broken Gods Before and After the Conquest of Mexico. *Current Anthropology* 49: 803–836.

Haubold, Johannes, Giovanni B. Lanfranchi, Robert Rollinger, and John Steele (editors)

2013   *The World of Berossos: Proceedings of the 4th International Colloquium on "The Ancient Near East between Classical and Ancient Oriental Traditions," Hatfield College, Durham, 7th–9th July 2010.* Harrassowitz Verlag, Wiesbaden.

Las Casas, Bartolomé de

1958   *Apologética história*, edited by Juan Pérez de Tudela, vol. 1. Biblioteca de Autores Españoles, Madrid.

Lockhart, James (editor)

1993   *We People Here: Nahuatl Accounts of the Conquest of Mexico.* University of California Press, Berkeley.

López de Gómara, Francisco

1553   *La Conquista de Mexico.* Miguel Capila, Zaragoza.

López Luján, Leonardo

2005   *The Offerings of the Templo Mayor of Tenochtitlan.* University of New Mexico Press, Albuquerque.

2014   Echoes of a Glorious Past: Mexica Antiquarianism. In *World Antiquarianisms: Comparative Perspectives*, edited by Alain Schnapp, pp. 273–294. The Getty Research Institute, Los Angeles.

Mason, Peter

2001   *The Lives of Images.* Reaktion Books, London.

Mendieta, Jerónimo de

1945   *Historia Eclesiástica Indiana*, edited by Joan de Domayquia, vol. 1. Salvador Chávez Hayhoe, México D.F.

1997   *Historia Eclesiástica Indiana: A Franciscan's View of the Spanish Conquest of Mexico*, edited by Felix Jay. Edwin Mellen Press, Lewiston.

Miller, Peter N.

2012   Writing Antiquarianism: Prolegomenon to a History. In *Antiquarianism and Intellectual Life in Europe and China, 1500–1800*, edited by Peter N. Miller and François Louis, pp. 27–57. University of Michigan Press, Ann Arbor.

Momigliano, Arnaldo

1950   Ancient History and the Antiquarian. *Journal of the Warburg and Courtauld Institutes* 13: 285–315.

More, Anna

2012   *Baroque Sovereignty: Carlos de Sigüenza y Góngora and the Creole Archive of Colonial Mexico.* University of Pennsylvania Press, Philadelphia.

Motolinía, Toribio de

1971   *Memoriales, o libro de las cosas de la Nueva España y de los naturales de ella*, edited by Edmundo O'Gorman. Universidad Nacional Autónoma de México–Instituto de Investigaciones Históricas, Mexico D.F.

1985   *Historia de los indios de la Nueva España*, edited by Georges Baudot. Castalia, Madrid.

Nagel, Alexander, and Christopher S.Wood
2010   *Anachronic Renaissance*. Zone Books, New York.

Orozco y Berra, Manuel (editor)
1979   *Códice Ramírez: manuscrito del siglo XVI intitulado "Relación del origen de los indios que habitan esta Nueva España, según sus historias"*. Editorial Inovación, Mexico D.F.

Phelan, John L.
1970   *The Millennial Kingdom of the Franciscans in the New World*, 2nd revised ed. University of California Press, Berkeley.

Robelo, Cecilio Agustín
1980   *Diccionario de mitología nahuatl*, 2 vols. Editorial Inovación, México D.F.

Romm, James
2001   Biblical History and the Americas: The Legend of Solomon's Ophir, 1492–1591. In *The Jews and The Expansion of Europe to the West, 1450 to 1800*, edited by Paolo Bernardini and Norman Fiering, pp. 27–46. Berghahn Books, New York.

Russo, Alessandra
2011   Cortés's Objects and the Idea of New Spain: Inventories as Spatial Narratives. *Journal of History of Collections* 23: 229–252.

Schnapp, Alain
1996   *The Discovery of the Past: The Origins of Archaeology*. Translated by I. Kinnes and G. Varndell. British Museum Press, London.

Schroeder, Susan, Anne J. Cruz, Cristian Roa-de-la-Carrera, and David E. Tavárez (editors)
2010   *Chimalpahin's Conquest: A Nahua Historian's Rewriting of Francisco López de Gómara's "La conquista de Mexico"*. Stanford University Press, Stanford.

Shelton, Anthony Alan
1997   Cabinets of Transgression: Renaissance Collections and the Incorporation of the New World. In *The Cultures of Collecting*, edited by John Elsner and Roger Cardinal, pp. 177–203. Reaktion, London.

Smith, Michael E.
1984   The Aztlan Migrations of the Nahuatl Chronicles: Myth or History? *Ethnohistory* 31: 153–186.

Temple, Nicholas
2001   Heritage and Forgery: Annio da Viterbo and the Quest for the Authentic. *Public Archaeology* 2: 151–162.

Tigerstedt, E. N.
1964   Ioannes Annius and *Graecia Mendax*. In *Classical, Mediaeval and Renaissance Studies in Honor of Berthold Louis Ullman*, edited by Charles Henderson Jr., vol. 2, pp. 293–310. Edizioni di Storia e Letteratura, Rome.

Torquemada, Juan de
1975   *Monarquía indiana*, edited by Miguel León-Portilla, vol. 1. Universidad Nacional Autónoma de México, México D.F.

Umberger, Emily
   1987   Antiques, Revivals, and References to the Past in Aztec Art. *RES: Anthropology and Aesthetics* 13: 62–105.
Weiss, Roberto
   1969   *The Renaissance Discovery of Classical Antiquity.* Basil Blackwell, Oxford.
Yaya, Isabel
   2008   Wonders of America: The Curiosity Cabinet as a Site of Representation and Knowledge. *Journal of the History of Collections* 20: 173–188.
Zimmermann, T. C. Price
   1995   *Paolo Giovio: The Historian and the Crisis of Sixteenth-Century Italy.* Princeton University Press, Princeton.

Rivaling Elgin: Ottoman Governors and Archaeological Agency in the Morea

Emily Neumeier

In the sprawling ancient sculpture galleries of the British Museum, a contemporary visitor may come across the monumental reconstruction of an architectural façade—the portal to the so-called "Treasury of Atreus" (Figures 7.1 and 7.2). This *tholos* or "beehive" tomb was originally constructed between 1350 and 1250 B.C. in Mycenae, today a major archaeological site in modern Greece perhaps best known for its legendary association with King Agamemnon (Wace 1926; Gere 2006; Moore et al. 2014).

In London, the museum curators have employed a minimalist display for the tomb's architecture in order to emphasize two ornamented columns, now broken into several pieces, which once framed the doorway of the subterranean burial chamber. Similar to other fine examples of sculpted marble situated in adjacent galleries, these fragmented columns serve as didactic objects, imparting knowledge about the impressive building practices of the Mediterranean during the Bronze Age. Yet these objects also stand as the material evidence of another moment in history—the early days of modern archaeology, when, in the late eighteenth and nineteenth centuries, an increasing number of Europeans traveled throughout the globe in search of antiquities. The majority of the Greek sculpture collection in the British Museum was gathered precisely during this period, a great age of acquisition when the British government assembled, as one scholar boasted, "the most comprehensive and important collection of ancient sculpture to be found anywhere in the world" (Jenkins 1992: 13).

Beyond these layers of institutional and disciplinary history, however, the columns from Mycenae are significant in that they bespeak another, more often overlooked, aspect of the early history of classical archaeology: the role of the modern inhabitants of ancient Greece, particularly local elites, in the appreciation and acquisition of such objects. For these columns were not

Figure 7.1. View of the Treasury of Atreus display at the British Museum, Room 6 (photograph by Taylan Güngör).

first uncovered by celebrated British travelers such as Lord Elgin or Charles Cockerell, but by another individual whose name is barely known today: Veli Pasha, the Ottoman governor of the Morea.

The eldest son of the notorious Tepedelenli Ali Pasha, Veli got his own shot at fame in the first years of the nineteenth century. In 1807, he was appointed governor general [*vali*] to the Ottoman province of the Morea, some fifteen years before the Greek revolution of 1821. Stationed at his post in Tripoli, Veli Pasha found himself in the midst of what has been memorably described as a "scramble for the past" (Bahrani et al. 2011), when the territories ruled by the Ottoman Empire emerged as one of the primary arenas for European archaeological exploration. It seems that the governor likewise came down with an acute case of marble fever. He became directly involved in some of the most significant discoveries of the day, including excavations at Argos and at the Temple of Apollo Epicurius at Bassae (Figure 7.3).

The expedition to Bassae, as well as other antiquarian efforts such as Lord Elgin's acquisition of the Parthenon sculptures or Stuart and Revett's publication of the *Antiquities of Athens*, have come to define the Western understanding of how Europe "discovered" ancient Greece, as well as the birth of scientific recording and archaeological excavation. Introducing an Ottoman governor as a protagonist in this drama provides an opportunity

Figure 7.2. Reconstruction drawing of the Treasury of Atreus façade from Mycenae (© Trustees of the British Museum).

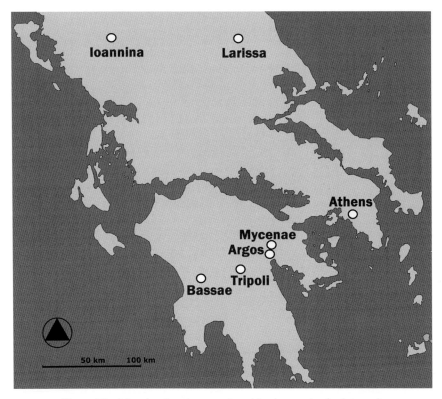

Figure 7.3. Map showing sites mentioned in the text (author's image).

to revise this narrative and think critically about how we can approach and frame the origins of Greek and Roman archaeology.

Ottoman Antiquarianism

The story of Veli Pasha lies at the juncture of two fields of scholarship—namely, Ottoman history and the history of archaeology. These two disciplines have traditionally been kept apart due to national identity and heritage politics, yet this situation has begun to shift, evidenced by a recent string of publications that work to situate the rise of archaeology within the Ottoman context (Shaw 2003; Bahrani et al. 2011; Holod and Ousterhout 2011; Çelik 2016). This move to destabilize the ever-growing pantheon of Europeans who have dominated the history of classical and Near Eastern scholarship emerges from a wider effort to address the link between political ideology and the fields of archaeology and anthropology (Trigger 1989; Schnapp 1993; Kohl and Fawcett 1995). Archaeology has likewise proven to be a particularly ripe topic for postcolonial critique, with scholars working to locate the indigenous or subaltern voices who speak back to hegemonic discourses of the past (Liebmann et al. 2008; Murray 2013). The historian of archaeology Alain Schnapp has recently reflected that one of the most notable results of probing deeper into the history of antiquarianism and archaeology has been the ability to "free ourselves of the notion that archaeologists, in the disciplinary sense of the term, have exclusive monopoly over archaeology" (Schnapp 2008: 394).

The recent publications that propose to examine archaeology from an Ottoman perspective, however, overwhelmingly focus on the second half of the nineteenth century, when the empire established its own imperial museum, launched excavations, and passed laws regulating antiquities—in effect crossing "a crucial line between being the field of western archaeological exploration and an actor in that field" (Bahrani et al. 2011: 13). Meanwhile, the handful of scholarly efforts examining what we could call Ottoman antiquarianism in the eighteenth and early nineteenth centuries—precisely when Veli Pasha was active—primarily look to evaluate "indigenous" and "alternative" archaeologies, investigating how non-elite, local inhabitants coexisted with and interpreted the past (Hamilakis 2008, 2011; Anderson 2015). These non-elite interpretations of ancient ruins were embedded in the routines of daily life, and often took on a mystical or superstitious nature, with locals ascribing magical powers—and, thus, life itself—to figural sculpture. It is just this type of ancient sculpture that was most prized by the Europeans. Any attempts by or on behalf of foreigners to remove these kinds of statues were often met with strong resistance from the local population, making archaeological sites "not only contact zones in the colonial sense, but also conflict zones" (Hamilakis 2011: 51).

This historiographic emphasis on a dynamic of transgression and resistance makes an explicit distinction between the pre-modern archaeology of local inhabitants and the modern archaeology of European foreigners, setting up an oppositional relationship between indigenous and colonial, or, in this case, crypto-colonial, actors. The case study of Veli Pasha complicates this paradigm by introducing a third group of stakeholders who played an important role in these cross-cultural, trans-imperial encounters: Ottoman provincial elites. Veli Pasha's high political status as governor of the Morea province also reminds us that, while the European travelers who came to this region in the eighteenth and nineteenth centuries were a small group of men with a similar education and class background, the "locals" whom they encountered could hardly be subsumed under a single language, class, or creed. Rather, the inhabitants of the area in question made up an entire social and political ecosystem that was distinctively Ottoman.

To say a few more words about this "ecosystem" and the administrative apparatus of the Ottoman provinces, we can note that, in the pre-modern period (which can be placed before the *Tanzimat* modernization reforms beginning in the 1840s),[1] these territories were governed by a small class of administrators (always Muslim), who were in the eighteenth and nineteenth centuries usually from the area, but still appointed to their position by the central authorities. Veli Pasha and his father, Tepedelenli Ali Pasha, can be considered part of this class of provincial power-holders. Besides these governors and their retinues consisting of scribes and military officers, one would also find in the Ottoman provinces, and especially in the Balkans, a class of elite notables including wealthy and educated merchants, mostly Christians who had spent some time abroad studying in Venice or Vienna; the clergy (both Muslim and Christian); and the headmen of villages or neighborhood communities (McGowan 1994; Barkey 2008: 242–255). The rest, and the majority, of the population consisted of the *re'aya*: the tax-paying subjects of the Ottoman Empire. When we speak about European encounters with the "indigenous" population in the Morea or Boeotia, therefore, we are principally referring to this last group, the (mostly Christian) villagers who lived among or nearby the ruins of sites such as Delphi, Corinth, Mycenae, Bassae, Aegina, Olympia, etc., and who were primarily occupied with farming and shepherding, as well as the occasional stint as archaeological laborers.

It is important to delineate the social stratigraphy and political hierarchies in operation within the Ottoman Empire during the earliest days of classical archaeology, because there is a vast difference between how ordinary people versus the more educated elites approached the ancient past, even though both discourses could be considered "emic" or "local." While the non-elite inhabitants of the region maintained a more vernacular view of the materiality and temporality of antiquity, governors such as Veli Pasha and his father Ali Pasha took up antiquarian practices of excavation and collecting that were not only provoked by the arrival of European archaeologists, but also fueled by the more long-standing intellectual interests of the members of the so-called Greek Enlightenment at their own courts.

What's more, Veli Pasha deviates from the portrait that we currently have of Ottoman officials in this period, characterized as generally indifferent to the European interest in locating and exporting ancient materials, "resulting in an almost systematic compliance with western demands" (Eldem 2011: 282). This is not to say that Veli Pasha objected to European archaeologists working in the area under his jurisdiction—if anything, he encouraged them—but he was hardly indifferent to the enterprise, content to observe from the sidelines. Rather than leave the business of excavations to foreign antiquarians, Veli Pasha got caught up himself in the hunt for ancient sculpture and, most significantly, initiated his own archaeological investigations. By examining the numerous examples of Veli Pasha's own antiquarian pursuits, this essay demonstrates that, even in the earliest days of classical archaeology, there were some Ottoman elites who exercised both their economic means and political authority to rival Europeans in their search for antiquity.

Excavations at Mycenae and Argos

As outlined above, it was at Mycenae that Veli Pasha made one of his first forays into archaeology. According to a local oral tradition, Veli Pasha first learned of the site from an elderly Muslim man from Nafplion, who told the governor that he knew of several statues hidden in "the tomb of Agamemnon" (Schliemann 1878: 49). Other archival sources confirm that, in the summer of 1810, Veli Pasha was hard at work at Mycenae, primarily engaged in excavating a *tholos* tomb, the same monument today known as the Treasury of Atreus (Hunt and Smith 1916: 281; Angelomati 2000: 108–109). Lord Elgin himself had ordered a first round of exploratory excavations of this tomb beginning in 1802, but, by the time Veli Pasha arrived, the entranceway had been filled in again (Leake 1830: II: 173) (Figures 7.4 and 7.5). Veli had this entire area cleared, in the process finding more pieces from the two half-columns of green serpentine that decorated the entrance. These are the architectural fragments that can now be seen on display at the British Museum.

Before the columns arrived in London, however, they underwent a circuitous journey. Just a few weeks after Veli Pasha's excavations, Howe Peter Browne, the 2nd Marquess of Sligo, arrived in Tripoli to pay his respects to the Ottoman governor at his official residence. Veli Pasha received Lord Sligo cordially, and, as was common at such meetings, the vizier and his guest exchanged gifts. Lord Sligo offered Veli Pasha two large cannons that were being held on his ship, and, in return, the governor presented a set of guns, a gold-embroidered costume in the Albanian style, a horse, and two ancient columns "which he said would last longer than the horse or clothes would" (Beinecke Library, Yale University, OSB MSS 74 Box 1, Folder 1, Lord Sligo to the Marchioness of Sligo, Tripoli, 3 August 1810).[2] Pleased with this gift, Lord Sligo ultimately transported the columns back to his estate in Ireland. There, they were eventually forgotten and left to linger until 1904, when they were located by the Marquess's grandson and donated to the British Museum (Finn 2002: 8).

Veli Pasha not only exposed the interior and entrance-way to the Treasury of Atreus, but he also broke ground on another nearby tumulus, quite likely at the advice of William Gell, a British artist and antiquarian, who, reading the ancient Greek geographer Pausanias, predicted the presence of another

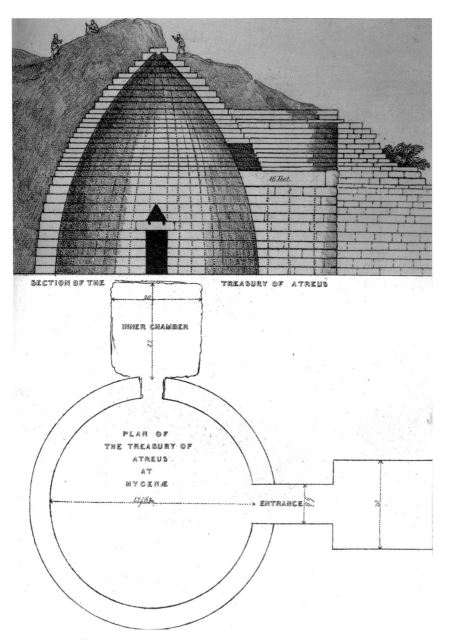

Figure 7.4. William Gell's cross-section and ground plan of the Treasury of Atreus, 1810, reproduced as Plate 4 in Gell 1810.

Figure 7.5. William Gell's view of the entrance to the Treasury of Atreus, 1810, reproduced as Plate 5 in Gell 1810.

tomb outside the city walls (Gell 1810: 34). In the end, the governor opened a trench and located another, smaller *tholos* tomb, what is now known as the Tomb of Clytemnestra, which Heinrich Schliemann went on to excavate more thoroughly in the 1870s (Moore et al. 2014: 78; Turner 1820: I,288; Angelomati-Tsougaraki 2000: 109). The fact that Gell may have guided Veli Pasha's excavations points to an interesting inversion of the roles that one typically sees in narratives of colonial encounter. Instead of the "indigenous" population serving as informants or guides to the colonial explorer, here it is the European visitor who guides the local governor in his archaeological pursuits.

Although this chapter will not be able to address the full range of Ottoman elites involved in investigating antiquity, it should at least be stressed that there were also other agents—usually Greek-speaking Christians with some wealth and education—who also played an important role in these archaeological discoveries. For example, Lord Elgin is traditionally credited with the discovery of the Treasury of Atreus in Mycenae, but, after his departure from the site, he hired a merchant and archon from Argos named Vlassopoulos to organize and oversee the actual excavations that led to the uncovering of other marble slabs from the façade, which are today located directly next to Veli Pasha's columns in the British Museum display (Hunt *et al.* 1916: 213; Gell 1810: 69).

Shortly before his time in Mycenae, Veli Pasha had also commenced digging in the nearby village of Argos in the early summer of 1810 (Hunt and Smith 1916: 281; Angelomati-Tsougaraki 2000: 104, 109). Today a modern town located about ten kilometers from the eastern coast of the Peloponnese, Argos boasts the remains of an ancient agora and adjacent theater in good condition. It was here that:

> Veli Pasha, Governor of the Morea, caused an excavation to be made near the theatre, and discovered sixteen marble statues and busts, in good style and preservation, particularly one of Venus and another of Aesculapius. They were not quite half the size of life. Several gold medals of the Emperor Valens were also found in a sepulchre near the same spot [Conder 1830: 49].

Similar to his efforts at Mycenae, Veli Pasha also employed the services of an Englishman—unnamed in the sources—who assisted the governor with drawing up an itemized register of all of the major finds at Argos. This register is lost now, but it was seen by William Gell in 1810, who mentioned it in his own travel account:

> I saw a list of statues found by an English gentleman, in company with [Veli] Pasha, on the eastern coast of Laconia, on the borders of Argolis, which, though highly ludicrous in itself, from the pompous style in which the several fragments were set forth, was sufficient to show that the field was very productive. This list began in full-mouthed Greek:—one Venus, without a head; one draped Minerva, without head, arms, or feet; one Apollo, wanting one leg, &c. &c. [Gell 1823: 364–365].

It is almost impossible now to determine the original configuration or purpose of this collection of statues in ancient times; yet the sculptures may have served some kind of votive or commemorative purpose in the city's agora, located directly next to the theater.

Unfortunately, we know little about the current whereabouts of these sculptures, although there is a clue from a letter that Lord Elgin received from one of his agents in September 1810, stating that Veli had sold some sculptures from Argos to "Messrs. Knight and Fazakerly" (Hunt and Smith 1916: 281). This is no doubt a reference to Henry Gally Knight (d. 1846) and John Nicholas Fazakerly (1787–1852), who travelled together to Greece in 1810. It is tempting to link Veli Pasha's finds in the theater of Argos with a Hellenistic statue of a marble kore now located in the British Museum, which was donated by Knight and Fazakerly in 1818 (Pryce 1892: 71–72).[3] The sculpture fits the description of what Gell refers to as the statue of a draped Minerva having lost its head, arms and feet, and being "not quite half the size of life" at a height of 0.535 meters (Figure 7.6). North and Fazakerly first saw the statues that Veli Pasha had found at Argos in the governor's palace in Tripoli, situated in a long passage where Veli said he kept sculpture that "he collected for his English friends" (quoted in Angelomati-Tsougaraki 2000: 111, 114). Knight and Fazakerly bought the whole lot of statues for the sum of 500 pounds. After having exported these sculptures back to the United Kingdom shortly thereafter with the assistance of one

Figure 7.6. Marble Kore, Hellenistic Period (© Trustees of the British Museum).

of the pasha's agents, perhaps Knight and Fazakerly donated one of their purchases to the British Museum.

When North and Fazakerly visited Veli Pasha in Tripoli, the governor also related to them that he still had a few sculptures from Argos waiting in Nafplion to be transported, and that he was expecting to renew his excavations after the harvest. (Angelomati-Tsougaraki 2000: 111) It is not clear whether or not Veli Pasha ever followed through with these intentions and returned to Argos for more archaeological exploration. We do know that he at least returned to Nafplion to retrieve the rest of his finds, as François Pouqueville, the French consul to Ioannina, mentions that Veli Pasha had gifted to a member of his father Ali Pasha's court a statue of Apollo "in the manner of the Belvedere" as well as a head of a gorgon that had been found in Argos (Pouqueville 1826: 5: 206; Leake 1835: 1: 223; Panagiotopoulos 2000: 1: 692).[4]

The Expedition to the Temple of Apollo Epicurius

Veli Pasha at first concentrated his energy on exploring the ancient remains of the Argolid, with his men moving from site to site, likely following tips or advice from villagers who volunteered information once they learned the vizier was interested. Yet, perhaps the most intriguing offer for locating antiquities presented itself about a year later, in the early days of the summer of 1812, this time on the opposite side of the Morea in the western mountains of Arcadia. It was around this time that George Gropius appeared in the governor's court to procure permission to excavate the Temple of Apollo Epicurius at Bassae. Gropius was representing the loosely-formed "Society of Friends," a mixed group of European antiquarians who had met in Athens and decided to pool their resources in their mutual mission to locate, document, and, ideally, extricate ancient sculpture from Ottoman lands. Fresh from successfully excavating a series of spectacular marbles from the Temple of Aphaea in Aegina—which eventually found their way to the Glyptothek in Munich—this same group decided to head to the remote mountains of the western Peloponnese in search of Bassae, a temple said to have been built by Iktinos, the architect of the Athenian Parthenon (Cockerell 1903: 51–57) (Figure 7.7). The Europeans undertook an initial reconnaissance and drawing survey in 1811, then decided to return the following year to excavate, which is how Gropius found his way to Veli Pasha's court.

To the great annoyance of the aspirant excavators, the governor was not satisfied with the standard remuneration that was usually offered by Europeans in exchange for a *buyuruldu* (order), but was only willing to grant the permission to excavate if he could join the mission as a financial backer and stakeholder. In his memoir from Bassae, one of the other members of

Figure 7.7. View of the Temple of Apollo Epicurius, Bassae, in Stackelberg 1826, Plate 11 (Gennadius Library, Athens).

the team, Peter Brøndsted, bemoans that the "sums of money were not the most cumbersome part of the contract. Worse was His Highness's capricious idea that he wanted to be a party to the enterprise." Brøndsted was concerned that Veli Pasha's enthusiasm might pose a further potential hindrance for removing statues from Ottoman soil, a task that proved to be quite difficult in the case of Aegina (Brøndsted 1861: 6; Cockerell 1903: 53–54; Hamilakis 2011: 53). Meanwhile, yet another member of the "Society of Friends," Otto von Stackelberg, maintained a more positive outlook on the situation, insisting in his account that Veli Pasha's passion for antiquities was actually to the team's advantage in negotiations: "Fortunately, ever since the sale of some antiquities which he had found in the Treasury of Atreus at Mycenae, the Pasha had picked up the hobby of excavations; so when Mr. Gropius came to him with the proposal, he aroused the Pasha's interest in taking part in the excavation himself" (Stackelberg 1826: 13, translation mine). In exchange for providing half of the excavation costs up front, Veli Pasha was promised half of the archaeological material—by which was meant the figural sculpture—that would be found, with the Europeans retaining the right of first refusal to purchase the governor's share of the marbles at the conclusion of the dig.

The governor of the Morea was not able to join Gropius and the rest of his team for the excavations at Bassae, so he sent one of his agents, a Greek-speaking Christian by the name of Vasilakis, to represent him and his interests at the site. Because the temple was situated in a remote mountain location—known to locals as "the columns" (τους στύλους)—upon their arrival the group set about building themselves primitive accommodations from the boughs of nearby oak trees. They named their encampment "Francopolis" (Cockerell 1903: 217). Vasilakis, whom Brøndsted later described as "an insignificant slave, with no spirit or heart," took up the job of paying the local workers, who were mostly from the village of Andritsaina. He was responsible for maintaining a register of names and working hours of the men. Brøndsted writes:

> This task which certainly was not without its difficulties has been assigned to him for two reasons: partly to keep him occupied because he was miserably bored and completely incapable of taking part in our delight in the marble amazons and heroes who day by day were descending in greater numbers to us from the night of the past, partly because of prudence which other circumstances imposed: Since the Pasha's own participation in our undertaking could not be avoided, His Highness would, of course, be more likely to trust the information given in the report on the expenses incidental to the excavation project if the most important of these passed through the hands of his own servant [Brøndsted 1861: 6–9].

Brøndsted also relates in his account an episode concerning Vasilakis and the local villagers co-opted as excavation laborers, whereby a fist-fight broke out over the amount of wages a particular worker was owed; Vasilakis was said to have dealt with the man and his friends "in a condescending and uncharitable way, he may even have hit a few of them." What followed was a confused skirmish, with Vasilakis fetching his pistols and discharging them in the air. The melée concluded when Vasilakis pursued one of the workers up the hill into the peristyle of the temple, only to be flung himself against one of the blocks of the architrave "with such violence that his loins and sides gave him pain long after" (Brøndsted 1861: 10).

While this anecdote as related by Brøndsted certainly indulges in the topoi of Orientalist sensationalism—the purity of ancient civilization and genius marred by ignorant brutality—the description of Vasilakis and his interactions with the archaeologists as well as the local workers serves to reiterate the complexity of the "colonial-indigenous" encounter. Although the European archaeologists at Bassae were not, strictly speaking, colonizers, they were certainly engaged in the imperial impulse of locating and appropriating valuable resources (in this case, antiquities) from far-flung regions and having them transported back to their respective centers in Western Europe. At the excavation site, Brøndsted witnessed tensions and violence erupt due to an asymmetrical power dynamic among and within the "indigenous" population itself. Despite a common language and religious confession, there was a gulf of difference between Veli Pasha's agent Vasilakis, who was both literate and wealthy (he seems to be the only one on the site who owned pistols), and the relatively poor and uneducated workers from the local village. These local politics playing out among the stones of the Apollo temple demonstrate that the epistemic model of foreign vs. local is insufficient when trying to understand the perspectives and motivations of the various actors involved in these early excavations.

The European archaeologists also resented Vasilakis for his position of power, as his mission of surveillance provided a constant reminder that they were only there by the good will of the governor. This situation naturally bred insecurity among the foreign antiquarians, and Brøndsted, for one, reacted by belittling the pasha's agent in his account as completely indifferent to the antiquities being unearthed at the temple, unworthy, as it were, of wisdom descending from the "night of the past." The Danish archaeologist also levelled similar accusations at Veli Pasha himself:

> How the excavation progressed had presumably been already reported from time to time to the Pasha by his servant, Vasilachi, to whom reference has repeatedly been made; but the incompleteness of this ignorant person's reports or the Pasha's own unimaginative ignorance, or both in conjunction, were, no doubt, the reason why the Pasha made known to us his most inconvenient demand of having a great many of the recovered idols (as they were termed) brought to him in Tripolizza where it would please his Highness to inspect them personally. The unpleasant demand could not but be complied with, whence a number of damaged Amazons and centaurs, carefully packed and transported by seven or eight mules, had to make their way, well over a day's journey, to Tripolizza and back again to the temple. However, the traveling excursion of the fragmentary heroes did, no doubt, result in one good thing, namely that the Pasha—who presumably did not feel too well at ease in this idol chaos—became more inclined to renounce his share in the discoveries against a sum of money [Brøndsted 1861: 12].

This disparagement of Veli Pasha as ignorant and incapable of appreciating the wonders of antiquity becomes a common trope in several of the later narratives of the Bassae excavations. The son of Charles Cockerell, who was part of the initial 1811 survey of the site but could not be present for the excavations the following summer, recalls in a 1903 edition of his father's journal that:

Veli Pasha, the Governor of the Morea, has sanctioned the explorations on the understanding that he should have half profits; but when he had seen the sculptures he was so disappointed that they were not gold or silver, and so little understood them, that he took the warriors under shields for tortoises, allowing that as such they were rather well done [Cockerell 1903: 219].

Deploying a rhetoric of the ignorant native is a well-established tactic of eighteenth- and nineteenth-century European travelers who sought to justify the removal of archaeological material from their local context. The fact that these kinds of travel accounts frequently stress in detail the archaeologists' efforts to acquire official permission from the Ottoman authorities could be understood as a pre-emptive response to any question about the ethical or legal validity of their enterprise. Pointing out European claims to cultural superiority vis-à-vis the Oriental "other" is by now nothing new, but it is worth raising here because this argument is one of the primary reasons that individuals such as Veli Pasha have disappeared from contemporary narratives of the early days of classical archaeology. It is easy to imagine that Veli Pasha in particular was seen as a threat by the likes of Brøndsted or Cockerell due to his special interest in ancient sculpture. Surely one of the reasons that the Bassae team opted to ship to the governor in Tripoli some of the more "damaged" sculptures, besides minimizing the risk of breakage for the choicer marbles, was because they did not want Veli Pasha, who after his previous experiences clearly held the capacity to judge the quality of ancient marbles, to decide that he wanted to keep his share of the finds. To their great relief, the European excavators were ultimately able to buy Veli Pasha out (Cooper 1992: 13). The collection was then put up for an open auction in Zakynthos, where it was ultimately sold to the British crown, thus securing the famous temple frieze for the British Museum.

Shortly after the excavations at Bassae, Veli Pasha was removed from his position in the Morea and transferred north to serve as the governor of Larissa (Ott. *Yenişehir Fener*) (Panagiotopoulos 2000: 2: 239). In his new post, the governor continued to keep himself abreast of all developments with regards to locating ancient materials. When the French artist Louis Dupré, who is responsible for some of the most famous imagery of Ali Pasha and his court, paid Veli Pasha a visit in his new palace, during their audience the governor "spoke about the Lion of Chaeronea, which has just been discovered, the bas-reliefs of Thespiae, as well as some other monuments" (Dupré 1825: 23, translation mine). All of these sites were located within the confines of the governor's new territory. Veli Pasha also continued to maintain a collection of marbles in his residence, similar to the sculptures he kept on display in Tripoli. In a letter dated 1818, the English diplomat

Arthur Carrighan recalled a meeting he had with the governor during his journey through the area:

> The example of excavating which I thought had originated with [Ali Pasha] was it seems set him by this son Veli, who made considerable excavations in the Morea his former Pachalick, among the objects of the fine arts he found four statues or busts which he presented to Lord Guilford then. Mr. North and I were surprised to find he recollected the names of the Deities and Personages represented by these stones. He also gave a good account of same basse relieves *still in his own possession*, and which he calls "quadri in marmor" or pictures in marble. He is a handsome man of very agreeable cast of countenance, and possessed of considerable powers of conversation [St. John's College Library, Cambridge, GBR/0275/Carrighan, Letter from Arthur Carrighan to Thomas Maitland, Thessaloniki, 20 June 1818, emphasis added].

From Carrighan's statement, we can gather a number of important points. First of all, Veli Pasha, in addition to his native languages of Greek and Albanian, could converse with foreign visitors directly in Italian, atypical for an Ottoman governor and a skill usually found principally among scribes or interpreters in the retinue of the provincial court, who had either spent time studying abroad or were from one the (ex-Venetian) Ionian Islands. Second, it seems that the governor continued to keep a collection of marbles for himself in Thessaly. Carrighan unfortunately does not provide us with enough information to determine whether or not the mentioned reliefs were brought from Veli Pasha's post in the Morea, or if he had acquired them after his arrival in the north. At any rate, the fact that the governor could recall in great detail the statues he had located in Argos several years ago and continued to collect such objects calls into question the claims of the foreign excavators at Bassae that Veli Pasha was unfamiliar with and even resistant to the concept of figural sculpture on any grounds of religion or superstition.

Veli Pasha's Motivations and Archaeological Agency

What can be made of Veli Pasha and his pursuit of "pictures in marble"? The provincial governor is most notable because he stands apart from the constellation of actors as described by the more recent scholarship on archaeology in the Ottoman Empire—i.e., the imperial center and foreign antiquarians (Eldem 2011). Because of his political position, Veli Pasha should be considered as a representative of the state, but it should also be emphasized that he was part of a new class of provincial power-holders, which began to emerge throughout the empire in the eighteenth century, who were outside of the centralized system that groomed the sultan's administrators within the palace court. It remains problematic, therefore, to equate Veli Pasha's interests with those of the Ottoman state. This particular political dynamic may be the reason that Veli Pasha's archaeological activities remain invisible in the Ottoman archives. The cases of Elgin's removal of the Parthenon sculptures or the French acquisition of the Venus de Milo were adjudicated at the highest levels of the central government in Istanbul (Eldem 2011: 289–293, and 326, fn. 44) and, consequently, left behind a paper trail in the archives primarily in the form of imperial decrees (*hatt-ı hümayun*). Yet other contemporaneous efforts to excavate and export sculpture, most notably the extraction of the Aegina and Bassae marbles, seemed to have been dealt with on a more *ad hoc* basis at the local administrative level, with apparently little or no consultation with the Ottoman center or foreign ambassadors. It likewise seems unlikely that Veli Pasha would have written to Istanbul to acquire permission to perform his own excavations at Argos or Mycenae.

The Ottoman state archives as well as the archives of the Imperial Museum (today the Istanbul Archaeological Museum) most certainly remain an underused resource that may offer local perspectives on Western claims to antiquity. Yet this information will be restricted mostly to the second half of the nineteenth century, when the organization of archaeological excavations within the empire became more bureaucratized and subject to scrutiny at the highest levels of state. That is why some of the best places to search for information about Veli Pasha's interactions with European travelers as well as his own excavations are still published Western travel accounts, as well as private or diplomatic correspondence. The recent revisionist scholarship on archaeology in the Ottoman world has quite rightly criticized earlier academic studies for relying too heavily on the published travel accounts of European antiquarians, reporting the information within these "normative texts" with little to no consideration of the imperialist ideologies operating in the background (Bahrani et al. 2011: 38). As I have tried to demonstrate, however, it remains possible to read against the text and detect traces of the actions and motivations of local actors in these foreign sources, especially when one can compare multiple accounts of the same sequence of events, as is the case with Bassae. Within these texts, it is also sometimes possible to find references to local documents and correspondence that are now gone. For example, when Brøndsted had left the Morea and was visiting Veli's father Ali Pasha in Preveza, Ali Pasha asked if he was "one of those Mylords" with whom his son had been excavating, because Veli Pasha "wrote to [him] of the marbles he found in the Morea" (Brøndsted 1999: 63–64). From this passage, we know that Veli Pasha had been keeping his father informed in their correspondence on his archaeological activities, even if he had not been writing to the officials of the Sublime Porte in Istanbul.

Veli Pasha's interest in archaeology seems to have been born in direct response to the arrival of European travelers such as Lord Elgin. Unlike the indigenous archaeologies of non-elite locals, which clearly pre-date such foreign initiatives, Veli Pasha appears to have only been turned on to what Stackelberg describes as his new "hobby" in conjunction with his European interlocutors. Considering how assiduously the governor kept track of the movements of foreigners in his territory (Cockerell 1903: 81), it is very likely that he was aware of Lord Elgin's initial excavation activities in Mycenae. As outlined above, it was in 1810 that Veli Pasha decided to try his own hand at digging up ancient sculpture. It is this jump from bystander to active participant that most interests me about Veli Pasha, how he fully exploited what could be considered his "archaeological agency." Bound up within this term is an acknowledgement of the fact that the governor, by virtue of his political position, was not subject to the same constrictions of physical mobility (either for his own person or the sculptures in question) and funding that confronted his European visitors at every turn. The wide degree of latitude that Veli Pasha enjoyed in his own antiquarian endeavors further throws into question how effective a colonial/ indigenous model is when discussing archaeology in the Ottoman provinces, at least for this earlier period.

There is no question that the governor was in part motivated by monetary considerations. Both Veli Pasha and his father commanded large swaths of territory, maintaining their political positions by collecting taxes for the central government and meeting the expenses of keeping a provincial court through the annual revenues generated by their own private estates of agricultural land; historians have claimed that both Ali and Veli Pasha were in their own time some of the greatest private landowners in the empire (Skiotis 1971: 221). With this enormous and complex economic machine operating in the background, both father and son naturally remained alert to all potential avenues of financial gain. The hunt for antiquities in the Ottoman Empire could to a certain degree be ascribed to an awareness that there was a market emerging for such objects, where sculptures became a valued commodity.

In the case of Bassae in particular, Veli Pasha approached the foreign request for permission to excavate as a business proposition, countering with his own demand to be part of the deal, leveraged against his own financial stake in the venture, as well as his ability to ensure the cooperation of local headmen and villagers. As mentioned, at the conclusion of the excavation, the "Society of Friends" bought out Veli Pasha's share of half the marbles, to the tune of 3,000 dollars (Cooper 1992: 13).[5] In the end, this group of European excavators sold the entirety of the marbles—the famed Phigaleian Frieze—to the British government for 60,000 dollars (Cooper 1992: 23). Looking at these numbers, it seems that Veli Pasha did not win the better part of this deal. Even so, to put these numbers into some perspective, it may be helpful to note that, at about the same time that the governor brokered this deal with Gropius in Tripoli, Veli

Pasha maintained his own estate of villages in the wider region that generated an annual revenue of about two million Ottoman *kuruş* (piaster), or about £100,000, although this was still apparently not sufficient to meet the expenses of maintaining his court and troops in the Morea. (North, in Angelomati-Tsougaraki 2000: 110). Using historic conversion rates,[6] we can translate Veli Pasha's annual revenue of £100,000 to 455,600 dollars, a number that, even if an approximate value, dwarfs the 3,000 dollars Veli was said to have received for the Phigaleian marbles. With this sum, therefore, being really just a drop in the bucket of the governor's finances, it remains difficult to claim that the governor was pursuing antiquities purely as a monetary venture.

In the same way that early European antiquarians who traveled to Ottoman Greece were driven both by pecuniary interest and a genuine desire to advance humanistic knowledge, it is reasonable to allow Veli Pasha the same depth of character and mixed motivations in his search for ancient sculpture. Marble sculptures certainly proved their worth as both economic commodity and diplomatic leverage, but it seems that, at least for Veli Pasha, he was equally captivated by the fragments of an ancient civilization practically littered at his feet.

Once we become open to the idea of Veli Pasha as an antiquarian, an individual dedicated to the collection and study of ancient artifacts, it is not difficult to find various details in Western travel accounts or archival material that characterize the governor's abiding interest in the past. Multiple Europeans mention that Veli Pasha had made a trip to Athens around 1810 or 1811, "by way of satisfying himself as to what could be the motive of coming so far to see such a place; it appears that he was much struck with the ruins, and the effect of the whole" (Gell 1823: 364; see also Cockerell 1903: 61). A short time later, Ali Pasha, speaking with another English traveler in Ioannina, "asked … how long we had left Athens, whether any discoveries had been made there lately by excavations, and mentioned the pleasure which his son Vely Pasha had received by his visit to that beautiful city" (Hughes 1820: 1: 448). Ali Pasha relates this information with the pride and bemusement of any parent who admires but does not quite understand their child's enthusiasm for the latest trends or technologies of the day. Yet, as Arthur Carrighan notes in his letter cited above, it was Veli's example that drew his father's attention to archaeological excavations. Eventually, Veli Pasha's activities in the Morea would inspire his father Ali Pasha to take up his own archaeological pursuits further north, most notably at the ancient Roman city of Nikopolis (Brøndsted 1999: 69–74).

Besides his frequent consultation with foreign visitors for advice and information regarding antiquity, Veli Pasha also made use of the growing corpus of literature on ancient Greece that was becoming more readily available. Frederick North relates that the governor had ordered Pausanias's

Description of Greece to be translated into modern Greek, and requested the Englishman to procure him a copy for that purpose (Angelomati-Tsougaraki 2000: 123). William Gell confirms that Veli Pasha "absolutely undertook to read, or cause to be read to him, Pausanias, that he might be enabled, as well as the milords, to judge where statues, or other precious relics of antiquity, might be probably concealed" (Gell 1823: 364). And when North visited Veli Pasha in Tripoli, he noted that the governor was at the moment employed in reading a modern Greek translation of Oliver Goldsmith's *History of Greece* (Angelomati-Tsougaraki 2000: 111). Veli Pasha's copy of the book was most likely an 1806 translation, printed in Vienna, by the scholar Dimitrios Alexandridis, who had added his own third section on Byzantine history to the volume (Alexandridis 1806). Veli Pasha had a reputation for being the most cultivated of Ali Pasha's sons; his brother, Muhtar Pasha, another provincial governor, was more interested in military operations and hunting. The pious endowment for Veli Pasha's congregational mosque complex in Ioannina makes provisions for a library; not one of the five mosque complexes built by his father featured such an institution (Vakıflar Genel Müdürlüğü, Ankara, Vakfiye Defter 629, page 743, entry 491, AH 11 Cemâziyelevvel 1219/CE 18 August 1804).

To what extent, then, could Veli Pasha be considered singular in his passion for antiquities? While the governor possessed the wealth and political authority to undertake an unusually active interest in unearthing ancient sculpture, he nevertheless could still be considered as coming from a culture of Ottoman notables, many of whom were educated in central Europe but returned to centers like Ioannina and Veli Pasha's own court in Thessaly, who at the time were engaging in a kind of hybrid antiquarianism, drawing upon the information brought by foreign travelers while forming their own intellectual tradition based on a classical education (Kitromilides 2013). The Alexandridis translation of Goldsmith's *History of Greece* mentioned above, printed in Vienna and ultimately intended for this group of Greek-speaking notables in the Balkans, is a good example of this kind of trans-imperial cultural hybridity. This flourishing of local elite interests in the ancient past, typically referred to as the "Greek Enlightenment," cannot be simply reduced to a burgeoning of Greek nationalism. Letting Veli Pasha step back into the spotlight of history even more firmly emphasizes that this phenomenon was not exclusive to Christians. His example encourages us to begin to seek other instances of alternative archaeologies that do not fit into the mold of European universalism or Greek nationalism. For example, in the early eighteenth century, Mahmud Efendi, a native of the Morea and *kadi* (chief justice) of Athens, wrote *Tarih-i Medinetü'l-Hükema* (History of the City of the Philosophers), an Ottoman treatise on the heart of ancient Greece, reportedly with the help of two Christian monks and at the behest of the Muslim governor of Nafplion, who enjoyed listening to the stories Mahmud

Efendi told him about ancient Greece when they met (Tunalı 2012). In this context, Veli Pasha appears to be the natural result of a complex constellation of different communities, both foreign and local, that each had their own unique relationship with antiquity according to their education and political interests. While both Christian and Muslim villagers often approached ancient ruins, particularly figural sculpture, with a superstitious belief in their apotropaic capabilities, the elite classes held a more academic interest that was informed by a variety of intellectual traditions.

Conclusion

In the online database of the British Museum's collection, most archaeological material has some brief information about the excavation of the object; the website credits, for example, the discovery of the sculptures from Bassae to an international group of antiquarians, naming among others Charles Cockerell (who was not actually present for the excavation; he was in Sicily at the time). As for the columns from Mycenae, the entry for these objects makes no mention of Veli Pasha, with the section on acquisition only recognizing the donation from Lord Sligo's son in 1905.[7] Highlighting this kind of discrepancy in how a modern museum presents the record of excavation and acquisition serves to illustrate a wider question within the booming field of the history of archaeology: the tendency to forget the role played by local actors in archaeological discovery. As early as 1821, eleven years after Veli Pasha's archaeological venture, a French traveler describes the leadership at the excavations at Mycenae as a joint partnership between Lord Sligo and Veli Pasha, with Sligo supposedly removing and transporting the columns that he himself played a part in finding (Laurent 1821: 145). By 1904, when the British Museum keeper Cecil Sharp travelled to the former residence of the Marquess of Sligo in order to examine the potential donations to the museum, Veli Pasha had disappeared completely from the story of the columns' discovery. Writing to the board of trustees, Sharp noted that "these are evidently the columns which were excavated by the second Marquis of Sligo about 1812, in the so-called 'Treasury of Atreus'" (Finn 2002: 9). Thus, about a century after the modern discovery of the columns at Mycenae, the precise details of how they came to light had become distorted, with Veli Pasha fading from the scene, and Lord Sligo, who had been at most a casual bystander, promoted by later historians to excavation director. I do not want to suggest that the elision of Veli Pasha's role in the columns' provenance is due to malicious intent; I bring up this example more to reflect on the casual assumptions and omissions that often occur when constructing historical narratives about archaeology. Who "deserves" to feature in these narratives, and to what aim?

The case studies outlined above demonstrate that Veli Pasha cultivated his antiquarian pursuits with an eye to the interests of foreign visitors to his territories, aspiring to locate and amass a collection of stones "as well as the milords." Unfortunately, with the available evidence it is less certain to what extent the governor mobilized these excavations or the display of these finds in his palaces to validate his own political or ethnic claims by forging connections with the past (although his father Ali Pasha would eventually generate his own self-image as the "new Pyrrhus," the great Hellenistic king of Epirus). At any rate, Veli Pasha has most likely been lost in the history of archaeology because his story fulfills no contemporary narrative of cultural or political identity. Today, what does it mean to anyone that a Muslim governor of an Ottoman province, born in what is now Albania and ruling over what is now part of Greece, took up a love of the classics alongside Lord Elgin or Byron? To return to the question of how we construct narratives of archaeology, David Lowenthal has pointed out that what we describe as history is often heritage in disguise:

> Legends of origin and endurance, of victory and calamity, project the present back, the past forwards; they align us with forbears whose virtues we share and whose vices we shun … History explores and explains pasts grown ever more opaque over time; heritage clarifies pasts so as to infuse them with present purposes [Lowenthal 1997: xv].

It is no secret that the history of archaeology is deeply enmeshed with heritage politics. Moving forward, it is clear that the European encounter with the Ottoman authorities in the Morea as well as Athens was much more multi-faceted than a meeting between two worlds. But where can we go from here to better characterize the nature of this exchange? At the present, any discussion of the early days of archaeology in Ottoman Greece is inevitably overshadowed by the fierce contemporary debate between Greece and the United Kingdom over the restitution of the Parthenon statues. Lord Elgin and his marbles are always hovering in the back of our minds. This essay has set out to join a more general call to resist the notion that the only relationship with the past that is legitimate, or, at least, worthy of study, is one that is forged strictly within the confines of Western Europe. If we begin to investigate the broader question of what antiquity meant to the early modern subject of the Ottoman Empire, both elite and non-elite, we will be able to detect previously unknown trajectories for alternative archaeologies of the classical world.

Notes

1. For a critical reappraisal of these reforms and a review of the relevant literature, see Abu-Manneh 1994.

2. This archival material has been made available by Peter Cochran, published on his personal website, accessed June 15, 2016, https://petercochran.wordpress.com/the-marquis-of-sligo/.

3. Acquisition number 1818,0509.1, http://www.britishmuseum.org/research/collection_online/collection_object_details.aspx?objectId=407833&partId=1&searchText=Gally+Knight&page=1, accessed June 15, 2016. On the British Museum website, however, the kore is reported as being acquired in Athens, not Argos. Upon further inquiry, a curator at the museum suggested that this information may be considered uncertain, as the archival letters recording the donation of the statue do not mention the provenance: E-mail correspondence with Thomas Kiely, March 30, 2016. My thanks to the staff of the British Museum for their assistance in this matter.

4. We also know from Pouqueville that around the same time Veli Pasha ordered that a large tomb in the ancient agora of Phlius, a site that is located a few kilometers northwest of Mycenae and Argos, be opened up, and took away from there several pieces of ancient marble decorated with inscriptions: Pouqueville 1826: 5: 310.

5. Additionally, Brøndsted claims that "the Pasha [Veli] received, in addition to the repayment of this disbursement incidental to the excavation enterprise, to which he had been a party, a further payment of 5000 Spanish piasters against his renouncing claims to these ancient marbles": Brøndsted 1861: 13. Cockerell reports that Veli Pasha accepted £400 for his share of the Bassae marbles: Cockerell 1903: 219–220.

6. Historical currency conversion is always problematic, but one source happens to give the conversion rate of 1 pound = 4.556 dollars for Zante in 1815, the same year that the marbles were auctioned on the island: *Encyclopaedia Britannica* 1824: 89.

7. See mentioned objects from the British Museum collection online: one part of the Bassae sculptures, also known as the Phigaleian frieze, no. 1815,1020.1, http://www.britishmuseum.org/research/collection_online/collection_object_details.aspx?objectId=461761&partId=1&searchText=bassae+sculptures&page=1; and the columns from the Treasury of Atreus, Mycenae, no. 1905,1105.1-3, http://www.britishmuseum.org/research/collection_online/collection_object_details.aspx?objectId=457905&partId=1&searchText=column+Mycenae&page=1, both accessed June 15, 2016.

References

Abu-Manneh, Butrus
1994   The Islamic Roots of the Gülhane Rescript. *Die Welt des Islams* 34: 173–203.
Alexandridis, Dimitrios
1806   Ἰὁλδσμίϑ Ἰστορία τῆς Ἑλλάδος ἀπό τῆς πρώτης καταβολῆς τῶν Ἑλληνικῶν πραγμάτων ἄχρι τῆς ἁλώσεως τῆς Κωνσταντινουπόλεως ὑπό τῶν Ὀϑωμανῶν [Goldsmith's History of Greece, from the First Origins of the Greeks until the Ottoman Conquest of Constantinople]. Sraimvleios Press, Vienna.
Anderson, Benjamin
2015   "An Alternative Discourse": Local Interpreters of Antiquities in the Ottoman Empire. *Journal of Field Archaeology* 40: 450–460.

Angelomati-Tsougaraki, E.
2000   *Τα ταξίδια του Λόρδου Guilford στην Ανατολική Μεσόγειο* [The Journey of Lord Guilford in the Eastern Mediterranean]. Academy of Athens, Athens.

Bahrani, Zainab, Zeynep Çelik, and Edhem Eldem (editors)
2011   *Scramble For the Past: A Story of Archaeology in the Ottoman Empire, 1753–1914.* SALT, Istanbul.

Barkey, Karen
2008   *Empire of Difference: The Ottomans in Comparative Perspective.* Cambridge University Press, Cambridge.

Brøndsted, Peter Oluf
1861   *The Excavation of the Temple at Phigaleia,* anonymous English translation located at the Gennadius Library, Athens, after the article "Udgravningen af Templet ved Phigalia," edited by M. Hammerich. *Nordisk Universitets-Tidsskrift* 7(1): 64–86. Copenhagen.
1999   *Interviews with Ali Pacha of Joanina in the Autumn of 1812; with some Particulars of Epirus, and the Albanians of the Present Day,* edited by Jacob Isager. Aarhus University Press, Aarhus.

Çelik, Zeynep
2016   *About Antiquities: Politics of Archaeology in the Ottoman Empire.* University of Texas Press, Austin.

Cockerell, Charles
1903   *Travels in Southern Europe and the Levant, 1810–1817,* edited by Samuel Cockerell. Longmans, Green and Co., London.

Conder, Josiah
1830   *The Modern Traveller: Greece.* J. Duncan, London.

Cooper, Frederick
1992   *The Temple of Apollo Bassitas: The Architecture, Volume 1.* The American School of Classical Studies at Athens, Princeton.

Dupré, Louis
1825   *Voyage à Athènes et à Constantinople, ou, collections de portraits, de vues et de costumes grecs et ottomans.* Dondey Dupré, Paris.

Eldem, Edhem
2011   From Blissful Indifference to Anguished Concern: Ottoman Perceptions of Antiquities, 1799–1869. In *Scramble For the Past: A Story of Archaeology in the Ottoman Empire, 1753–1914,* edited by Zainab Bahrani, Zeynep Çelik and Edhem Eldem, pp. 281–330. SALT, Istanbul.

Encyclopaedia Brittanica
1824   *Supplement to the Fourth, Fifth, and Sixth Editions of the Encyclopaedia Britannica: Volume 5.* Archibald Constable and Company, Edinburgh.

Finn, Christine
2002   A Little Souvenir: The Marquess and the Mycenaean Columns. *Oxford Journal of Archaeology* 21: 1–12.

Gell, William
1810   *The Itinerary of Greece with a Commentary on Pausanias and Strabo and an Account of the Monuments of Antiquity at Present Existing in That Country.* T. Payne, London.

1823   *Narrative of a Journey in the Morea*. Longman, Hurst, Rees, Orme and
                Brown, London.

Gere, Cathy
    2006   *The Tomb of Agamemnon: Mycenae and the Search for a Hero*. Profile Books,
                London.

Hamilakis, Yannis
    2008   Decolonizing Greek Archaeology: Indigenous Archaeologies, Modernist
                Archaeology and the Post-Colonial Critique. In *A Singular Antiquity:
                Archaeology and Hellenic Identity in Twentieth-Century Greece*, edited by Dimitris
                Damaskos and Dimitris Plantzos, pp. 273–284. Benaki Museum, Athens.
    2011   Indigenous Archaeologies in Ottoman Greece. In *Scramble For the Past: A
                Story of Archaeology in the Ottoman Empire, 1753–1914*, edited by Zainab
                Bahrani, Zeynep Çelik and Edhem Eldem, pp. 49–70. SALT, Istanbul.

Holod, Renata, and Robert Ousterhout (editors)
    2011   *Osman Hamdi Bey and the Americans: Archaeology, Diplomacy, Art*. Pera
                Museum, Istanbul.

Hughes, Thomas Smart
    1820   *Travels in Sicily, Greece and Albania*. 2 volumes. J. Mawman, London.

Hunt, Philip, and A.H. Smith
    1916   Lord Elgin and His Collection. *The Journal of Hellenic Studies* 36: 163–372.

Jenkins, Ian
    1992   *Archaeologists and Aesthetes in the Sculpture Galleries of the British Museum,
                1800–1939*. British Museum Press, London.

Kitromilides, Paschalis
    2013   *Enlightenment and Revolution: The Making of Modern Greece*. Harvard
                University Press, Cambridge, MA.

Kohl, Philip, and Clare Fawcett
    1995   *Nationalism, Politics and the Practice of Archaeology*. Cambridge University
                Press, Cambridge.

Laurent, Peter
    1821   *Recollections of a Classical Tour Through Various Parts of Greece, Turkey and
                Italy (Made in the Years 1818 & 1819)*. W.B. Whittaker, London.

Leake, William
    1830   *Travels in the Morea*. 3 volumes. John Murray, London.
    1835   *Travels in Northern Greece*. 4 volumes. J. Rodwell, London.

Liebmann, Matthew, and Uzma Z. Rizvi (editors)
    2008   *Archaeology and the Postcolonial Critique*. AltaMira Press, Lanham, MD.

Lowenthal, David
    1997   *The Heritage Crusade and the Spoils of History*. Viking, New York.

McGowan, Bruce
    1994   The Age of the *Ayans*, 1699–1812. In *An Economic and Social History of the
                Ottoman Empire, 1300–1914*, edited by Halil İnalcık and Donald Quataert,
                pp. 637–758. Cambridge University Press, Cambridge.

Moore, Dudley, Edward Rowlands, and Nektarios Karadimas
    2014   *In Search of Agamemnon: Early Travellers to Mycenae*. Cambridge Scholars
                Publishing, Newcastle upon Tyne.

Murray, Tim
    2013   Antiquarianism *of* and *in* Preliterate Societies: Colonial and Postcolonial
                Contexts. In *World Antiquarianism: Comparative Perspectives*, edited by
                Alain Schnapp, pp. 11–34. Getty Research Institute, Los Angeles.
Panagiotopoulos, Vasilis, and Demitris Dimitropoulos (editors)
    2007–2009   Αρχείο Αλή Πασά: συλλογής I. Χώτζη: Γενναδίου Βιβλιοθήκης της Αμερικανικής
                Σχολής Αθηνών: έκδοση, σχολιασμός, ευρετήρια [The Ali Pasha Archive: The I.
                Chotzi collection of the Gennadius Library, American School of Classical
                Studies at Athens: Text, Commentary, and Indexes]. Neohellenic Research
                Institute, Athens.
Pouqueville, François
    1826   *Voyage de la Grèce*. 5 volumes. Firmin Didot, Paris.
Pryce, F.N., and A.H. Smith
    1892   *Catalogue of Greek Sculpture in the British Museum*. British Museum Press,
                London.
Schliemann, Heinrich
    1878   *Mycenae: A Narrative of Researches and Discoveries at Mycenae and Tiryns*.
                Scribner, Armstrong & Company, New York.
Schnapp, Alain
    1997   *The Discovery of the Past*. Harry N. Abrams, New York. (originally
                published 1993 as *La conquête du passé*. Carré, Paris.)
    2008   Between Antiquarians and Archaeologists: Continuities and Ruptures. In
                Histories of Archaeology: A Reader in the History of Archaeology, edited by
                Tim Murray and Christopher Evans, pp. 392–405. Oxford University Press,
                Oxford.
Shaw, Wendy
    2003   *Possessors and Possessed: Museums, Archaeology, and the Visualization of History
                in the Late Ottoman Empire*. University of California Press, Berkeley.
Skiotis, Dennis
    1971   From Bandit to Pasha: First Steps in the Rise to Power of Ali of Tepelen,
                1750–1784. *International Journal of Middle East Studies* 2: 219–244.
Stackelberg, Otto Magnus von
    1826   *Der Apollotempel zu Bassae in Arcadien und die daselbst ausgegrabenen
                Bildwerke*. Andreäischen Schriften, Frankfurt.
Trigger, Bruce
    1989   *A History of Archaeological Thought*. Cambridge University Press,
                Cambridge.
Tunalı, Gülçin
    2012   Another Kind of Hellenism? Appropriation of Ancient Athens via Greek
                Channels for the Sake of Good Advice as Reflected in *Tarih-i Medintü'l-
                Hukema*. Unpublished Ph.D. dissertation, Ruhr University Bochum.
Turner, William
    1820   *Journal of a Tour in the Levant*. 3 volumes. John Murray, London.
Wace, A.B.J.
    1926   The Date of the Treasury of Atreus. *The Journal of Hellenic Studies* 46: 110–120.

"… that we trusted not to Arab notions of archaeology": Reading the *Grand Narrative* Against the Grain

Eva-Maria Troelenberg

… in comparison between older photographs or travel accounts and the current state of things, we have to note a rapid decay of the ruins. Particularly endangered are the antique buildings near Circassian colonies, such as Amman and Jerash, and then in the Druse villages of the Hauran. In Suweda we met some stonemasons as they were just demolishing and breaking up the last ashlars from a large beautiful tomb, which had been complete until recently, and in Amman, where a station of the new Mecca railway is being erected during these months … we witnessed how the Nymphaeum, a colossal and unique building of the Imperial period, once of highest splendor, was assaulted so that a Circassian house could be built from its ashlars. We cannot expect any remedy against such actions of the population on the part of the local government. Its provincial organs are too ignorant to understand why educated Europe is interested in antiquities, the devout Mohammedan considers the destruction of pagan things a pious deed and the Syrian social politics greet with pleasure that old masonry gives way to new, more useful buildings [Bundesarchiv (BArch) vol. 15, Sheet 66].

This assessment is taken from a letter written in the spring of 1903 by the German archaeologist Otto Puchstein, whose excavations in the Middle East were undertaken in close cooperation with the emerging Royal Museums in Berlin. When he wrote this letter, Puchstein was working at the Roman temple site of Baalbek in Lebanon, at the time an autonomous province within the Ottoman Empire (Mertens 1991; Petersen 2008). Puchstein's letter argues for a more systematic mining of the region, with the purpose of securing artworks and antiquities. Accordingly, it was addressed to the general director of the Berlin Museums, Richard Schöne, to provide ammunition for Germany's active role in the race for antiquities, which was carried out among Western nations during this period as a strategy of indirect imperialism

(Makdisi 2011). Schöne in turn sent a copy of the letter to the ministry of foreign affairs—it was thus an official matter of German cultural politics (Marchand 2009: 387–426).

The entire letter, especially if considered within its politico-historical context, is a typical example of how roles and agencies were usually understood and assigned when Western interests over ancient sites and monuments encountered local practices, and how the ensuing methods of archaeology suggested and defined a seemingly clear-cut civilizational difference. However, upon closer examination, even this short passage, notwithstanding its unambiguously chauvinist claim and conclusion, does hint at a somewhat more complex constellation: "Western" exploration obviously considers the Muslim "other" as its ultimate counterpart, but below the surface of this binary there are multilayered dynamics playing out between centers and peripheries and, moreover, between different social groups such as Druse and Circassian minorities, local Bedouins and Ottoman authorities. Their respective interests range from practical urbanistic-logistic to ideological and intellectual factors.

Taking its cue from the complex dynamics involved in this passage, this essay primarily seeks to further complicate the notion of "Western" versus "local" or "indigenous" agencies – or of emic versus etic perspectives: I want to support the argument that such categories run the risk of cementing simplified binaries. At the same time, the nature of our methods and sources inherently privilege these binaries, especially because the binary of literate versus pre-literate and illiterate societies immediately places the academic writer on one side of the equation. For instance, Tim Murray has broken up the seemingly self-evident interrelation between illiteracy and the "indigenous" category—yet the nexus between power and knowledge as represented in the written word remains unavoidable (Murray 2013). This predicament holds true not only when applied to our contemporary academic discourse, but also when considering the situation on the ground in the late nineteenth century, which saw the early decades of an increasingly systematic perception and appropriation of ancient and early Islamic sites in the Middle East. Of course, this argument is based on a number of recent studies particularly interested in the historiography of archaeology, which have pointed towards new directions in thinking about methodological limitations and epistemic conditions of archaeology as a discipline growing out of antiquarian culture. They have shaped an increasing awareness for a multitude of trajectories and alternative agencies (see, for instance, Trigger 1984; Atalay 2006; Hamilakis 2008; Challis 2008: 101–113; Anderson 2015).

Against the background of these recent studies, the various social groups and agents mentioned in the letter quoted above raise the question if and how "the Druse" or "the Circassians" can speak for themselves, and how we can detect their voices beyond the archives of mainstream or "elite" archaeology. It becomes clear that, inherently to the task, the identification, availability, or accessibility of sources to illuminate the picture is a major challenge. It is a challenge for several academic fields such as archaeology, art history, anthropology, or the disciplines of regional studies that require concerted interdisciplinary work, and aim to produce fundamentally new types of historiography, beyond the established categories of source study.

What I would like to do here is much more modest, but should be considered one step on this path—namely, to scratch the surface of what is largely considered the "Grand Narrative."[1] Can there be an alternative reading, a reading against this narrative's own grain? Again, refraining from binary categories, the purpose of this experiment is not so much to find an antithesis or an opposite of antiquarianism or later archaeological practices between the lines of its own sources and methods, but rather to expand the awareness of its multivocality (Habu et al. 2008; Hodder 2008; Anderson 2015: 456).

I will attempt this by a close reading of an illustrative source from the 1870s—the very period that saw an increasing specialization and differentiation between the realms of archaeology, antiquarianism, and history (Levine 1986; Bahrani et al. 2011: 25–28). My case in point is a travel account by the British traveler Henry Baker Tristram, which is mostly known because it contains the first lengthy description of the so-called "desert castle" of Mshatta, including the monument's first art-historical assessment by James Fergusson. Mshatta is an early Islamic structure built in the mid-eighth century A.D. and located in the steppe of Moab east of the Jordan River. Today the site is located about 20 miles south of the modern city of Amman and near the Queen Aliyah Airport. At the time of its discovery this was in the periphery of the Ottoman Empire. A large part of this monument's splendidly ornamented façade is on display in the Museum of Islamic Art in Berlin today (Figures 8.1 and 8.2).[2]

Using the case of Mshatta as a point of reference, I will look at Tristram's book, particularly considering how it spells out the relation between the well-known categories of Western exploration and erudition, and the less recognized contribution of Near Eastern protagonists—specifically that of one individual Bedouin—to the discovery and interpretation of antiquities. This kind of information on local protagonists is often blatantly present in such accounts, but considered peripheral at best to the success-stories of archaeological discovery. I will use the directed and asymmetrical, yet detailed and—within the limits of its particular narrative—multifaceted gaze of this proto-academic source. It directs our attention to an additional voice, and thus contributes to a more differentiated notion of "Western" vs.

Figure 8.1. Bedouin shepherd near the ruin of Mshatta, March 1900 (photograph by Gertrude Bell, © The Gertrude Bell Archive, Newcastle University).

Figure 8.2. Mshatta in the Islamic Department of the Pergamonmuseum, Berlin, after 1932 (ZA SMB, Archivische Sammlung).

"local" agencies. This example will also reveal how privileges of interpretation may be read along particular lines of social distinction as much as along a fundamental "East–West" divide. It thus offers an insight into how the agencies of institutionalized archaeology and heritage discourse were constituted while academic debate took its course from the last quarter of the nineteenth century onwards, ultimately also paving the way for the literal appropriation of archaeological materials.

"Unknown to History, Unnamed in the Maps": Authority and Consensus

In 1873, the seasoned British traveler Henry Baker Tristram published his travel account entitled *The Land of Moab: Travels and Discoveries on the East Side of the Dead Sea and the Jordan*, a panoramic literary document of a journey he had undertaken two years earlier. It is worth noting that the initial purpose of Tristram's trip had been an inquiry into the flora and fauna of the region, and into the remains of Biblical history—a combination of interests that was not uncommon at that time, and hints at the kind of proto-scientific universalist erudition which did not yet ask for strict divisions between *historia*, *artificialia*, and *naturalia*. However, in his book he introduces the ruin of Mshatta (Figure 8.3) as one of his main discoveries, allegedly hitherto "unknown to history, and unnamed in the maps" (Tristram 1873: 212). In fact, a number of travelers had at least mentioned Mshatta before, and Austen Henry Layard dedicated a short passage to it in his memoir, claiming that he had seen it already around 1840 (Layard 1887: 114–115). Yet it was indeed Tristram who first acknowledged the artistic importance of the monument and considered it worthy of a lengthy description and of an attempt at art-historical categorization. His claim to be the first to "map" the monument clearly indicates how much importance was attached to the ability to document places and monuments in writing so as to put them on the map of world history, especially for Western readers and observers.

Tristram presents a paradigmatically colonial biography of the Victorian era. After having studied theology and ancient philology in Oxford and Durham, he became a military cleric for the British fleet in the Bahamas, spent several winters in Algeria, and then began traveling the Eastern Mediterranean, mostly motivated by natural scientific interests (A. G. 1908: xlii–xliv). Accordingly, even at the advanced stage of his life and career, he remained an amateur even by the standards of his own time when it came to the discovery of antiquities and their classification: this in itself was also quite typical for early explorers (Levine 1986).

PART OF WEST WING WALL OF EXTERNAL FACADE OF PALACE AT MASHITA.
FROM A PHOTOGRAPH.

Figure 8.3. Detail of the ornamented façade of Mshatta, woodcut after photograph by Buxton, published in Tristram 1873, pl. 38.

Tristram's gaze, which we may characterize as proto-academic from today's point of view, reveals interesting insights and creates interrelations that may appear surprising to us today, at first glance. For instance, in the realm of ornithology, Tristram's greatest success in Jordan was the discovery and description of a starling native to the Kidron Valley near Jerusalem, subsequently known as the *amydrus tristrami*. This creates a strange and to date largely forgotten relation between a type of bird and a monument like Mshatta. The ornamental relief of Mshatta features a stylistically and iconographically broad variety of leaves, scrolls, and animals, among them a number of birds that Tristram describes with the taxonomic gaze of the natural scientist: "There are upwards of 50 animals in all sorts of attitudes, but generally drinking together on opposite sides of the same vase. Lions, winged lions, buffaloes, gazelle, panthers, lynx, men ... peacocks, partridges, parrots and other birds ..." (Tristram 1873: 215). Furthermore, Tristram states with a certain tone of scholarly satisfaction (though drawing erroneous conclusions concerning the historical classification of the monument): "The birds and beasts are fully represented, and not, as in Arab sculpture, melting into fruit or flowers, but correctly drawn" (Tristram 1873: 215). This statement at the same time mirrors how criteria of Western art and image concepts such as mimetic naturalism fed into his judgement along with a scientific-scholarly gaze.

The fact, however, that Tristram recognized the limits of his own judgement in the face of a monument like Mshatta is an interesting indicator of the growing awareness of disciplinary specialization in this period. This was largely characterized by the voices of "amateurs on the way to expertise," as James Turner describes the development of art history's miscellaneous beginnings throughout the nineteenth century in relation to other, mostly philological disciplines, particularly in the English-speaking world (Turner 2014: 313–315). Tristram therefore resorted to the kind of expertise that would extract the monument from its immediate context and instead place it in a larger perspective of architectural history. He asked for the advice of the art historian James Fergusson. The resulting art historical assessment of Mshatta warrants some attention in the context of my argument, as it provides an interesting comparative backdrop to local narratives.

Fergusson was largely perceived as "an architect and archaeologist, instinctively rather than by education" (Goldsmid 1886: 113) by his contemporaries—and yet at that time he was already the most renowned specialist on so-called "Eastern" architecture. Since 1845, Fergusson had published systematically, focusing on previously largely unknown monuments of India, but also searching for universal principles of a world architecture (Goldsmid 1886: 113–115; Craig 1968: 140–152). Against this background, Fergusson seemed predestined to provide an assessment of Mshatta's position as a monument situated on the geographical crossroads between Europe and Asia. He thus contributed an entire chapter to Tristram's book in which he suggests a pre-Islamic date for the monument, classifying it as a commission for the Sasanian king Khosrau II (AD 590–628) (Fergusson 1873). Fergusson assumed that the figural representations on the façade could not have been reconciled with a common contemporary understanding of the so-called "ban on images," thus using and supporting the idea of Muslim culture as hostile to imagery and art in general.

Fergusson's attribution of Mshatta to Khosrau also corresponds to a historiographic tendency of his age to write world history as the history of great persons. Khosrau is one of the protagonists in Edward Gibbon's *The Decline and Fall of the Roman Empire*, which had been published between 1776 and 1788 and contributed significantly to a common understanding of historical periodization and the significance of late antique culture (Gibbon 1887). Partaking of such a narrative, a figure like Khosrau may not have been central, but nevertheless familiar to an educated Western audience.

To provide an even more tangible narrative context, Fergusson introduces another historical persona. He relates the construction of Mshatta to the love triangle between Khosrau, his beautiful wife Shirin and the builder Ferhad, who, according to tradition, leaped to his death due to his unfulfilled love for Shirin. This episode originates in ancient Persian literature, and was later popularized also in the West through accounts related to the Arabian Nights (Baum 2003: 72–107). For Fergusson, the most relevant information from this episode is that Ferhad had been an important consultant for construction projects before he fell in love with Shirin. Therefore, it seems self-evident for the historian Fergusson to link Ferhad's name to the construction of Mshatta: "We may, perhaps, assume that it was by his [i.e., Ferhad's] advice, and partially under his inspiration, that Mashita attained the prominence which undoubtedly belongs to it" (Fergusson 1873: 381). He even produces some possible evidence in the form of a rock relief near Shiraz, which he believes might depict Ferhad working on the Mshatta façade (Troelenberg 2016: 38)—but he also recognizes that this might be a bold leap, blurring the lines between fiction and fact. Fergusson therefore concedes: "It might be going too far to assert that this palace was actually executed by or under the direct superintendence of Ferhad, but it certainly looks as if he inspired the design" (Fergusson 1873: 371).

In any case, Mshatta was now connected to the name of a prominent ruler, and even to an artistic master—the monument was thus no longer lost in the anonymity of what was perceived in a somewhat essentialist way as "oriental" or "eastern" art practice in those days. Fergusson's attribution of Mshatta to the Sasanian period was to be proven wrong by a much less romantically inclined architectural analysis a few decades later. The early Islamic date for Mshatta was established by Ernst Herzfeld in 1910, and has been largely accepted by the academic community ever since (Herzfeld 1910; Troelenberg 2016: 105–121). Viewed with the benefit of hindsight, Fergusson's first assessment is based on scarce evidence and a good deal of speculation. Its contemporary validity was largely based on its proximity to an established cultural horizon of Western educated elites. It links an enigmatic monument to the agency of some protagonists of ancient history who can stand paradigmatically for romantic popular notions of Ancient Near Eastern empires.

This is very much in line with Tristram's own historiographic take on things, which was characterized by a teleological concept of decline and fall, narrating the history of civilizations with a clear East-West trajectory. The thread of history, Tristram claims, had been interrupted for the region east of the Jordan river with the end of Khosrau's reign. According to him, this thread was only taken up again by modern Western exploration: "Retired from the route of armies, it [the region of Moab] has been without fortress, town, or inhabitants, to invite a conqueror: inaccessible to ordinary troops from the west, it has remained without the record of one single event on its soil; and its eastern plains untrodden by European foot till yesterday" (Tristram 1873: 226–227). In this worldview, the Bedouins who had populated the region up to his day remained anachronistic testimonies to Biblical history, not really contemporary interlocutors. Already in the preface to his book, Tristram states that

> … there is scarcely a passage in Holy Writ, in which Moab is mentioned, and which was not in some degree illustrated during the journey … Arab society also is in a more primitive and simple state than where affected by intercourse with other nationalities in the rest of Syria. The [members of the Bedouin tribe] Beni Sakk'r are true Midianites in all their habits: the minor tribes reproduce perhaps the nearest parallel to the state of Canaan at the time of the Israelitish conquest, which can be found in the present day [Tristram 1873: 5].

According to this, the Bedouin's only merit was that they did not have any drive to settle, and thus hardly needed any building material, which meant that they left ancient buildings and ruins largely untouched—but also that they lacked any competence considering the value and classification of their heritage. It is a typically Orientalizing concept of temporality as a means to define cultural difference (Fabian 2002; Anderson 2015: 453, 458).

The underlying premise is that a sense of history and of the cultural dimension of any given discovery could only be appreciated by civilized man, who inevitably seemed to be an educated Westerner from a certain social stratum. Accordingly, the world literally only existed if captured, read, and described by his gaze. Philippa Levine has shown for the case of Great Britain how this notion developed during a process of increasing professionalization of history, archaeology, and antiquarianism during the nineteenth century. Even within the frame of national historiography and heritage definition, this was related to an ever tighter closing of social ranks, excluding the voice of the local, the vernacular, the un-academic (Levine 1986; Saitta 2007). It is a conversation kept between socially and professionally authorized experts and their audiences who together constitute a community of consensus over certain "Grand Narratives." This overarching consensus enables distribution of specialized tasks, and even allows for differences, conflicts, and debates, as it unites all interlocutors within one academic community. Interestingly, as Peter N. Miller reminds us, the history of European antiquarianism is at the same time not detached from the realm of emotions. Passion, imagination, and a sense of longing are recurrent standard tropes, feeding into a poetic notion of the discipline (Miller 2013). Indeed, if we look, for instance, at

Fergusson's fantasies involving Shirin and Ferhad, we may assume that he used the privilege of a generous poetic license—which he could afford due to his professional and social position. Examples like these thus allow us to glance behind the professionalized rhetoric of disinterestedness.

Altogether, this strong social codification of an emerging "authorized heritage discourse" (Smith 2006; Waterton and Smith 2009; see also Anderson 2015: 450) is an even more important inherent factor when we deal with the antiquarian and archaeological gaze abroad in an expanding colonial world, and with its subsequent techniques of intellectual and material appropriation. This authorized—and authoritative—heritage discourse leads directly from the realm of interpretive privilege to claims to physical ownership of monuments and other items of cultural heritage. Consequently, it is thus a question relevant for museum discourses on property and restitution as well. The very example of Mshatta, which would be partly shipped to Berlin a few decades later, confirms it (although this episode must remain outside the scope of the present essay). Suffice it to say that the most authoritative voices in this discourse do not, by definition, put much emphasis on such questions of social privilege (e.g., Cuno 2009). In this dimension, questions of social distinction become intertwined with categories of cultural and aesthetic difference, and an authoritative discourse on cultural heritage can become functional within the constitution of social relations between colonial agents of different ranks, settlers, local elites, and the broader native population (Brummett 2014; Anderson 2015).

"Zadam Himself, Intelligent Though He Be (…)": Tracing the Bedouin's Voice

Returning to our case study, it becomes clear that what we have observed so far is in line with the typical narrative of asymmetric knowledge production. In Tristram's book, we see empire at work in all its historiographic authoritarianism. The travel account confirms this categorical asymmetry even further when the author speaks explicitly about his interaction with locals. When he describes how he spots the ruin of Mshatta on the horizon, and how he decides to visit it against the advice of his local guide, he clearly uses this incident to establish an explicit difference between the ignorant and the savant, personified in the contrast between his Bedouin guide and himself with his entourage of determined explorers:

> Zadam had told us that it stood beyond the great Hadj road, and was, he believed, a ruined khan, built by Saladin (to whom everything great, and not clearly Christian or Roman, is here referred); but that it contained nothing particular, and was just like … any other isolated ruin we had seen … Though assured

that we should not be repaid for our labour, we had no intention of leaving any ruin unvisited, and fortunate were we, that we trusted not to Arab notions of archaeology [Tristram 1873: 211].

Similarly superior attitudes of explorers and archaeologists have been described for many other cases, for instance the German excavations at Pergamon (Bilsel 2007). Zadam, it must be noted, is a recurrent figure throughout Tristram's travel account, often referred to as the person who literally guides the way through the vast steppe. A typical episode in Tristram's book begins like this: "Next day Zadam advised us to move to Ziza, where he promised we should find very fine ruins, never yet visited by any European" (Tristram 1873: 192). However, many of Tristram's comments seem to confirm the Bedouin's ignorance about more sophisticated matters concerning antiquities and heritage.

One important instance occurs when the travel group encounters the remains of the so-called "Moabite Stone", a fragmentary basalt stele from the Iron Age bearing Phoenician inscriptions. Originally located near present-day Dhiban, its partly reconstructed fragments today are kept in the Louvre and commonly referred to as the "Mesha Stele" (Figure 8.4). Due to its inscriptions, this stone was instantly recognized as an important source for the interests of philological antiquarianism at the time of its discovery (Ginsburg 1871; The Journal of Anthropology 1871).[3] It had been found intact only a few years before Tristram and his entourage stood in front of its shattered remains (Figure 8.5). In 1868, the Anglican Missionary Frederick Augustus Klein had been led to its site by the very same Zadam. Negotiations over the stele's transfer to either Berlin or Paris immediately ensued after the object's publication in Western journals.[4] The "Moabite Stone" provides one of many examples for German-French rivalries in the Middle Eastern antiquities race (Marchand 2009; Trümpler 2008). Attention by Western explorers obviously also exacerbated the conflicting interests of local groups and Ottoman authorities. While the Ottomans were leaning towards favoring the German side's claim for ownership, a squeeze of the inscription, executed by local inhabitants, was secured for the French party.

Shortly thereafter, the stone was broken into pieces by the local population—apparently by sedentary villagers, or Bedouins who had become sedentary, at least if we are to believe the testimony of one contemporary commentator who explains what happened after the French consul tried to buy the stone directly from "the Arabs":

They disputed among themselves its ownership, although it seems to have been used as a charm by the tribe; and at length they heated the stone and then threw cold water upon it to split it into pieces, so that each family might have a

Figure 8.4. Reconstruction of the Mesha Stele, basalt stone, ca. 800 B.C., Musée du Louvre AO 5066 (© RMN-Grand Palais [Musée du Louvre]/Mathieu Rabeau).

limestone, and there is no trace of any basalt, but what has been carried here by man.   Still there are many basaltic blocks, dressed, and often with marks of lime on them, evidently used in masonry; and we

No. 9.   RUINS OF DHIBAN, WHERE THE MOABITE STONE WAS FOUND.

found a few traces of carvings on other stones. The place is full of caverns, cisterns, vaulted underground storehouses, and rude semi-circular arches, like the rest.

The basalt would seem to have been the favourite material of the earlier Cyclopean builders, as in Bashan, and then to have been used up by the constructors of the later town, which cannot be much

Figure 8.5. Remains of Dhiban, location of the Mesha Stele ("Moabite Stone"), woodcut after photograph by Buxton, published in Tristram 1873 (London edition), p. 133.

fragment to place in its granary, as a charm to bless their crops [The Journal of Anthropology 1871: 350].

Tristram himself refers to a dispute among the Bedouin tribe of the Hamideh which led to the stele's destruction (Tristram 1873: 148). When Tristram inspects the site where Klein had found the stele, he reflects about its provenance, assuming that it must have been reused as a building block already in antiquity, maybe by the Romans, and that it was only exposed again by an earthquake in the 1830s—an event for which he refers to the oral testimony of Arab inhabitants of the region (Tristram 1873: 149–150). Nevertheless, he concludes with a summary statement that confirms his notion of the timelessness, as well as lack of historical awareness and competence of the "Orientals." This notion becomes even stronger as these lines could be equally directed at the provincial Romans, unaware of the significance of an ancient Oriental inscription, or at the contemporary local population who in his view had privileged superstition over philology when they destroyed the stone: "It would be strangely out of keeping with Oriental habits and ways, if the new-comers had had any reverence for the lapidary records of their predecessors; still more so if, unable to decipher these records, they had respected them" (Tristram 1873: 150). By way of contrast, he describes his own professional antiquarian practice, equipped with the modern means of photography, sextant, and compass.

The notion of superstition as an argument to disqualify the Bedouin voice becomes even more explicit, with even more personal references to Zadam, when the party visits a tower—which they recognize as an early Christian church tower—and which still stands among the ruins near Umm er-Rasas, the ancient Kastron Mefaa (Piccirillo 1994: 65, fig. 21). Tristram recounts several legends that circulated in local Arabic folklore around this tower. He even describes how he witnessed these superstitions being immediately related to the activities of his travel party, namely his photographers. This episode again opens up a striking contrast between the modern means of capturing the world and the backward belief of the Bedouins:

> Another legend is to the effect that, before the Christians were driven out by the faithful, they deposited enormous treasures in the top of this tower, and left it in the care of a Jinn. This Jinn has prevented its being overthrown by earthquakes, while all around has fallen, and has filled up the staircase, so that none can ascend. Our party, however, were openly accused to having dealings with the Evil One and many of the Arabs declared that when Buxton and Johnson went to photograph the tower they were seen looking over the battlement, and had been lifted up there by the sprite. The tale spread, and Zadam himself, intelligent though he be, firmly believed it, remarking that the Jinn might guard and prevent the Bedouin

from touching the treasure, yet that Westerners, having greater minds, might overcome the guardian spirit of the place, and get it out [Tristram 1873: 161–162].

In a quite subtle way, Tristram's narrative even puts the confirmation of the superiority of the enlightened foreign perspective into the mouth of the Bedouin himself. Altogether, here we see another variety of labeling the local voice as ignorant and irrational (Anderson 2015: 457). As Christopher Pinney (2012) has shown in a different context, this particular interrelation between local or "indigenous" superstition and the modern medium of photography is a current trope of anthropological writing in the nineteenth century.

If we take a broader look at the entire travel account, however, it becomes clear that Zadam must have played a crucial role for the success of Tristram's journey in more than one way. In fact, there are several passages in which Tristram cannot but recognize Zadam's role, beginning with the account of an official contract "… signed and sealed by him [Zadam] in the presence of the English consul, by which he had agreed to be our guard, and to take us through all the country north of Kerak for forty days, for the moderate sum of £60 sterling" (Tristram 1873: 104). In merely technical terms, the Bedouin does appear like an equal contract partner, and, later on, Tristram also does not fail to mention that entire parts of the expedition would not have been possible without Zadam's local competence—or rather authority—be it because he guided the way, or because he knew how to smooth out problems with local inhabitants which would have endangered the undertaking otherwise. Accordingly, Zadam's last appearance at the very end of the book is an appraisal of the mission accomplished, describing the travel party's safe "return to civilization", as one of the running titles towards the end of his accounts reads (Tristram 1873: 373).

> Zadam looked in an ecstasy of quiet triumph as he rode over the slippery pavements of Jerusalem, having fulfilled his promise that he would never leave us till he had ridden by our side up Christian Street … As we sat at dinner that evening, in Hornstein's comfortable hostel, with Zadam for our guest, his best Arab costume setting off his handsome face and figure, while he complacently quaffed his Champagne, which of us felt not some tinge of regret that our wanderings in the land of Moab were ended [Tristram 1873: 375–376]?

This assessment is however as condescending as it is affectionate. Zadam remains a "guest" within the realm of civilization, a handsome picturesque reminder of the adventure that the "Land of Moab" had been for the explorers—in one word, an object for ethnographic observation, while intellectual agency and historical awareness have remained reserved for Tristram and his kind throughout the journey.

This confirms the strong sense of social and cultural difference which fed into the self-image of Western explorers at that time, even if Tristram was obviously aware of the noble Bedouin lineage of his guard. In fact, his "Zadam" is identical with the person modern historians refer to as Sattam Al-Fayez, the son of the head of the Beni Sakhr tribe at that time (Abujaber 1989: 177–196; Rogan 1999: 79–82; Van der Steen 2014: 189).[5] As we have seen above, Tristram explicitly characterized this Bedouin tribe as "true Midianites," fallen out of time. In fact, the Beni Sakhr were at the time the most powerful social group originating on Transjordanian soil. The tribe lived in tense relation with both the Ottoman authorities and with new settler groups such as the Circassians, who came to the Ottoman Empire in several waves of migration during the late nineteenth century, thus changing and challenging traditional social orders (Rogan 1999; Shami 2009). Even more so, the members of this Bedouin tribe were major players within the local social pecking order. A figure like Sattam Al-Fayez would not only help to understand the fundamental lay of the land in the sense of a territorial or topographic pathfinder: he would also be an important gatekeeper (or gate-opener) for Western explorers within the complex society of the region, as M. Talha Çiçek (2016) has shown for the neighboring region of the Hejaz during the same period.

This information should help us to read Tristram's narrative against its own grain. In fact, Zadam's own awareness of his position shines through in many instances. For example, when Tristram complains about "the Arab's" disinterest in repairing things during the visit to a dilapidated Khan, we also learn that "certainly, as Zadam observed, it is not the business of the Bedouin to repair these places, as it is not they who would use them; and the central government, he shrewdly added, would have to send more soldiers than workmen for the task" (Tristram 1873: 186–187). And during the survey of the heavily spoliated buildings in the abandoned village of Ziza, near the ruin of Mshatta, it is actually only the interplay of information provided by Tristram and Zadam together that unfolds an entire historical panorama for the reader. The Englishman begins with a conventional philological explanation of the name of the village that can be traced back to Latin sources from Roman antiquity. He then describes a number of buildings, dating their origins from Roman times to the "Saracenic" period (Tristram 1873: 202)—once more drawing a historical line of decay leading to the present dilapidated state of affairs, represented by a "Saracenic" building which once had been a strong fortress, containing a large number of spolia from earlier periods, but now was being used as a cemetery and falling apart. Nonchalantly, Tristram folds in some historical data provided by Zadam:

> This castle, we are told, was occupied, during the war of Mehemet Ali, by a garrison of Egyptians, left here by Ibrahim Pasha, who did much damage to the

ruins of Ziza, and wantonly destroyed a very perfect building in the town, and several perfect Christian churches. Zadam assured us that, before the Egyptian invasion, the large buildings inside the town had their roofs entire, and were often used as places of shelter [Tristram 1873: 208].

Here we find a clear indication of the importance of a more recent historical event which had left its imprint on local village life, on the state of built heritage, and on the mind and memory of the Bedouins. Zadam refers to the Ottoman-Egyptian wars that had been fought in this region one generation earlier, around 1830–1840.

This recent date for the destruction and abandonment of the village not only adds a more differentiated periodization to Tristram's own rather general notion of a persisting, largely uncivilized and eventless "Saracenic period." It also reflects an awareness of the conflicting roles and interests of different social groups. Zadam's explanation demonstrates the Bedouins' particular point of view, which consequently identifies the Egyptian invader as the villain in his version of history. In merely systematic terms, it almost seems to prefigure what a professional archaeologist like Otto Puchstein would write several decades later about the positions of different social groups towards the built heritage of the region: we only need to look at the opening quote of this essay for comparison. What is of course missing in Zadam's testimony is the polemical hint to some general "oriental" indolence that the Western archaeologist uses to draw a binary notion of an active and intelligent "us" versus a mute and ignorant "them" in the end.

Conclusion

If, based on these preliminary observations, we can begin to think about the voice of the Bedouin on its own terms, we may recognize hitherto obscure interrelations and reassess the value of certain information that has been considered largely as peripheral to the "Grand Narrative." From this perspective, for instance, Tristram's statement that the Bedouins attribute everything that is not clearly Roman to Saladin may be much more than just a sign of their historiographic disinterest or incompetence. On the contrary, related to an extended picture of local agency and historical awareness, it points to the question concerning what function the figure of Saladin can have played in the Bedouins' memory.[6] How may this have been related to a local invention of tradition at this specific moment of the modern era, a time when local social structures were increasingly the source of conflicts between rising settler movements and central authorities? And, ultimately, did this affect the Bedouins' relation to the tangible heritage of the region, and hence to the Western explorers whom they encountered at these sites in increasing numbers?

And what about the numerous allusions to local practices relegated to the realm of "superstition" and "folklore", not worthy of intellectual consideration? As Yannis Hamilakis (2006: 306–307) has shown for the case of Ottoman Greece with the example of apotropaic re-uses of marble slabs from the Parthenon, this kind of re-use was part of a larger Mediterranean vernacular culture. Related to this, Benjamin Anderson (2015) has hinted at examples of resistance against the removal of Greco-Roman antiquities on the part of the local population in Ottoman Greece. Although my example draws on a different geographical and cultural context, it might be worth considering whether Zadam's initial refusal to lead Tristram to Mshatta could also be read as an act (or at least attempt) of resistance, exactly because this building with its outstanding appearance may have had a particular function and meaning for local Bedouin culture.

It becomes obvious here that my close reading of one source can only open a path for questions. A thorough research project to provide solid answers would not only have to consider systematically other travel accounts from the same period so as to identify further evidence for the function and attitude of Zadam; it would also have to include investigations into archival material, reading also the documents of institutions such as the Ottoman administration or the Palestine Exploration Fund against their own grains, so as to complete the picture further. Finally, it would have to weigh the applicability of oral history and anthropological research for heritage studies. In any case, any possible "alternative" notion then should not necessarily be seen as diametrically opposed to the Western antiquarian's interest. As we can clearly detect already, aesthetically appealing and outstanding remains of the past were invested and charged with a certain symbolic value by local populations. Even if the decay, dispersal or even active destruction of monuments and objects have to be counted into the equation, local actions and narratives nevertheless constitute an alternative practice.

In sum, we cannot compare positions like those of Henry Baker Tristam and James Fergusson on one side and Zadam on the other side in any taxonomic way—too different are their interests, their backgrounds, and of course their means of expression. Fergusson, who had not seen Mshatta *in situ*, gets to write his own chapter in Tristram's book, while what we know about or from Zadam is filtered, altered and edited by Tristram, who uses his own poetic license on more than one occasion. Therefore a text like this travel account certainly cannot be understood as a possible source of future methods. Its inherent epistemological limits and problems have been addressed throughout this essay. Systematically deconstructing them would be one of the interdisciplinary challenges mentioned at the outset. For the purpose of my argument, this text rather was targeted in an attempt to outmaneuver our literary culture's own authoritative claim. It revealed how Fergusson's claim about Ferhad and Zadam's attribution to Saladin are, if not directly comparable, then certainly worth being put into relation with each other: both of them are constructed and directed historical narratives with a valid purpose within their respective contexts, yet neither of them has a claim to an objective truth. What we have seen is thus an example of how the antiquarian methods of the past can and should be revisited, in a sense of critical continuity with the pre-history of current heritage studies, while opening new, inclusive ways to "move with the time" (Waterton and Smith 2009: 11) beyond authoritarian, socially exclusive discourses.

Notes

1. I use this term with reference to its use and definition by Lyotard (1984). In this essay, published in its French original in 1979, thus almost simultaneous with Edward Said's critical assessment of "Orientalism," Lyotard introduced the notion of the "Grand Narrative" as characteristic of a normative, teleological concept of modernity, as opposed to the more fractured and multiple narratives of postmodernism.

2. The quote at the beginning of this essay also belongs to the administrative and diplomatic repercussions of the acquisition process of Mshatta for Berlin. The discovery and musealization of the Mshatta façade are the subject of my monographic study (Troelenberg 2016). I have not addressed the role of Zadam in Tristram's narrative in the book in detail, but I have used some sequences from the book as points of departure, esp. chapter 2, pp. 27–48. I have discussed one draft of this essay with Emily Neumeier and Alison Boyd; I thank both of them as well as the editors of this volume for valuable input.

3. See also the stone's description on the website of the Louvre: http://cartelfr.louvre. fr/cartelfr/visite?srv=car_not_frame&idNotice=21796 [accessed April 6th, 2016].

4. Klein was also a member of Tristram`s travel party, but had to leave before they reached the site of the Mesha Stele.

5. For the sake of continuity, I will henceforth refer to this person as "Zadam", as he is frequently thus named in the historical sources I use.

6. For the function of the role of Saladin in the collective memory of contemporary Syria and Iraq, see Heidemann (2013).

References

Abujaber, Raouf Sa'd
   1989   *Pioneers Over Jordan: The Frontier Settlement in Transjordan, 1850–1914.* I. B. Tauris, London.

A. G.
   1908   Obituary of Fellows Deceased, Henry Baker Tristram, 1822–1906. *Proceedings of the Royal Society of London, Series B, Containing Papers of a Biological Character* 80: xlii–xliv.

Anderson, Benjamin
2015   "An Alternative Discourse": Local Interpreters of Antiquities in the
              Ottoman Empire. *Journal of Field Archaeology* 40: 450–460.

Atalay, Sonya
2006   Archaeology as Decolonizing Practice. *American Indian Quarterly* 30:
              280–310.

Bahrani, Zainab, Zeynep Çelik, and Edhem Eldem (editors)
2011   *Scramble for the Past: A Story of Archaeology in the Ottoman Empire,
              1753–1914.* SALT, Istanbul.

Baum, Wilhelm
2003   *Schirin. Christin, Königin, Liebesmythos: eine spätantike Frauengestalt–
              historische Realität und literarische Wirkung.* Kitab, Klagenfurt.

Bilsel, Can
2007   Marbles Lost and Found: Carl Humann, Pergamon, and the Making of
              an Imperial Subject. *Centropa* 7: 121–135.

Brummett, Palmira
2014   You Say "Classical", I Say "Imperial", Let's Call the Whole Thing Off:
              Empire, Individual, and Encounter in Travel Narratives of the Ottoman
              Empire. *The Journal of Ottoman Studies* 44: 21–44.

Challis, Debbie
2008   *From the Harpy Tomb to the Wonders of Ephesus: British Archaeologists in the
              Ottoman Empire 1840–1880.* Bloomsbury Academic, London.

Çiçek, M. Talha
2016   Negotiating Power and Authority in the Desert: the Arab Bedouin and the
              Limits of the Ottoman State in Hijaz, 1840–1908. *Middle Eastern Studies*
              52: 260–279.

Craig, Maurice
1968   James Fergusson. In *Concerning Architecture: Essays on Architectural Writers
              and Writing*, edited by John Summerson, pp. 140–152. Allen Lane, London.

Cuno, James (editor)
2009   *Whose Culture? The Promise of Museums and the Debate over Antiquities.*
              Princeton University Press, Princeton and Oxford.

Fabian, Johannes
2002   *Time and the Other: How Anthropology Makes its Object.* Columbia
              University Press, New York.

Fergusson, James
1873   The Persian Palace of Mashita. In *The Land of Moab: Travels and Discoveries
              on the East Side of the Dead Sea and the Jordan*, edited by Henry Baker
              Tristam, pp. 378–395. Harper & Brothers, New York.

Ginsburg, Christian D.
1871   *The Moabite Stone: A Facsimile of the Original Inscription. With an English
              Translation, and a Historical and Critical Commentary.* Reeves & Turner,
              London.

Gibbon, Edward
1887   *The History of the Decline and Fall of the Roman Empire.* Murray, London.

Goldsmid, Frederic
1886   Obituary: James Fergusson. *Proceedings of the Royal Geographic Society and Monthly Record of Geography,* New Monthly Series 8: 113–115.

Habu, Junko, Clare Fawcett, and John M. Matsunaga (editors)
2008   *Evaluating Multiple Narratives: Beyond Nationalist, Colonialist, Imperialist Archaeologies.* Springer, New York.

Hamilakis, Yannis
2006   Stories from Exile: Fragments from the Cultural Biography of the Parthenon (or "Elgin") Marbles. *World Archaeology* 31: 303–320.

2008   Decolonizing Greek Archaeology: Indigenous Archaeologies, Modernist Archaeology and the Post-Colonial Critique. In *A Singular Antiquity: Archaeology and Hellenic Identity in Twentieth-Century Greece,* edited by Dimitris Damaskos and Dimitris Plantzos, pp. 273–284. Benaki Museum, Athens.

Heidemann, Stefan
2013   Memory and Ideology: Images of Saladin in Syria and Iraq. In *Visual Culture in the Modern Middle East: Rhetoric of the Image,* edited by Christiane J. Gruber and Sune Haugbolle, pp. 57–81. Indiana University Press, Bloomington and Indianapolis.

Herzfeld, Ernst
1910   Die Genesis der islamischen Kunst und das Mshatta-Problem. *Der Islam* 1/2: 27–63, 105–144.

Hodder, Ian
2008   Multivocality and Social Archaeology. In *Evaluating Multiple Narratives: Beyond Nationalist, Colonialist, Imperialist Archaeologies,* edited by Junko Habu, Clare Fawcett, and John M. Matsunaga, pp. 196–200, Springer, New York.

Layard, Austen Henry
1887   *Early Adventures in Persia, Susiana, and Babylonia.* Murray, London.

Levine, Philippa
1986   *The Amateur and the Professional: Antiquarians, Historians and Archaeologists in Victorian England, 1838–1886.* Cambridge University Press, Cambridge.

Lyotard, Jean-François
1984   *The Postmodern Condition: A Report on Knowledge.* Manchester University Press, Manchester.

Makdisi, Ussama
2011   The "Rediscovery" of Baalbek: A Metaphor for Empire in the Nineteenth Century. In *Scramble for the Past: A Story of Archaeology in the Ottoman Empire, 1753–1914,* edited by Zainab Bahrani, Zeynep Çelik, and Edhem Eldem, pp. 257–279. SALT, Istanbul.

Marchand, Suzanne L.
2009   *German Orientalism in the Age of Empire: Religion, Race, and Scholarship.* Cambridge University Press, Cambridge.

Mertens, Dieter
1991   Otto Puchstein. In *Archäologenbildnisse: Porträts und Kurzbiographien von klassischen Archäologen deutscher Sprache,* edited by Reinhard Lullies and Wolfgang Schiering, pp. 118–119. Verlag von Zabern, Mainz am Rhein.

Miller, Peter N.
2013   A Tentative Morphology of European Antiquarianism, 1500–2000. In *World Antiquarianism: Comparative Perspectives*, edited by Alain Schnapp, pp. 67–87. Getty Research Institute, Los Angeles.

Murray, Tim
2013   Antiquarianism of and in Preliterate Societies: Colonial and Postcolonial Contexts. In *World Antiquarianism: Comparative Perspectives*, edited by Alain Schnapp, pp. 11–34. Getty Research Institute, Los Angeles.

Petersen, Lars
2008   Die Orientreise des deutschen Kaisers 1898 und die Ausgrabungen in Baalbek. In *Das Große Spiel: Archäologie und Politik zur Zeit des Kolonialismus (1860–1940)*, edited by Charlotte Trümpler, pp. 398–409. DuMont, Köln.

Piccirillo, Michele
1994   Le Rovine. In *Umm al-Rasa, Mayfa'ah 1: Gli Scavi del Complesso di Santo Stefano. Studium Biblicum Franciscanum Collectio maior 28*, edited by Michele Piccirillo and Eugenio Alliata, pp. 55–67. Jerusalem Franciscan Print Press, Jerusalem.

Pinney, Christopher
2012   *Photography and Anthropology.* Reaktion Books, London.

Rogan, Eugene L.
1999   *Frontiers of the State in the Late Ottoman Empire: Transjordan, 1850–1921.* Cambridge Middle East Studies 12. Cambridge University Press, Cambridge and New York.

Saitta, Dean J.
2007   *The Archaeology of Collective Action.* University Press of Florida, Gainesville.

Shami, Seteney
2009   Historical Processes of Identity Formation: Displacement, Settlement, and Self-Representations of the Circassians in Jordan. *Iran & The Caucasus* 13: 141–159.

Smith, Laurajane
2006   *Uses of Heritage.* Routledge, London.

The Journal of Anthropology
1871   Review of *The Moabite Stone: A Facsimile of the Original Inscription, with an English Translation, and a Historical and Critical Commentary*, edited by Christian D. Ginsburg. *The Journal of Anthropology* 1: 349–354.

Trigger, Bruce G.
1984   Alternative Archaeologies: Nationalist, Colonialist, Imperialist. *Man* n.s. 19: 355–370.

Tristam, Henry Baker
1873   *The Land of Moab: Travels and Discoveries on the East Side of the Dead Sea and the Jordan.* Harper & Brothers, New York.

Troelenberg, Eva-Maria
2016   *Mshatta in Berlin – Keystones of Islamic Art.* Kettler, Dortmund.

Trümpler, Charlotte (editor)

2008   *Das Große Spiel: Archäologie und Politik zur Zeit des Kolonialismus (1860–1940)*. DuMont, Köln.

Turner, James

2014   *Philology: The Forgotten Origins of the Modern Humanities*. Princeton University Press, Princeton and Oxford.

Van der Steen, Eveline

2014   *Near Eastern Tribal Societies during the Nineteenth Century: Economy, Society and Politics between Tent and Town*. Routledge, New York.

Waterton, Emma, and Laurajane Smith

2009   There is No Such Thing as Heritage. In *Taking Archaeology out of Heritage*, edited by Emma Waterton and Laurajane Smith, pp. 11–27. Cambridge Scholars Publishing, Cambridge.

Archival Sources

BArch (Bundesarchiv) R 901 37702; *Auswärtiges Amt Abt. IIIb Akten betreffend: Die wissenschaftliche Erforschung von Kleinasien*.

— 9 —

Forgetting Athens

Benjamin Anderson

The comparative study of antiquarianisms is in its infancy, and certain fundamental questions have yet to be systematically debated, much less answered. The most crucial question regards the basis for comparison: what shared characteristics unite varieties of "antiquarianism" and thus permit their comparison with each other?

One possible response is to adopt the practices of the early modern European antiquaries as the basis for comparison. This response produces a double challenge: first, to recover those practices from the marginalization and misunderstanding to which they have been subjected by later historians and archaeologists; and second, to abstract from them core principles that reveal "the divergent and distinctive contours" of similar traditions practiced in other regions (Miller 2012: 104). In this response, only those antiquarianisms would be compared whose contours are sufficiently *similar* to European antiquarianism to facilitate the comparison: for example, those traditions that are practiced in highly stratified societies by elites whose ability to undertake scholarship depends on the manual labor of others; and whose primary expressions are written treatises intended to edify future generations.

A second response, fully reconcilable with the first but potentially more capacious, is to posit "the antiquarian" as "a figure common to all literate cultures," who may also exist in other contexts: "we also need to address the question of antiquarian behavior in prehistoric cultures as well as in contemporary hunter-gatherer tribes attempting to deal with their past" (Schnapp 2013: 1). Here the antiquarian practices of "literate cultures" establish the standard to which various practices observed among "prehistoric cultures" and "contemporary hunter-gatherer tribes" (two groups that, a few decades ago, many scholars would have collapsed into the single category of "primitive peoples") are to be compared.

Although this second response may seem more inclusive than the first, it is also susceptible to an ethical critique. As Alfredo González-Ruibal writes in his contribution to this volume, it would be repugnant to posit the existence of "antiquarianism" (especially if defined by implicit analogy to the practices of western Europeans post-1500) as yet another standard against which to measure the relative evolution, or indeed the humanity, of various cultures and societies. To do so is to raise *el demonio de las comparaciones* ("the specter of comparisons"), that mechanism discovered by the narrator of Filipino novelist's José Rizal's *Noli Me Tángere* (1887) through which all "gardens are shadowed automatically … and inescapably by images of their sister gardens in Europe" (Anderson 1998: 2). A comparative study of antiquarianisms must not only avoid the overt assertion of western European supremacy, it must actively banish its specter, which tends to appear uninvited wherever a space is left for it.

The second response furthermore begs a question about the social position of "the antiquarian" within hierarchical societies. Is it, as González-Ruibal posits in this volume, a role naturally assumed by leisured elites? Counter-examples may be cited: eighteenth-century English usage distinguished "popular antiquities" from "classical" and "religious" varieties, and advocates of "popular antiquities" gave explicit voice to "class consciousness and class hostility" (Butler 1999: 332). But such distinctions are little discussed in recent comparative studies, as one reviewer notes:

> While "casual" indigenous practices are considered sufficiently respectable for inclusion [in a study of "World Antiquarianism"], what then of non-/sub-academic past collectors/investigators in western cultures? In this capacity we should think, for example, of ley-line hunters, Scandinavian farmers' "home museums," stamp collectors or historic airfield aficionados [Evans 2014: 1].

One may go further: not all "non-academic" practices are so quaint, apparently innocuous, as those listed; indeed some claim antiquarianism as a charged field of contest and of solidarity along multiple axes of difference (economic class, social status, gender, race, etc.) (see, for example, Smith 2006).

In short, although the second response may appear more inclusive than the first, it is susceptible to ethical and political objections that remain insuperable so long as a historically contingent manifestation of antiquarianism (e.g. the study of "classical antiquities" by early modern Europeans) is adopted, explicitly or implicitly, as the basis of comparison. If the comparative study of antiquarianisms wishes to investigate without prejudice different ways of approaching the material remains of the past, then it requires a definition of "antiquarianism" that does not rely on analogy to western European practice. We need a theoretical definition that can be assessed on the basis of its ability to advance the investigation, as opposed to a lexical definition that is determined by the term's historical usage.

In the first section of this paper I offer such a theoretical definition. However, I am myself an intellectual descendant of the European antiquaries, and a professional academic employed by a private university in a settler-colonial state. Even if one were to grant my best intentions, my definition might well be an *idolum specus*, embodying the interpretive reflexes and prejudices inherent to my class and native tradition. For this reason, the proposed definition would need to be tested in a variety of circumstances and modified by a variety of interlocutors before it could provide a legitimate basis for a comparative study of antiquarianisms.

However, there is at least one test that I can perform myself. A robust theoretical definition of antiquarianism should be able to reveal *non-antiquarian* practices, not only among "the so-called primitives, people 'without history,' supposedly isolated from the external world and from one another" (Wolf 2010: 4), but also in hierarchical societies. Most crucially, it should be able to identify elements of the heretofore normative early modern European antiquarian tradition that are "antiquarian" according to customary usage of the term, but not for the purposes of comparative study. Accordingly, in the third and fourth parts of this paper I offer such a test case, arguing that eighteenth-century European "antiquarianism" included a form of Romantic forgetting that is, according to the proposed theoretical definition, fundamentally non-antiquarian. This case study focuses on a French painter's view of the ruins of Athens, and thus on what might seem to be a paradigmatically "antiquarian" product. However, the painting betrays little concern with the stuff of antiquarianism proper: objects.

A Working Definition

Antiquarianism is the attempt to understand the past through interaction with objects that exist in the present.

On the basis of this definition, the comparative study of antiquarianisms would only be of interest if different milieux were to exhibit various modes of interaction with objects with the intention of understanding the past. This is demonstrably the case. For example, in 1753, the British antiquaries James Stuart and Nicholas Revett visited Thessaloniki, where they developed an interest in an old two-storey stone structure whose upper level incorporated multiple life-size carved figures doubling as supports ("caryatids"). By following their own mode of engagement, Stuart and Revett hazarded to identify the remains of an ancient theater, but they also recorded the result of an alternative mode of engagement ("the vulgar tradition of the place") according to which the structure was a balcony that once connected two palaces, and the caryatids the members of a royal retinue who had been petrified by magic (Anderson 2015: 454–455).

If we assume that time is linear and unidirectional, then such propositions about the past are unverifiable, but they can attain relative degrees of plausibility within clearly defined parameters.[1] For example, few of Stuart and Revett's intellectual heirs would accept their proposal that the stone monument in Thessaloniki once formed part of a theater. According to the parameters of argument in classical archaeology, scholars now prefer to understand the structure as a fragment of a Roman portico, which may have stood within an agora or a forum (e.g., Guerrini 1961; Baldassare 1976). However, as those parameters are intrinsic to a specific mode of engagement ("classical archaeology"), they possess value for the comparative study of antiquarianisms only as data about that mode, not as standards of proof. In fact, the comparative study of antiquarianisms is not concerned to adjudicate between divergent claims about the past produced by different modes of interaction on the basis of a common object. It remains agnostic about the past whose investigation is the primary concern of the various traditions that it compares.

If comparative antiquarianism cannot be anchored in any given understanding of the past, then it will have to be anchored by objects instead: different modes of interaction can be thought of as engines that generate propositions in response to the qualities of objects.[2] Comparative study produces a richer understanding of the object than any single tradition can offer. For example, whereas medieval interpreters of an equestrian statue in Rome did not recognize the emperor whom it depicted, early modern scholars compared his physiognomy and hairstyle to the portraits on ancient coins to produce a plausible identification. However, modern viewers of the same statue have missed the exemplary qualities of the horse, to which medieval interpreters were particularly well attuned (Kinney 2002). The medieval "engine" responded to the horse, the early modern "engine" to the emperor. The two modes of interpretation are mutually enriching, jointly producing a "braided" form of knowledge (Atalay 2012: 207). To return once more to Thessaloniki: the classical archaeologist may be more adept at comparing the physical structure to other ancient monuments, but the local tradition reveals its sculptures' potential to evoke a terrifying captivity, which is missed when they are briskly identified as "caryatids," which threaten to become *idola fori*.[3]

Therefore, if we accept the definition of antiquarianism as the attempt to understand the past through interaction with objects that exist in the present, then the primary criterion for the inclusion of a given tradition within a comparative study of antiquarianisms would be its reliance upon and fidelity to objects. (The comparatist's job, then, would be to identify the underlying principles that cause a tradition to account for a given object in a particular way.) Of course, there are ways to understand the past that disregard or disavow objects (for example: those that abstract source texts from their material substrates; those that discover in human behavior and dreams the after-effects of repressed trauma), just as there are modes of interaction with objects that are not concerned to understand the past (transcendental accounts of the qualities of given materials, such as marble or gold; the appraisal of the monetary value of a given object within current market conditions). To exclude such practices from a comparative study of antiquarianisms entails no judgment on their value to human life or the common good. It merely marks the impossibility of their comparison along one particular axis.

Much of the foregoing may seem uncontroversial at best, banal at worst. But I suspect that if this primary criterion were rigorously applied, the resulting account of antiquarianism would be startlingly unfamiliar. By proceeding on the basis of a theoretical definition, comparative study would be compelled to include modes of interaction that, assuming a lexical definition, might seem too bizarre, such as the practice of smelling monumental remains to understand the distant past of a given site (on which see Felipe Rojas in Ch. 2 of this volume). Just as importantly, it would have to exclude aspects of the early modern European tradition that a lexical definition would allow.[4]

By way of an example, I offer a case for the exclusion of a particular strain in the late eighteenth-century representation of sites associated with classical antiquity. As my account is conceived as an exercise in antiquarianism, it engages an object (a painting of Athens) through a specific mode: "iconology," or "the discovery and interpretation of [those] 'symbolical' values … which are often unknown to the artist himself and may even emphatically differ from what he consciously intended to express" (Panofsky 1955: 31). The potential for a radical disjunction between intent and essence is crucial: for if the author of the painting in question understood his work as an engagement with the "classical" past through the contemporary fabric of Athens, I detect in it an underlying obliviousness to the particularities of that fabric.

The painting to be discussed acquires additional interest since it appears in its own right to present a kind of comparative study of antiquarianisms, in which two distinct groups of people interact with the material remains of the past in divergent fashions. Upon closer inspection the unfamiliar mode of engagement emerges not as an object of genuine interest but as a foil for the figure of the painter. The painting therefore serves not only as a test case for the differing results produced by the application of theoretical and lexical definitions of antiquarianism, but also as monitory example of the fine line that separates comparison from solipsism.

Cassas in Athens

A painting in watercolor and ink on paper, today in the Pera Museum in Istanbul, depicts an encounter in Athens (Figure 9.1). The picture belongs to a group of very similar views executed by Louis-François Cassas in the 1790s.[5] The scene depicted unfolds to the southeast of the Acropolis of Athens, before the Temple of Olympian Zeus ("Olympieion"), whose platform, columns, and entablature dominate the right foreground, framing a view to the Arch of Hadrian behind. Three additional columns, once part of the same temple, appear in the left middle ground, framing in turn the arches of the Odeion of Herodes Atticus at the base of the Acropolis. At far left, the Monument of Philopappos appears through a clearing in a thicket of trees, crowning the Mouseion Hill.

The Acropolis stands in the distant background, unobstructed and carefully delineated, just beneath the painting's geometric center (Figure 9.2). It is dominated by the husk of the Parthenon, hollowed out by the explosion of the previous century. Inside we see the mosque, a small domed mescid of square plan. The great rock outcropping is bracketed by two medieval towers: the so-called Frankish tower beside the Propylaea on the left, and the Belvedere tower on the right.

Like the Acropolis, the plain below is a palimpsest of the ancient, the medieval, and the contemporary. The remains of a small medieval structure (variously identified as a watchtower or a stylite's hut) perch atop the architrave of the temple, while scenes of contemporary life unfold below. At center, two women engage in conversation, and to the left, in front of the trio of columns, women link hands and dance to the music provided by a drummer and a flutist.

In the right half of the picture we may distinguish three groups of figures (Figure 9.3). Furthest from us, three men, recognizable by their hats as western European, cluster about the temple platform, two of them gesturing toward the monumental columns. A group of four stands closer to us. Two men in hats, one of whom wears the blue coat of a French officer, engage two local women in conversation. The woman on the left places her hand on the officer's upper arm. In the foreground, three men in turbans gather before a massive stone relief depicting a contest between a man and a centaur. Two of the turbaned figures crouch, of whom one inspects the relief to which the other points while looking at the third, standing figure and speaking.

Figure 9.1. Louis-François Cassas, View of the Acropolis of Athens from the Temple of Olympian Zeus, 103 × 67 cm. 1790s (Suna and İnan Kıraç Foundation Orientalist Paintings Collection, Pera Museum, Istanbul).

Figure 9.2. Detail of Figure 9.1.

Figure 9.3. Detail of Figure 9.1.

Born in 1756, and trained as an architectural draughtsman, Louis-François Cassas traveled to Rome at the age of 23. His drawings of antiquities attracted the patronage of the Comte de Choiseul-Gouffier, the French ambassador to Constantinople, and between 1784 and 1787 Cassas traveled throughout the Ottoman Empire, producing views primarily of the Greek and Roman sites. His only recorded visit to Athens dates to the very beginning of this trip. Choiseul-Gouffier intended to use his protégé's drawings to illustrate a sequel to his widely read travel narrative, the *Voyage pittoresque de la Grèce* (1782), but the aristocratic ambassador fled to Russia after the revolution of 1789, and the project was never completed. Cassas returned to Paris in 1791 (Gilet and Westfehling 1994).

As a product of the 1790s, Cassas's painting must represent an act of remembrance on the part of its author, a view of a city visited a decade previous, presumably aided by sketches and also by the views produced by other artists. However, in the following I wish to focus instead on its multiple points of engagement with discourses of forgetting. First, Cassas's view evokes a familiar narrative of the eighteenth-century western European "rediscovery" of a classical city that had been forgotten by its contemporary inhabitants— *quella smemorata Atene di un lunghissimo Medio Evo*, "that forgotten Athens of an extended Middle Age," to quote a recent retelling of the story (Settis 2014: 4). A second narrative, by contrast, would set Cassas's view not at the

Figure 9.4. View of the Acropolis of Athens from the Temple of Olympian Zeus, 2014 (author's photograph).

end but at the beginning of a history of forgetting. If we compare his painting to a snapshot taken in the summer of 2014 (Figure 9.4), we see that much has disappeared in the intervening centuries: the mosque, the Frankish tower, the small enclosure atop the temple. Thus Cassas provided unwitting testimony to the subsequent process of "forgetting the multi-temporal and multi-cultural life of the Acropolis" and other Athenian monuments (Hamilakis 2011b: 628)—even as he (likewise unwittingly) participated in that process by contributing to a western European cult of classical antiquity.

If I say nothing more about these two narratives, it is because Cassas's painting speaks more strongly still to a third, and less familiar, discourse of forgetting, one that is closely related to those intellectual and cultural tendencies that we now habitually group under the term "Romanticism." This third discourse emerges from the relations within and between the three groups of figures in the picture's right half, who are arranged in a strict symmetry (Figure 9.3). At far left, we find three local men; at far right, three foreign men. Both groups are discussing ancient remains, and thus present variations on two standard elements in the genre of "picturesque" views of archaeological sites, whose conventions were well established by the last decade of the eighteenth century. The first element is the group of gentlemen pointing at antiquities, as seen in the foreground of an early view of the excavations at Herculaneum, published to accompany Jean-Claude Richard de Saint-Non's *Voyage Pittoresque* (1781–82) (Figure 9.5). The second element is the group of men in turbans, a favorite trope of antiquarians' depictions of Ottoman lands, for example in James Stuart's view of the Erechtheion published in 1787 in the second volume of the *Antiquities of Athens* (Figure 9.6). Stuart characteristically represents the locals as indifferent to the ancient monument whose space they share.[6] In Cassas's view, by contrast, both turbaned locals at left and behatted visitors at right are engaged in the same activity: a discussion of old things. By maintaining a clear and uniform distinction in dress between the two groups, Cassas depicted two distinct conversations about antiquity.

The profound differences between European travelers' approaches to antiquity and those of Ottoman subjects had become an explicit theme in the travelers' accounts of the later eighteenth century. In his 1769 essay on Homer, Robert Wood recalled of his journey through Syria:

> In vain did we attempt to explain to the Arabs any fact recorded on the marbles, which we found there [i.e., at Tadmur, or Palmyra]; they treated the account of some of those buildings, which we read to them from the inscriptions, with great contempt, as the invidious contrivance of later times to rob Solomon the son of David (Solymon Ebn Doud) of the honour of having erected them [Wood 1769: xl].[7]

As we have already seen, Stuart and Revett gave a more detailed account of a local interpretation of a monument in Thessaloniki in the third volume of their *Antiquities of Athens* (1794), all the while dismissing it as "the vulgar tradition of the place."

When compared to these textual accounts, the relative position of the two lateral groups of interpreters in Cassas's painting is surprising. The three locals at left are foremost in the image, and their expressions are fully legible. By contrast, the three foreigners at right are distant, tiny, and faceless. This interest in the locals at the expense of the visitors is also maintained in the central group. While the two lateral groups are homogeneous, the central group is mixed in both origin and gender: two local women interact with two foreign men. Most surprising is the gesture of the woman at left, who initiates physical contact with the man in the officer's jacket. The woman's gesture is ambivalent: on the one hand, affectionate or even flirtatious; on the other hand, an attempt to interrupt or restrain. Its significance for the interaction between locals and foreigners emerges from the man's right arm, which falls slack in response, as if about to drop the object in his hand. This

Figure 9.5. Excavations at Herculaneum. Reproduced from Saint-Non 1782: 3 (Universitätsbibliothek Heidelberg).

Figure 9.6. View of the Erechtheion. Reproduced from Stuart & Revett 1787: Chapter II, Plate II (Cornell University Library).

latter resembles the measuring stick held by Cassas in a self-portrait from his own *Voyage Pittoresque*, published in 1799, where he uses it document the so-called "Tomb of Absalom" near Jerusalem (Figure 9.7). Thus we may connect the central to the lateral groups: the local woman dissuades the officer from joining his countrymen at the temple and measuring its constituent architectural elements. The customary western European mode of antiquarian engagement with ruins is interrupted by an encounter with a living culture.

Both in Cassas's painting of Athens (Figure 9.1) and in the engraving of his view of the Tomb of Absalom (Figure 9.7), the measuring stick marks a crucial difference between divergent approaches to ancient remains. According to its caption, the engraving depicts the *costume, sous le quel l'Artiste déguisé, a pu prendre à loisir les mesures du monument*—"the costume, disguised in which the Artist was able to take the measurements of the monument at leisure." The implication that Cassas worked in Jerusalem under conditions adverse to scholarship is reinforced by the threatening posture of the figure at right, who strides forward, pointing with his left hand and holding a musket in his right. The painter's solution, to adopt local dress, found ample precedent in the works of earlier travelers—as in Stuart's view of the Erechtheion, in which the artist depicts himself drawing, unobserved, in robe and skullcap (Figure 9.6). Local dress in these images allows the artist a position whence to "see and yet not be seen," like that adopted in the following century by "the photographer, invisible beneath his black cloth as he eyed the world through his camera's gaze" (Mitchell 1992: 306).

The measured architectural drawing of ancient buildings was, by Cassas's time, a century-old genre, whose conventions had been established in the 1680s by the work of Antoine Desgodetz. The images in the volumes published by Stuart and Revett and by Cassas alternated between disembodied "architectural" views presented in two-dimensional plans, sections, and elevations; and the "picturesque" engravings (e.g., Figures 9.6 and 9.7) in which monuments were depicted in perspective and surrounded by local anecdote (Watkin 2006: 26–35). Although some nineteenth-century photographers optimistically claimed to capture the "architectural" and the "picturesque" in a single image (Bohrer 2015: 103–104), ultimately the photograph only replaced the picturesque view, becoming the standard accompaniment to measured drawings in the scholarly documentation of architecture. However, the camera shares with the ruler a tacit claim to objectivity, so that today both standard modes of representation purport to depict the monument as it really is. The distinction between the picturesque and the architectural drawing, by contrast, maintains a clear division between the subjective perception of a monument at a specific moment in

TOMBEAU D'ABSALON,

situé dans la vallée dite de Josaphat, et taillé dans le roc.
costume, sous lequel l'Artiste déguisé, a pu prendre à loisir les mesures du monument.

Figure 9.7. View of the "Tomb of Absalom." Reproduced from Cassas 1800: Plate 30 (Universitätsbibliothek Heidelberg).

time, cluttered with the accidental and the extraneous, and the objective representation of its quantifiable and trans-temporal form.

By the late eighteenth century, the distinction between the two types of views could be expressed within the systematic terms of Kant's critical philosophy. The third critique argued for the universality of disinterested judgments of taste, which were by definition indifferent to the material existence of an object:

> Dagegen ist das Geschmacksurtheil bloß contemplativ, d.i. ein Urtheil, welches, indifferent in Ansehung des Daseins eines Gegenstandes, nur seine Beschaffenheit mit dem Gefühl der Lust und Unlust zusammenhält [Kant 1908(1790): 209].

> By contrast, the judgment of taste is purely contemplative, that is, a judgment which, indifferent in respect to the existence of an object, only associates its nature with the experience of pleasure and displeasure.

Although the travelers' measured drawings derived from a much older tradition, in the late eighteenth century they provided the nascent science of archaeology with a technique for abstracting immaterial form from material objects (Arnold 2003: 40–43), thus sustaining a disciplinary claim to salutary indifference, or "disinterestedness" (Marchand 1996).

To return to Cassas's painting: if the encounter between the woman and the officer merely stages the distraction of a draughtsman from his natural task, then its primary valences would be monitory and erotic (here are the delights and dangers of the East). However, it attains a subtler significance within an emergent Romantic philhellenism that accorded an explicit role to contemporary Greek communities and other Ottoman subjects. The clearest expressions of this new attitude are found in the first volume of Friedrich Hölderlin's epistolary novel *Hyperion*. The novel follows its eponymous hero, a young Greek, through a series of encounters: first with the sculptor Adamas, who comes from away and awakens in Hyperion the desire to learn about antiquity; then with Alabanda, a military conspirator from Smyrna; and finally with Diotima, a woman with whom Hyperion visits Athens. There she addresses the hero with a speech that could serve as a caption for Cassas's painting:

> Ich bitte dich, geh nach Athen hinein, noch Einmal, und siehe die Menschen auch an, die dort herumgehn unter den Trümmern, die rohen Albaner und die andern guten kindischen Griechen, die mit einem lustigen Tanze und einem heiligen Mährchen sich trösten über die schmähliche Gewalt, die über ihnen lastet … [Hölderlin 1957(1797): 88].

> I beg you, go once more into Athens, and look also at the people who go about there amongst the ruins, the rough Albanians and the other good, child-like

Greeks, who with a merry dance and a holy tale console themselves for the humiliating power that oppresses them …

Hyperion himself both celebrates *die sechszehn Säulen, die noch übrig stehn vom göttlichen Olympion* ("the sixteen columns that still remain standing from the divine Olympieion") and scorns *zwei brittischen Gelehrten, die unter den Altertümern in Athen ihre Erndte hielten* ("two British scholars who reaped their harvest among the antiquities of Athens"), the latter surely a reference to Stuart and Revett (Hölderlin 1957[1797]: 86).

Within the context of Romantic philhellenism, Cassas's view loses its monitory aspect and becomes instead an exemplary reminiscence, in which the painter, nearing forty, looks back on his first visit to Ottoman lands. The mode of engagement with antiquity in which he was trained as an architectural draughtsman in Rome proves insufficient to his encounter with the actual site. The French officer is forced to forget the Athens of the great leather-bound folios of Stuart and Revett, and to confront a living city instead. The beauty that arrests him is not of the crumbling temple, but of a living woman. Instead of donning native disguise in order to draw and measure, the artist allows himself to appear fully other, to attract attention. He lets his ruler fall.

This disruption of the customary is mirrored by the foremost group. The three men show themselves little concerned with the encounter unfolding behind them, directing their attention instead to an ancient relief half-buried in the soil and shrubs. One points and speaks with a worried expression, while another gazes as if transfixed. The arrival of the foreigners and their enthusiasm for old stones has caused a familiar part of the landscape to become an object of wonder. In short, Cassas presents us with a double moment of becoming-strange. Or to put this account in the terms of the present volume: the painting depicts the generative potential of an encounter between distinct antiquarian traditions.

Cassas in the Mirror

To discover in Cassas's painting a relevance to contemporary archaeological theory should give us pause. Perhaps he was remarkably prescient; or perhaps we are embarking on a previously trodden path. Indeed, many of the concerns of the present discourse around comparative antiquarianism were anticipated by late eighteenth-century, or "Romantic," antiquarianism. This earlier moment was marked, on the one hand, by a "democratic" impulse that "levels distinctions between the learned and popular reception of ancient objects," which is shared between Cassas's painting and by many of the contributions to the present volume (Heringman and Lake 2014: 1).

On the other hand, Romantic antiquarianism was deeply invested in "the power of representations to transform or displace the things themselves" (Heringman and Lake 2014: 4). This too appears in Cassas's painting, and with implications for the apparently "democratic" approach to the engagement with antiquity. For what might first appear as an appreciation of alternative modes of engagement with antiquity on closer inspection reveals a profound solipsism.

To understand this aspect of the painting, we must turn our attention once more to the figures depicted, this time heeding their embeddedness within contemporary visual codes. In the account that we have developed, the blue-coated officer serves as a proxy for Cassas, if not indeed as a self-portrait. But how are we to understand the other figures? It can easily be shown that the locals in the scene are not so much individuals as types,[8] derived both from the printed accounts of travelers and from the "costume albums," often produced by Ottoman artists, that served "to decode the social structure of a foreign society for the traveller, and to help locate the place of individual 'locals' within this structure" (Schick 1999: 628).

Some of these types are generic, as with the dancers and musicians in the left half of the image, who recall a scene depicted and described in Choiseul-Gouffier's *Voyage pittoresque*. Observing a folk dance on Paros, Choiseul-Gouffier remarks on its "surprising conformity" with the dances of the ancient Greeks, and states that its function is to distract its modern practitioners from their present condition:

> Le goût de la danse a toujours été le même chez les Grècs; le malheur & la servitude n'ont pû leur faire perdre l'amour naturel qu'ils ont pour le plaisir: un moment de fête leur fait oublier leur misère [1782: 68].

> The Greeks have always maintained the same taste for the dance; unhappiness and servitude have not been able to make them lose their natural love of pleasure: a festive moment makes them forget their misery.

As later for Hölderlin, so already for Choiseul-Gouffier: the dance serves as a temporary distraction from Ottoman rule (indeed, the earlier passage was likely a direct source for the later). Cassas's painting evoked the same conceit, thus engaging a pre-existing set of western European tropes about the manners and customs of the Greeks.

Other types seem intended to evoke more specific occupations within Ottoman society, as among the figures in the painting's right half. For example, the two women who initiate the central encounter, with their long tresses and low necklines, resemble nothing so much as the "Turkish dancers" of the contemporary costume books (Figure 9.8). Surely one did

Figure 9.8. So-called Diez Album, "Danseuse Turcque," 22 × 37 cm, ca. 1790 (British Museum, 1974,0617,0.12.2.21).

Figure 9.9. "Hamale: portefaix," 38 × 25 cm, 1786 (Médiathèque E. & R. Vailland, Bourg-en-Bresse, MS 65, No. 134).

not encounter such entertainers on an afternoon's visit to the Olympieion; their presence here indicates that this scene lies as much in the painter's fantasy as in Ottoman Athens. Other figures were drawn from the same stock: for example, the standing figure in the foremost group, with his drooping mustaches, long musket, open vest and baggy trousers, is a near twin to a figure depicted in a manuscript owned by Joseph Gabriel Monnier (Figure 9.9). Monnier was, with Cassas, a member of Choiseul-Gouffier's mission to Constantinople (Paviot 1982). Perhaps both images depict the same man, an actual servant employed by the French ambassador, but in Monnier's album he is labeled as an occupational type (*hamale*, "porter"), and it is likely that his counterpart in Cassas's painting is meant to play the same role.

Indeed, real people must stand behind all of these images, filtered through various degrees of abstraction: behind Choiseul-Gouffier's merry Greeks, and behind the female dancers and porters of the costume books and of Cassas's painting. However, they do not appear in these contexts on their own terms, or even as individuals, but as generalized types that drive someone else's story. As we have seen, it is quite possible to understand Cassas's view sympathetically: as a retrospective reflection on the painter's first encounter with Hellenism's promised land, in which the desire to approach the antiquities in a scientific fashion is interrupted by an encounter with a living culture. Still, all of this remains at the level of allegory, and serves at best to critique the practice of a previous generation of travelers, like Hölderlin's Romantic critique of the *zwei brittischen Gelehrten*. Alternative modes of engagement do not exist here autonomously, but as stock figures in a foreign drama. This is not so far from the role of the "indigenous archaeologist" in some present-day accounts, whose concerns turn out to mirror those of contemporary academic discourse: "the agency of archaeological objects," for example, and "multisensory engagement with materiality" (Hamilakis 2011a: 62). Perhaps this is an accurate image, perhaps an *idolum theatri*; but surely it is less interesting to discover confirmations of our own hunches, than to learn something new.

Cassas's painting might, then, point to an impasse: can modes of antiquarian practice with ambitions to universal applicability, such as those practiced in early modern Europe and by many contemporary archaeologists, interact with local modes without subsuming the singularities of the latter into a new "Grand Narrative" (such as that invoked by Eva-Maria Troelenberg in Ch. 8 of this volume)? But as I have argued above, this problem is easily overcome. So long as there is a common object of interpretation, the diversity of approaches and opinions can be understood to activate various potentialities that co-exist within that object. Thus it is not so much the generic character of Cassas's local actors that sets his image outside of the sphere of antiquarianism, as the generic character of its central object. Much in this painting is faithfully depicted. Indeed, the entire scene has been structured to encourage maximum visibility: of Philopappos through the foliage, Herodes Atticus and Hadrian through the Olympieion's columns, the Acropolis unobstructed. Yet all of these merely serve the action as a backdrop. Only one object fully participates in the drama: the massive relief in the foreground (Figure 9.3).

If this object is revealed to nearly its full extent, and the "porter" is 180 cm tall, then the relief would measure roughly 225 cm H × 100 cm W × 50 cm D. While all surfaces appear to be finished, only one is sculpted. Two simple horizontal strips of molding, one at top and the second ca. 75 cm from the bottom, frame a square field carved in relief. At picture left appears a male figure, nude but for a cloak that billows behind him, whose right arm extends out of frame; at picture right a centaur, fully contained with the relief, a stray limb above his haunches. Man and centaur face each other in combat, and the man's left arm extends as if to throttle his opponent, whose right arm is raised and bent in defense.

The contest evokes the centauromachies on the south metopes of the Parthenon; furthermore, as the battle of Lapiths and Centaurs is conventionally understood as an allegorical representation of the conflict between civilized peoples and barbarians, it may also provide a sinister gloss on the cultural encounter unfolding in its immediate vicinity.[9] However, the object depicted cannot be a stray bit of the great temple. The width of the Parthenon metopes varies between ca. 110 and 130 cm, and each is slightly broader than high (Brommer 1967: 162–165): roughly square, in other words, and in marked contrast to the vertically elongated object in Cassas's painting. Cassas surely inspected the south metopes on site (they are visually distinguished from the triglyphs in his depiction of the Parthenon [Figure 9.2] as inset fields marked by squiggles) and in Stuart and Revett. He will have seen that the centauromachies of the south metopes regularly represent two complete figures locked in combat, and present no analogue to the arm extending out of frame or the stray limb on the opposite side. Finally, while elements of Cassas's relief do appear on the south metopes— the billowing cape, the throttling arm—none of the actual reliefs depict the precise configuration depicted in the painting.

The comparison is pedantic, but with purpose. Just as Cassas's dancers and porters serve as types, not as portraits, so too his relief serves as a cipher for antiquity, not as a representation of an actual thing. His painting, in other words, frames a discourse within which "we" interact with "them" over "antiquities," but within which the only fully defined agent is that of the artist himself.

Forgetting Athens

We cannot know what led Cassas to invent the object in the foreground of his image: perhaps the desire to create a composition in which the wedge of the relief neatly complements the three groups of figures, perhaps a mutation of memory, perhaps a will to license. But the gesture, in which the parameters of a certain discourse lead the author to invent an object that is required, not to respond to an existing one, is so commonplace as to be banal. In scholarship it is ubiquitous as "the desire to find confirmation of a theory … in a given monument rather than to analyse a specific artefact" (Lolla 2003: 16).

Any mode of antiquarian practice will systematically ignore or exclude something: a historical era, a class of people, an aspect of human experience: such are the *idola tribus*. But different modes can still be placed in conversation, and serve to fill each other's lacunae, so long as they obey the limitations imposed by their objects of inquiry:

> We must reconcile ourselves to the stones,
> Not the stones to us.
> [MacDiarmid 1993: 151]

The object is required as a *tertium comparationis* that enables comparison of different modes of engagement without prejudice, collapsing the arbitrary distance that accidents of history and the resulting hegemonies might place between traditions. Although comparatists, like the traditions that we study, have no unmediated access to the object "as such," its centrality allows comparative antiquarianism to enter into "the logic of emancipation," which requires "the third thing that is owned by no one, whose meaning is owned by no one, but which subsists between" all who approach it (Rancière 2009: 14–15). In the absence of honest engagement with an object, a given tradition can only be understood according to its own hermetic terms, however elegant and well-tuned those might be.

To summarize: Cassas's painting is both representative of a certain "period attitude" toward antiquity, and a representation of an encounter between distinct antiquarianisms. Consideration of these two aspects results in two interrelated hypotheses. First, the painting shares with multiple strands of late eighteenth-century thought (Kantian aesthetics, Romantic philhellenism) an indifference to the material existence of its central object. Second, its staged encounter between antiquarianisms issues in solipsism: the encounter with a generic other as a valuable experience for a young man abroad.

Neither hypothesis could be sustained as a general claim about the study of the past in late eighteenth-century western European circles. A systematic evaluation of the sources would unquestionably reveal the existence of multiple competing attitudes toward the material existence of objects; and perhaps (although here the source material is likely to be much thinner) toward the existence of multiple antiquarianisms as well. However this may be, we can now characterize Cassas's painting as representative of an attitude that is fundamentally non-antiquarian according to the definition advanced at the beginning of this paper; and this despite its apparent interest in those most canonical of antiquities, the ruins of Athens. This demonstration points to the potential rewards of pursuing the comparative study of antiquarianisms on the basis of a theoretical, not a lexical definition. Cassas's painting attests the existence of a variety of systematic forgetting that partakes neither of the "primitive" nor of nineteenth-century capitalist "modernity" (cf. Connerton 2009), but is positioned at the heart of the "age of antiquaries."

Ideally, a comparative study of antiquarianism anchored in objects should aid in the recognition and preservation of real difference between traditions. If we seek out traditions that resemble those familiar to us, we run the risk of finding them: radically misunderstanding their nature and context in pursuit of the false analogy. However, if we seek concrete instances of response to objects and attempt to understand them on their own terms, we are less likely to be led astray. The exercise will surely enrich our understanding of the objects, some of which have been run through our own engines so many times, and with such diminishing returns, that they threaten to inspire fatigue in place of wonder. More than enough interpretations of the sculptures of the Parthenon have been generated according to the conventions of classical archaeology. Yet I am far from understanding their effect on a seventeenth-century Ottoman traveler:

> Whatever living creatures the Lord Creator has created, from Adam to the Resurrection, are depicted in these marble statues around the courtyard of the mosque. Fearful and ugly demons, jinns, Satan the Whisperer, the Sneak, the Farter; fairies, angels, dragons, earth-beasts; the angels that bear up the throne of God and the ox that bears up the earth; sea-beasts, elephants, rhinoceri, giraffes, horned vipers, snakes, centipedes, scorpions, tortoises, crocodiles, sea-sprites; thousands of mice, cats, lions, leopards, tigers, cheetahs, lynxes; ghouls, cherubs, Gabriel, Israfil, Azrael, Michael; the Throne, the Bridge, the Scales; and all creatures that will arise in the plain of resurrection and be assigned their places—those in the fires of hell depicted grieving and mourning and tormented by serpents and demons; and those in the gardens of paradise depicted in marble enjoying the pleasures of the houris and gilman ... If you do not travel to Athens yourself and see it with your own eyes, you can have no idea what it was like in ancient times [Dankoff and Kim 2010: 285].

Acknowledgments

I first spoke on Cassas's painting at a colloqium at the Clark Art Institute ("New Antiquity III: Conditions of Visibility"); my thanks especially to Elizabeth McGowan and Richard Neer for key questions. I continued to worry it in successive guest lectures for Cheryl Finley's "Introduction to Visual Studies" at Cornell, before attempting to put it to rest at Brown. In the event, further questions from Peter Miller, Emily Neumeier, and Felipe Rojas provoked further considerations and revisions. And surely more remains to be said—but not by myself, except to thank the Joukowsky Institute and the John Carter Brown Library for hosting a memorable weekend, and an antiquarian taxi driver for hosting an impromptu tour of historic Providence.

Notes

1. Also within cyclical accounts of time, as among the Maya, it is not so much events as structures that repeat: thus "wars might occur in each cycle, but the leaders and the warriors would not be the same personalities in any two cycles" (Bricker 1981: 7). The type of verification provided by recurrence is therefore similar to that provided by notions of "plausibility" within linear chronologies.

2. I borrow the "engine" metaphor from cognitive science (e.g., Haugeland 1981). In its starkest form, the claim would be that modes of engagement function as formal systems that generate propositions by applying a fixed series of rules to the objects presented to them: thus mode A will always respond to object B with proposition C. Perhaps this is not how things really work. However, to conceive of unfamiliar modes of engagement in this fashion compels us to seek the ways in which they, quite literally, make sense of objects. It thus becomes more difficult to exclude them from comparative study as "superstition" (in the old language) or as "radically other" (in the new).

3. Felipe Rojas remarks (personal communication): "A label such as 'caryatid' tends to become an end in itself and thus to lose hermeneutic power. There are many other examples from archaeological discourse: obviously 'palimpsest' and the like, but also apparently self-evident terms such as 'tomb' or 'midden.'" My claim here is that attention to unfamiliar modes of interaction provides a way to disrupt this routinization. It helps us to be surprised.

4. And compare the discussion by Steve Kosiba in Ch. 5 of this volume of the Inca understanding of the *wak'a*: not an object in the present through which the past was known, but an object from the past through which present social aims are authorized. According to my working definition, the associated practices would not constitute "antiquarianism." But many recent North American and European practices would be excluded on the same criterion (consider, e.g., twentieth-century engagements with the Holy Crown of Hungary).

5. For the similar views, see: Orléans, Musée des Beaux-Arts, No. 348 (Gilet and Westfehling 1994: 113, No. 64), signed "L. F. Cassas" with date, 1792; Tours, Musée des Beaux-Arts, Inv. AF 58-11-1 (Gilet and Westfehling 1994: 113, No. 65); Athens, Benaki Museum, Inv. no. 40166 (Delivorrias and Georgoula 2005: 112); Attingham Park, Shropshire, National Trust NT 607888, signed with initials.

6. The accompanying description renders their indifference explicit: "The Turkish Gentleman smoking a long pipe, is the Disdár-Agá, he leans on the shoulder of his son-in-law, Ibrahim Agá, and is looking at our labourers, who are digging to discover the Base, and the steps of the Basement under the Caryatides. He was accustomed to visit us from time to time, to see that we did no mischief to the Building; but in reality, to see that we did not carry off any treasure; for he did not conceive, any other motive could have induced us, to examine so eagerly what was under ground in his Castle" (Stuart and Revett 1787: 19).

7. The Arabs had the Bible on their side (2 Chronicles 8: 4).

8. Here again, Cassas's image is very different from the superficially similar views of Stuart and Revett, since the latter often explicitly represent named individuals: see the caption cited in note 6 above.

9. Or not; for the ancient authors, as still for the *Encyclopédie*, the Lapiths were far from civilized themselves. The understanding of the Parthenon metopes as metaphors for Hellenic-Persian contest has a whiff of Art History; Tarbell 1920 is refreshing.

References

Anderson, Benedict
1998   *The Spectre of Comparisons*. Verso, London.
Anderson, Benjamin
2015   "An Alternative Discourse": Local Interpreters of Antiquities in the Ottoman Empire. *Journal of Field Archaeology* 40: 450–460.
Arnold, Dana
2003   Facts or Fragments? Visual Histories in the Age of Mechnical Reproduction. In *Tracing Architecture: The Aesthetics of Antiquarianism*, edited by Dana Arnold and Stephen Bending, pp. 30–48. Blackwell, Malden.
Atalay, Sonya
2012   *Community-Based Archaeology: Research With, By, and For Indigenous and Local Communities*. University of California Press, Berkeley.
Baldassare, Ida
1976   Contributo alla precisazione cronologica de "las Incantadas" di Salonicco. *Studi miscellanei* 22: 23–35.
Bohrer, Frederick N.
2015   Doors into the Past: W.J. Stillman (and Freud) on the Acropolis. In *Camera Graeca: Photographs, Narratives, Materialities*, edited by Philip Carabott, Yannis Hamilakis, and Eleni Papagyriou, pp. 95–112. Centre for Hellenic Studies, King's College London, Publications 16. Ashgate, Farnham.
Bricker, Victoria Reifler
1981   *The Indian Christ, the Indian King: The Historical Substrate of Maya Myth and Ritual*. University of Texas Press, Austin.
Brommer, Frank
1967   *Die Metopen des Parthenon*. Philipp von Zabern, Mainz am Rhein.
Butler, Marilyn
1999   Antiquarianism (Popular). In *An Oxford Companion to the Romantic Age: British Culture 1776–1832*, edited by Iain McCalman, pp. 328–338. Oxford University Press, Oxford.
Choiseul-Gouffier, Marie-Gabriel-Auguste-Florent
1782   *Voyage pittoresque de la Grèce*. Paris.
Dankoff, Robert, and Sooyong Kim (translators)
2010   *An Ottoman Traveller: Selections from the Book of Travels of Evliya Çelebi*. Eland, London.
Delivorrias, Angelos, and Electra Georgoula (editors)
2005   *From Byzantium to Modern Greece: Hellenic Art in Adversity, 1453–1830*. Alexander S. Onassis Public Benefit Foundation, New York.

Evans, Christopher
    2014   Review of *World Antiquarianism: Comparative Perspectives*, edited by Alain
                     Schnapp. *Bulletin of the History of Archaeology* 24, p.Art. 18. DOI: http://
                     doi.org/10.5334/bha.2418.

Gilet, Annie, and Uwe Westfehling (editors)
    1994   *Louis François Cassas, 1756–1827: Im Banne der Sphinx*. Philipp von
                     Zabern, Mainz am Rhein.

Guerrini, Lucia
    1961   *Las Incantadas* di Salonicco. *Archeologia classica* 13: 40–70.

Hamilakis, Yannis
    2011a   Indigenous Archaeologies in Ottoman Greece. In *Scramble for the Past: A
                     Story of Archaeology in the Ottoman Empire, 1753–1914*, edited by Zainab
                     Bahrani, Zeynep Çelik, and Edhem Eldem, pp. 49–69. SALT, Istanbul.
    2011b   Museums of Oblivion. *Antiquity* 85: 625–629.

Haugeland, John
    1981   Semantic Engines: An Introduction to Mind Design. In *Mind Design*,
                     edited by John Haugeland, pp. 1–34. Cambridge, MIT Press.

Heringman, Noah, and Crystal B. Lake
    2014   Romantic Antiquarianism: Introduction. In *Romantic Antiquarianism*,
                     edited by Noah Heringman and Crystal B. Lake. Romantic Circles
                     Praxis Series. Electronic document, http://www.rc.umd.edu/praxis/
                     antiquarianism/praxis.antiquarianism.2014.heringman_lake.html, accessed
                     October 21, 2016.

Hölderlin, Friedrich
    1957[1797]   *Sämtliche Werke, Dritter Band: Hyperion*. Edited by Friedrich Beissner.
                     Kohlhammer, Stuttgart.

Kant, Immanuel
    1908[1790]   *Kants Werke, Band V: Kritik der praktischen Vernunft. Kritik der Urtheilskraft*.
                     Georg Reimer, Berlin.

Kinney, Dale
    2002   The Horse, the King and the Cuckoo: Medieval Narrations of the Statue
                     of Marcus Aurelius. *Word & Image* 18: 372–398.

Lolla, Maria Grazia
    2003   Monuments and Texts: Antiquarianism and the Beauty of Antiquity. In
                     Tracing Architecture: The Aesthetics of Antiquarianism, edited by Dana
                     Arnold and Stephen Bending, pp. 11–29. Blackwell, Malden.

MacDiarmid, Hugh
    1993   *Selected Poetry*, edited by Alan Riach and Michael Grieve. New Directions,
                     New York.

Marchand, Suzanne L.
    1996   *Down from Olympus: Archaeology and Philhellenism in Germany, 1750–1970*.
                     Princeton University Press, Princeton.

Miller, Peter N.
    2012   Comparing Antiquarianisms: A View from Europe. In *Antiquarianism and
                     Intellectual Life in Europe and China, 1500–1800*, edited by Peter N. Miller

and François Louis, pp. 103–145. Cultural Histories of the Material World. University of Michigan Press, Ann Arbor.

Mitchell, Timothy

1992   Orientalism and the Exhibitionary Order. In *Colonialism and Culture*, edited by Nicholas B. Dirks, pp. 289–317. University of Michigan Press, Ann Arbor.

Panofsky, Erwin

1955   *Meaning in the Visual Arts*. University of Chicago Press, Chicago.

Paviot, Jacques

1982   Les voyages de Joseph Gabriel Monnier (1745–1818): un officier du génie bressan à travers quelques évènements de la fin du XVIIIe siècle. *Les nouvelles annales de l'Ain*, pp. 75–124.

Rancière, Jacques

2009   *The Emancipated Spectator*. Translated by Gregory Elliott. Verso, New York.

de Saint-Non, Jean-Claude Richard

1782   *Voyage pittoresque, ou description des Royaumes de Naples et de Sicile*. Paris.

Schnapp, Alain

2013   The Roots of Antiquarianism. In *World Antiquarianism: Comparative Perspectives*, edited by Alain Schnapp, pp. 1–10. Issues & Debates. Getty Research Institute, Los Angeles.

Schick, Leslie Meral

1999   Ottoman Costume Albums in a Cross-Cultural Context. In *Art Turc/ Turkish Art: 10th International Congress of Turkish Art*, edited by François Déroche, Charles Genequand, Günsel Renda, and Michael Rogers, pp. 625–628. Fondation Max Van Berchem, Geneva.

Settis, Salvatore

2014   *Se Venezia muore*. Giulio Einaudi editore, Turin.

Smith, Laurajane.

2006   *Uses of Heritage*. Routledge, London.

Stuart, James, and Nicholas Revett

1787   *The Antiquities of Athens. Volume the Second*. John Nichols, London.

Tarbell, Frank B.

1920   Centauromachy and Amazonomachy in Greek Art: The Reasons for Their Popularity. *American Journal of Archaeology* 24: 226–231.

Watkin, David

2006   Stuart and Revett: The Myth of Greece and its Afterlife. In *James "Athenian" Stuart, 1713–1788: The Rediscovery of Antiquity*, edited by Susan Weber Soros, pp. 19–57. Yale University Press, New Haven.

Wolf, Eric R.

2010   *Europe and the People Without History*. University of California Press, Berkeley.

Wood, Robert

1769   *An Essay on the Original Genius of Homer*. London.

— 10 —

Coda: Not for Lumpers Only

Peter N. Miller

Before we can talk about comparative antiquarianism and whether it is possible, we have to talk about comparison and whether *it* is possible. In principle, of course, anything can be compared with anything else. In the seventeenth century, comparison was deemed so central as to appear the distinctive feature of the wise man. Pierre Charron, for example, wrote that the sage knew "to examine all things, to consider them individually, and then to compare together all the laws and customs of the world that can be known" (Charron 1625: 500). René Descartes, a few years later, in his *Rules for the Direction of the Mind* explained that "all knowledge whatsoever results from a comparison between two or more things. In fact," he continued, "the business of human reason consists almost entirely in preparing for this operation" (Descartes 1986: X: 440). On the other hand, in principle, no two things, experiences or mental states are ever *exactly* alike. And thus, Pierre Nicole, to stay in France, writing later in the seventeenth century, entitled a chapter of his *On Human Weakness*: "The difficulty of knowing things which one must judge by comparison of likenesses." The chapter begins: "The discovery of truth in most things depends on the comparison of appearances. But what is more misleading than that comparison?" (Nicole 1715: I: 30).

In practice, of course, comparison was and remains ubiquitous. Nicole might make the skeptic's observation, and we might even be sympathetic to it. But the fact is that when confronted with novelty the way Cortés or Columbus or Matteo Ricci or Galileo might have been, the only way forward is to try and make sense of the new and unknown by way of the old and familiar. Perhaps there is even a theory to be suggested that periods which saw "information overload" were more likely to be ones in which comparison was the more practiced. If this is so, then we should expect the later sixteenth and seventeenth centuries to have witnessed a great deal of comparing. Where there was a kind of intellectual "groping in the dark"—how John Aubrey described trying to make sense of Stonehenge—there was comparison. "These antiquities are so old," he continued, "that no books do reach them: so that there is no way to retrieve them but by comparative antiquity, which I have writ upon the spot, from the monuments themselves" (Aubrey 1980: I: 32).

But if comparison offered the prospect of understanding where before there was none, the very act of assimilation suggests the need to overlook some phenomena and pay close attention to others. Without fixing priorities the act of comparison will always produce a null set. The debate is ever joined over what features to put in the category that allows for comparison (two legs, six legs, eight legs) and what in the one deemed indifferent to a comparison (hairy, smooth, pied-colored). To those who object, comparison always comes at too high a cost: either of blurring difference or not paying enough attention to difference. In August 1857, thinking about the classification of species, Charles Darwin provided future comparatists with their language: "It is good to have hair-splitters and lumpers (Those who make many species are the 'splitters,' and those who make few are the 'lumpers')" (Darwin 1888: II: 105).

Darwin is imagining that splitting (and lumping) is an action that creates a map of connections between distinct elements as if at a single moment in time. But if we think carefully about this, the comparison that identifies connections (lumping) also allows for linking over time. Complex narratives—not ones that, say, follow a single person or family over generations—are dependent upon comparison to weld together their component parts. Think about Goethe's morphology. This was his attempt, grounded in fact on a comparison of bone structures, to identify patterns of development resulting from both internal change and the impact of external circumstances on that internal change. The genres of intellectual and cultural history are not so very different in that their continuities are discerned based on implicit comparison between ideas or forms over time. As important as these issues are to practicing scholars they are rarely the subject of sustained reflection, even by those who are actually performing comparison.

Since lumping and splitting are opposite sides of the same coin, a comparative history of scholarship—and in this special case, of antiquarianisms—not only raises issues relevant to the extensive but also the intensive. That means it can help us understand something about the global phenomenon, but also about the internal history of each of the traditions being compared. Recovering the long history of antiquarianism in Europe, for example, can have a real impact on thinking not just about antiquarianism between cultures, but about the broader shape of historical scholarship within each of them—i.e., of the place of antiquarianism relative to other forms of historical scholarship in Europe, in China, in the Americas, in the Islamic world.[2]

But back, now, to the question of whether there can be a "comparative antiquarianism"? What is involved in this is, first, establishing what "antiquarianism" is. Before turning to this issue, however, there is yet another question that has to be dealt with. It is represented in this volume by Alfredo González-Ruibal (Ch. 3): is the very premise of comparison hegemonizing? We might see this political argument as a version of the epistemological argument: that all comparison starts from some point and the choice of that one point inevitably favors one vision of the world over another.

This argument can, I believe, be answered. Even a little self-consciousness, judiciously applied, could wield comparison in different directions, taking in turn one's own terms as the touchstone and then those of the other. For instance, in this volume, Byron Hamann's essay (Ch. 4) refines the Spanish vision of antiquarianism by examining its application via the same format—the *Relación*—in both Iberia and New Spain. And then the essays of Steve Kosiba (Ch. 5) and Giuseppe Marcocci (Ch. 6) shine a spotlight onto the way Incas and Aztecs mediated access to the past through ruins. Kosiba looks at the way Inca ruins functioned for both Andean peoples and their Iberian conquerors in the colonial period, while Marcocci examines how Motolinía brought a European's eye and categories to the ruins of New Spain. These are wonderful contributions to the state of our knowledge and very sensitive excavations of long-suppressed voices. But to fully clear ourselves of González-Ruibal's warning we would want one more essay: using these newly accessed categories to illuminate Ibero-European concepts for understanding the past. The Spanish did, hegemonically and sometimes to tragic effect, use the Romans as their measure of the Inca. But we should use the Inca as a way of examining the Romans. It's the failure to make proper use of what is in principle a bi-directional tool that is the real flaw, but also the real hope. Comparison is not hegemonizing, because it is not in principle only a one-way street: it flows both ways.

But there is a deeper claim that is harder to dismiss, and that is that the very pose of comparison, far from respecting the views of the compared, actually demeans them. Respect for autonomy, therefore, might actually imply accepting the appearance of incommensurability (we're apples and oranges all the way down). This implies a very different ontology. Perhaps it is understandable as a quasi-utopian demand. But it deprives us of a generally used tool: science.[3] Indeed, for those who hold this view another question imposes itself: how will we understand the new without being able to resort to comparison? Or are we are only to be denied the application of this tool to the human, as opposed to the natural, sciences?

Let me put it another way. Around 1970, Fernand Braudel reported, a young Italian philosopher upon learning that the great *Mediterranean* was written in prison commented: "Oh, that is why it always struck me as a book of contemplation" (Braudel 1972: 453). Braudel's point was that real originality might have to be worked out in solitude. That the desire to be understood by others, as in a community, necessarily entails a translation that is not superficial at all, but occurs at the level of thought and origination. Establishing a ground of comparison might really take the edge off the new, the brilliant, the creative. But as the alternative is solipsism (the prison), we push on.

Putting this challenge aside, therefore, as not a question about antiquarianism at all, let us turn to the two definitions proposed by the book's editors in their separate contributions. Felipe Rojas (Ch. 1) reaches back for the original definition of "archaeologist" as someone with knowledge of "old things" and uses this broader category to stretch "antiquarian" so that it works equally well for Neolithic Anatolia and Mongol Samarkand. In this, I think we can see the continuing impact of Richard Bradley's powerful *The Past in Prehistoric Societies* (2002) on those working on the less deep past. Rojas is aware of the risk of "dilution" inherent in a broadened definition of archaeologist/antiquarian as someone interacting "with old things." That is why he proffers a new word, "archaeophilia," to encompass the widest possible range of practices, from the precision of the erudite analyst to the affective gesture of the artist or the practical applications of the shaman—or the contrary-to-fact tales of reincarnation implied in the story of the shield of Euphorbos/Pythagoras.

Rojas notes in passing the difficulty of applying the model of antiquarian practice derived from the work of scholars in the highly sophisticated intellectual cultures of Europe and China. The same set of circumstances that enable us to derive a precise definition from their historical reality also sets such a high evidentiary standard that no pre-literate society can meet it. Even some literate societies from which we lack a sufficient volume of surviving evidence might therefore not give us a comparably precise set of circumstances and therefore not meet a sufficient threshold to discuss and evaluate its antiquarianism. And yet, the reality of the insistent material past, in so many different times and places, seems to require us to do more than marvel or turn away in rationalistic despair.

The other editor, Benjamin Anderson (Ch. 9), also rejects a modeling based on the examples of early modern Europe and China, or even from other literate societies. For him, all of these represent accounts that reflect specific conditions of power and class. They cannot serve as definitions workable in a wider anthropological context. He proposes instead a definition of antiquarianism as the interaction with the past through objects that survive into the present. This is a definition whose lineage could be traced back to

R. G. Collingwood by way of Michael Shanks. And "interacting" instead of "studying" lifts the historical operation out of the purely erudite context and allows for an affective and imaginative engagement that might not express itself in the form of scholarship. He adds as an additional condition that a comparative approach to antiquarianism is only valuable if it also helps us see what is not antiquarian. Comparison, to come back to where we began, is in his view not forensic (i.e., aimed at establishing truth), but aesthetic (i.e. aimed at seeing the breadth of the human experience). Comparative antiquarianism is best viewed as an exercise in splitting. Anderson also provides us with a practical outcome: object-based accounts would, he writes, illuminate this pluralism of approaches precisely because the object is in principle inexhaustible.

Both Rojas and Anderson reject taking as a model "a historically contingent manifestation of antiquarianism (e.g., the study of 'classical antiquities' by early modern Europeans)." Making any contingency into a universal is a fraught enterprise, to be sure. But they seem to assume that this is the only way of operationalizing the historically localizable.

But what if there are other ways? What if, for example, we approached the case studies in this volume, on the different kinds of engagements with the material past found in colonial Latin America and the eastern Mediterranean basin, not as a benchmark but as a map of possibilities? As with the comparative study of the historical scholarship of early modern Europe and China, the self-consciousness and documentary richness that characterize these examples would not feed an exclusiveness but actually make possible a wider engagement. This is where the micro-historical richness of case studies such as Emily Neumeier's (Ch. 7), on the archaeological roles of the Ottoman governors of the Morea in the nineteenth century, is so valuable. For comparison becomes more valuable the more concrete its terms. And thus the more tactile our grasp of the past, the less it is beholden to accreted abstraction, the better placed we are to compare. In a similar vein, Eva-Maria Troelenberg has tried to tease out indigenous antiquarian attitudes amongst the Arab and Bedouin informants recorded by British and German archaeologists on either side of 1900. Working on seeing more clearly through that refracting layer Troelenberg (Ch. 8), like Neumeier, is engaged in the game of complication, which is perhaps above all what is needed to avoid clumsy lumping.

There is a further step, too, beyond history. We might also be able to address the problem of a comparative antiquarianism phenomenologically. In other words, we could study these examples in order to discern the deeper patterns of the practice. For instance, I have argued that antiquarianism worked by collecting objects, describing objects, and comparing objects.

These are, for the most part, not words that would have been used in this way by the historical actors we call antiquarians. (Yes, Nicolas Fabri de Peiresc [1580–1637], Momigliano's "archetype of all antiquarians" [1990: 54], talked a great deal about comparing and comparison, but only in terms of his research and not as a trait of his species.) And yet they are present in the historical phenomenon we call antiquarianism. Moreover, they are general enough features that we can hope to find them elsewhere. Similarly, we can find scholars in Europe and China experiencing the study of past objects found in the present through the affective lens of *tempus edax rerum* ("Time the destroyer of all things")—that brutal encounter of flesh and time. The words might be an ancient Roman's (Ovid, *Metamorphoses* XV: 234), and the painting of the emblematic scene might be a sixteenth-century Fleming's (Hermanus Posthumus), but it is equally present and at work in Song and Ming antiquarians. The phenomenological approach works because we are all mortal and because objects and humans have had a symbiotic existence emotionally and intellectually for at least a few hundred thousand years.

However, we need the detail provided by rich case studies to save us from the peril of banality lurking in this last sentence. Yes, we all die and, yes, we all live symbiotically with objects. But to make this the basis of a comparative antiquarianism makes for a very weak notion of antiquarianism. Rojas and Anderson are aware of this. Therefore, the richer the source base we have to work from, the greater the precision with which we can define collection, description, comparison, and reconstruction at a given time and place—and therefore how they might be present but working differently in other places and at other times. Again, precisely because Mesoamerican or sub-Saharan peoples may not have left us written sources, or at least the kind of written sources that are easily mined, we need the kind of detail the European or Chinese sources provide if we are to tease out whatever comparanda there may be—and then assess what is or is not similar. At the moment, it is clear that our greatest gap is the antiquarian understandings of the Arab and Islamic populations of North Africa, the Middle East, Iran, and Central Asia. As long as we remember that comparison can be for splitting, then the discovery of dissimilarity is still learning.

In the case of the Europe-China comparison, for example, what emerged clearly was the distinctiveness of the European turn to the visual. Where Chinese antiquarians paid most attention to the inscriptions on, say, vases, the Europeans were attentive to the forms of the vases. Chinese antiquarian books focused on inscriptions, the Europeans' increasingly on images. The differing roles of art and artists in the antiquarian enterprise followed from this. By the same token, Chinese antiquarians seemed more open to the poetic impact of the broken as a window into the human condition than the Europeans, who tended to keep scholarship and poetry apart.

In attempting something of this sort one has to be willing to operate at the level of suggestion rather than certainty, something scholars are often uncomfortable doing. As Paul Veyne noted, comparative history is a "heuristic device" that facilitates discovery rather than revealing anything in particular (1984[1971]: 124). And one point has to be kept in mind at all times: that all comparisons must be bi-directional. For instance, the model of early modern European antiquarianism can be useful to see what is similar and what is different in Chinese antiquarianism. But then we need to turn around and treat the shape of the Chinese antiquarian phenomenon as the norm or ideal type in order to assess where the Europeans diverged from it. Comparison undertaken in this way is far from a hegemonizing or patronizing approach. Indeed, it is one of the few sure-fire instruments we possess capable of cutting our own pretensions to normativity down to size. Comparison, then, may not be about either splitting or lumping but about skepticism. Its founding father may not be Darwin, but Montaigne.

And yet, what can we say about a moment in which comparative antiquarianism is on the intellectual agenda? What does it mean that historians are now interested in plural forms of interaction with the past as undertaken by actors of different sorts pursuing different goals? The yearning to break free of old intellectual constraints is often marked by neologism. Rojas's "archaeophilia" ought, then, to make us sit up and take notice.

More than three centuries ago, in the 1670s, we can identify a moment of linguistic explosiveness in the work of Jacob Spon, a medical doctor from Lyon and an antiquarian and traveller of some renown. His neologistic output has not been linked to his broader work, nor seen—as I think it should be—as a turning point in the history of antiquarianism.

Spon coined the term *archaeographia* in 1685, which he defined as "knowledge of the monuments through which the Ancients transmitted their religion, history, politics and other arts and sciences, and tried to pass them down to posterity" (Stark 1880: 1: 46). *Archaeographia* had eight parts: numismatics, epigraphy, ancient architecture, iconography (including sculpture), glyptography, toreumatography (the study of reliefs), bibliography, and angeiography, "a vast and prickly" field that included weights, measures, vases, domestic and agricultural utensils, games, clothing, "and a thousand other things whose study does not easily fit among the existing sciences." Spon gave names to some of these. "Deipnographia" was the study of dining customs, "dulographia" the study of slavery, and "taphographia" the study of funerary customs (Spon 1679: 70).

In the longer view, Spon stands between the idiosyncratic practices of antiquaries like Peiresc who came before him, and the systematicity of Mabillon, Montfaucon, Muratori, and Leibniz who followed immediately after. Spon was, like Peiresc, a southerner, and had actually gone to Aix-en-Provence and studied the Peiresc archive *in situ*. Unlike his predecessor, however, Spon published. Even more, as we have just seen, Spon stepped back and tried to conceptualize his practice on a second order. This, in turn, made possible the assimilation of that practice to other, broader historical enterprises and helped make the eighteenth century, as Momigliano wrote long ago, the "Age of the Antiquaries" (1950: 285).

If we can read neologism as a marker for a problem needing a solution impossible within the existing linguistic order, then we could view these antiquarianizing neologisms, both of Spon and now of Rojas, as a sign that the Kuhnian "normal science" of history is bursting at its seams. Spon helped give birth to a modern history that found a way to include both the evidentiary paradigm of the antiquarians and the story-telling of the hitherto rhetorically minded historians. Is something antiquarian happening to history today as well? Are we witnessing the birth of a neo-antiquarianism? I will end with this very speculative question.

"Neo-antiquarianism" is term I owe to Michael Shanks, a classical archaeologist, design thinker and performance artist.[4] His point in neologizing was to make the connection between the object-mindedness of the present age and that of a previous one and also to acknowledge that it is not exactly the same. The fact is that, even as antiquarianism as a form of historical scholarship became marginalized among professional historians in the nineteenth century, it persisted elsewhere: in local history, museums, collectors, artists, and writers. It even returned, unnoticed, in the form of the academic monograph that dominated twentieth-century English and German-language historical scholarship. And right now it is experiencing a flourishing in the work of visual artists such as David Macaulay, Mark Dion, Rosamund Purcell, Érik Desmazières, and Grisha Brushkin perhaps unequalled since the time of Piranesi, Abbé Barthélemy, and Sir Walter Scott. What neo-antiquarianism signals is the role of the artist in teaching the scholar to see beyond the confines of a disciplinary bibliography.

But there is one more thing. Once our instructors are artists then it is our hearts that are being engaged as much as (if not more than) our minds. It was Nietzsche, in his lecture course of 1871 who told his no doubt stunned auditors that archaeology was about "yearning" and then, in 1874, the readers of his second *Untimely Meditation*, on "The Advantage and Disadvantage of History for Life," that the antiquarian impulse helped people make their home in the world. Its "gifts and virtues" included, according to Nietzsche, empathy with past people and an instinctive way of reading texts, even broken ones. The example he gave of an embodied set of these antiquarian virtues was Goethe. When he stood in front of the monument to Erwin von Steinbach "the historical cloud cover spread between them tore, and for the first time he saw the German work again" emerging out of the German soul (Nietzsche 1980: 19). It is not so surprising that the Nietzsche who wrote this way felt increasingly out of step with the gifts and virtues of academic life. His turn from philology to philosophy was a step towards what in *Human, All Too Human*, his first work as a philosopher, he called "historical philosophy"— which might be just another variety of neo-antiquarianism. Following him in this direction, even if we start out more than a hundred years behind, is where we can go if we take comparison to be our primary means of making sense of the world, much as it was in the great age of the antiquaries.

Notes

1. For example, Schnapp 2013; Pollack et al. 2015.
2. On comparative history, the classic text is by Marc Bloch (1928); and note the review by William H. Sewell, Jr (1967). For bibliography see Schieder 1965: 195–219; Rothacker 1957. See further Miller and Louis 2012.
3. This extreme position is rejected by G.E.R. Lloyd (2014: esp. 222–224, 226). Lloyd is a special case: his *The Ambitions of Curiosity* (2002) is an almost unique example of a perfectly comparative history, equally balanced in all directions, and his early *Polarity and Analogy* treated comparison as an early epistemic category (1966: Ch. V).
4. For the next two paragraphs, see more fully Miller 2017.

References

Aubrey, John
   1980   *Monumenta Britannica or a Miscellany of British Antiquities*. Dorset Publishing Co., Milborne Port.

Bloch, Marc
   1928   Pour une histoire comparée des sociétés européennes. *Revue de synthèse historique* 46: 15–50.

Bradley, Richard
   2002   *The Past in Prehistoric Societies*. Routledge, London and New York.

Braudel, Fernand
   1972   Personal Testimony. *The Journal of Modern History* 44: 448–467.

Charron, Pierre
   1625   *De la sagesse*. Robert Fuge, Paris.

Darwin, Charles
   1888   *The Life and Letters of Charles Darwin*, edited by Francis Darwin. John Murray, London.

Descartes, René
   1986   *Oeuvres de Descartes*, edited by Charles Adam and Paul Tannery. Vrin, Paris.

Lloyd, Geoffrey E.R.
1966   *Polarity and Analogy: Two Types of Argumentation in Early Greek Thought.* Cambridge University Press, Cambridge.
2002   *The Ambitions of Curiosity: Understanding the World in Ancient Greece and China.* Cambridge University Press, Cambridge.
2014   On the Very Possibility of Mutual Intelligibility. *HAU: Journal of Ethnographic Theory* 4: 221–235.

Miller, Peter N.
2017   *History and Its Objects: Antiquarianism and Material Culture Since 1500.* Cornell University Press, Ithaca.

Miller, Peter N., and François Louis
2012   Introduction: Antiquarianism and Intellectual Life in Europe and China. In *Antiquarianism and Intellectual Life in Europe and China, 1500–1800*, edited by Peter N. Miller and François Louis, pp. 1–24. University of Michigan Press, Ann Arbor.

Momigliano, Arnaldo
1950   Ancient History and the Antiquarian. *Journal of the Warburg and Courtauld Institutes* 13: 285–315.
1990   *The Classical Foundations of Modern Historiography.* University of California Press, Berkeley.

Nicole, Pierre
1715   *Essais de morale.* Guillaume Desprez, Paris.

Nietzsche, Friedrich
1980   *On the Advantage and Disadvantage of History for Life*, translated by Peter Preuss. Hackett, Indianapolis.

Pollack, Sheldon, Benjamin A. Elman, and Ku-ming Kevin Chang (editors)
2015   *World Philology.* Harvard University Press, Cambridge.

Rothacker, Erich
1957   Die vergleichende Methode in den Geisteswissenschaften. *Zeitschrift für vergleichende Rechtswissencschaft* 60: 13–33.

Schieder, Theodor
1965   *Geschichte als Wissenschaft: Eine Einführung.* Oldenbourgh, Munich.

Schnapp, Alain (editor)
2013   *World Antiquarianism: Comparative Perspectives.* The Getty Research Institute, Los Angeles.

Sewell, William H.
1967   Marc Bloch and the Logic of Comparative History. *History and Theory* 6: 208–218.

Spon, Jacob
1679   *Réponse à la critique publiée par M. Guillet, sur le Voyage de Grèce de Iacob Spon.* Amanlei, Lyon.

Stark, Carl Bernhard
1800   *Handbuch der Archäologie der Kunst.* Wilhelm Engelmann, Leipzig.

Veyne, Paul
1984[1971] *Writing History: Essay on Epistemology.* Translated by Mina Moore-Rinvolucri. Welseyan University Press: Middletown.

Index

Figures in *italics;* n refers to note

A

Abandoned towns (*despoblados*), 51–52, 55–58, 62, 66, 75, 88
Aboriginal Australians, 21, 23–24
Acropolis of Athens, 189, *190*, 192, *192*, 202
Aegina
   ruins, 136
   statues, 146, 151
   Temple of Aphaea, 145
Agamemnon, 134, 140
Alexandridis, Dimitrios, 154
Ali Pasha (Tepedelenli Ali Pasha), 135, 139, 145, 149–151, 153–154, 156
Alternative archaeologies, 32–33, 138, 154, 156
Anäj (*also* Anag or Aneg), 39–40, *41*
Ancestor
   Dats'in, 39–40
   founding, 79, 88, 90, 110, 122
   Iberian Peninsula, 124
   Inca, 90
   living, 95
   mythical, 37, 79, 97, 120–122
   prestigious, 37
   Sith Shwala, 42
Andean
   past, 80, 82–83, 89, 96, 100n11
   people, 74, 76–78, 89, 93, *94*, 95–96, 212
Annals of Tlatelolco, 113–114
Annius of Viterbo, 110, 123–126, 128
Antiquarian (*also* "antiquary"), definition, 1, 5, 12, 36, 49, 186
Antiquities (Annius of Viterbo), 123–126
Antiquities of Athens (Stuart and Revett), 6n2, 135, 193, *194*, 195, 198, 203, 206n8
Aphaea, Temple of (Aegina), 145
Apollo Epicurius, Temple of (Bassae), 135, 145–150, *146*
Appropriation
   of antiquities of New Spain, 128

architectural, 60
imperial, 53
intellectual, 170
of land, 96
material, 165, 170
of Middle Eastern ancient and early Islamic sites, 162
Arabian Nights, 168
Arch of Hadrian (Athens), 189, 202
Archaeologies
   alternative, 32–33, 138, 154, 156
   at war, 51, 54, 67–68
   collaborative, 35
   indigenous, 4, 15, 32, 35, 40, 50, 61, 138, 152
Archaeographia, 216
"Archaeophilia", 5, 8–25, 213, 216
Archeologists, indigenous, 35, 202
Argos, 22–24, 135, 140–145, 150–151
Aristotle, 9, 17
Athena temple (Lindos), 23
Athens
   Acropolis, 189, *190*, 192, *192*, 202
   Arch of Hadrian, 189, 202
   Cassas's painting, 188–193, 195, 197–199, 201–204
   Erechtheion, 193, *194*, 195
   Frankish tower, 189, 192
   Odeion of Herodes Atticus, 189, 202
   Olympieion (Temple of Olympian Zeus), 189, 198, 201–202
   Parthenon, 22, 135, 145, 151, 156, 178, 189, 192, 203, 205, 207n9
   Philopappos, Monument of, 189, 202
   Veli Pasha's visit to, 153
Aubrey, John, 210–211
Aztec
   Empire, 109, 111, 113–114, 116, 118
   pictorial codices and maps, 66, 110–111, *112*, 117–119, *123*, 125–128, *127*

solar calendar, 111, *112*, 113
vision of time, 118, 128

B

Bachicao, Hernando, 88
Bassae
excavation, 152
sculptures (*also* Phigaleian Frieze), 151–153,
    155, 157n5, 157n7
Temple of Apollo Epicurius, 135, 145–150, *146*
Bedouins, 162, *164*, 169–179
Beer, 42, *92*, 93, *94*
Belief systems, Andean, 91, 99n3
Benavente, Count of, 117, 124
Benavente, Toribio de (*also* Motolinía), 109–128,
    212
Beni Sakhr tribe, 176
Berossos, 123
Binary, 4, 21, 52–53, 115, 162–163, 177; *see also*
    Distinction
Bones, 16, 35, 62, 81
Border thinking, 83
Braudel, Fernand, 212–213
Brøndsted, Peter Oluf, 146–149, 151
Browne, Howe Peter, 2nd Marquess of Sligo
    (Lord Sligo), 140, 155
Burckhardt, Jakob, 49
Busase, 42, *44*

C

Calendar, Aztec solar, 111, *112*
Camaxtli (god of war), 120
Capac Raymi ceremony, 91
Cape Iapygia, 17–19
Carrighan, Arthur, 150, 153
Cartari, Vincenzo, 125–126
Cassas, Louis-François, 189–204, *190–191*, *196*
Caves, 20–21, 81, 85
Ceremonial complex (Inca), 86, 90–91, 93
Ceremony
austral winter solstice, 91
beer drinking, *92*
Capac Raymi, 91
Central Mexican, 114, 118, 120
New Fire, 111–112, 117
public, 74
state, 81
Change, historical, 3, 34, 38–43, 74
Charron, Pierre, 210
Checa kin group, 78, 97
chicha (beer), *92*, 93, *94*
Chichimecs, 110, 118–119, 122
Chicomoztoc, 122, *123*, 125
Chimalpahin (Domingo Francisco de San Antón
    Muñón Chimalpahin Quauhtlehuanitzin), 125

China, 1, 16, 36, 211, 213–215
Choiseul-Gouffier, Marie-Gabriel-August-Florent,
    Comte de, 191, 199, 201
Cholula, pyramid of, 119, *120*
Chronology
calendrical, 36
cyclical, 112–113, 118, 129, 206n1
linear 118, 206n1
Renaissance tripartite schema of, 115
solar, 113
Cieza de León, Pedro, 75, 82
Circassian settlers, 161–163, 176
Clytemnestra, Tomb of, 142
Cockerell, Charles, 135, 148–149, 155, 157n5
Codex Vaticanus A (*also* Codex Vaticanus Latinus
    3738 or Ríos Codex), 125–126, *127*
Codices, pictorial, 110–111, *112*, 117–119, *123*,
    125–128, *127*
Coins, 1, 6n1, 14–16, 49, 63, 187
Colhua, 110, 119, 122, 129n3
Collective memory, 13, 36, 81, 100n11, 179n6
Collingwood, Robin George, 214
Colonization, 13, 74–75, 84–85, 91
Community
academic, 168–169
Andean mythological, 78
egalitarian, 38–39, 43
identity, 5, 78, 84
indigenous, 32, 35, 38, 40, 60
local, 4, 14, 35, 80
marginalized, 31
non-Western, 31–33
organization, 82
Ottoman, 139, 155, 197
prehistoric, 15
Roman Mediterranean, 19–20
rural, 62
Samburu, 36
subaltern, 33–35, 38, 42
Concept of temporality, 139, 169
Cortés, Hernán, 111, 114, 122, 125, 210
Creation myths, 37, 76, 78, 113
Critical heritage, 32, 38, 43, 156
Cult
Inca mummy, 97–98
of the Sun, 86–87
Culture, vernacular, 3, 13, 178
Cusco (*also* Cuzco), 61, 80–81, 84–85, 88,
    90–91, 95, 97, 99n3
Customs, 116, 121, 199, 210

D

Darwin, Charles, 211, 216
Dats' in people, 39–40
Decline and Fall of the Roman Empire (Gibbon), 167

Decommissioning practices (Andean), 93–94;
    see also Ruination practices
el demonio (Satan), 82, 114, 185, 205
Descartes, René, 210
Desgodetz, Antoine, 195
Dhiban, 171, 173
Dichotomy, 3–4, 43; see also Distinction
Diodoros of Sicily, 22
Discourse
    about the past, 97–98
    academic, 162, 202, 206n3
    alternative, 2
    authoritarian, 170, 179
    colonial, 83
    dominant, 2, 138
    elite, 139
    of forgetting, 191–192
    heritage, 32, 165, 170
    local, 4, 139
Distinction
    between communities, 78, 115, 122, 138
    between Iberia and America, 52–53
    between indigenous and colonial, 4–5, 115,
        122, 138, 147, 152
    between learned and popular, 198
    between literate and pre-literate, 3, 162
    between local and visitor, 138, 148, 193
    between past and present, 43
    between social groups, 165, 170, 185
    between subjective and objective, 195–197
    between Western and non-Western, 34, 162,
        164–165
    between written and oral history, 82–83
Divide see Distinction
Domination, 33–35, 43, 84
Dominican friars, 110, 123–125
Druse minorities, 162–163

E
Egalitarian communities, 38–39, 43
Elgin, Lord (Bruce, Thomas, 7th Earl of Elgin
    and 11th Earl of Kincardine), 135, 140,
    142–143, 151–152, 156
Elgin Marbles, 22, 156
Elites
    Andean, 66, 84
    antiquarians, 3, 12, 36–37, 49, 184–185
    (Western) educated, 139, 168
    Inca, 87, 90–91, 97
    leisured, 185
    local, 116, 134, 154, 170
    Ottoman (provincial), 138–140, 142, 154–156
Engagement, mode of, 32, 186–188, 191, 195,
    198–199, 202, 204; see also Interaction, mode of
Enlightenment, Greek, 139, 154

Enríquez, Luis, 88
Erechtheion (Athens), 193, 194, 195
Ethiopia, 2, 39–43
Euphorbos, shield of, 22, 213
Experts, 1–3, 19, 21, 40, 61, 169

F
Fake and forgery, 2, 5, 19, 110, 121–128
Fazakerley, John Nicholas, 143–145
Fergusson, James, 163, 167–168, 170, 178–179
Ferhad, 168, 170, 179
Fernández de Oviedo, Gonzalo, 124
Fiore, Joachim of, 115
Flood, 76, 78, 95, 99n3, 123–124
Folklore, 18, 35, 174, 178
Foundation myth, 11, 37, 79, 88, 90, 110
Franciscans, 5, 67, 110, 113–118, 125–126, 128
Frankish tower (Athens), 189, 192
Frederick II (Holy Roman Emperor), 37

G
Gell, William, 140–143, 141–142, 154
Genealogy
    Busase, 42
    (mythical) lineage, 39, 42, 65, 80, 110, 117,
        121–126
    Lisu, 39
    royal, 79–80
Geschichtskultur (culture of history), 31–32
Giants, 17–19, 123–126, 127
Gibbon, Edward, 167
Giovio, Paolo, 1, 6n2, 110–111
Goethe, Johann Wolfgang von, 211, 218
Goldsmith, Oliver, 154
Grand Narrative, 161–179, 202
Great Temple (Mexico City), 113
Gropius, George, 145–147, 152
Guide see Informant
Guilford, Lord (Frederick North), 144–145, 150,
    153–154
Gumuz people, 40

H
Hamideh (Bedouin tribe), 174
Hatun Kancha Raqay (waka), 86, 87, 88
Herakles (Hercules), 17–18, 63, 79
Herculaneum, 193, 194
Heritage
    authorized discourse, 32, 170
    critical, 32, 38, 43, 156
    institutionalized discourse, 165, 169–171
    management of cultural, 1
    non-Western, 33–36
    politics, 137, 156
    studies, 178–179

Herodotus, 3
Heroikos (Philostratos), 11–12
Herzfeld, Ernst, 168
Hierarchical societies, 36, 38, 139, 185–186
Historicity, 31, 34–36, 38, 43
Historiography, 31, 43, 74, 162–163, 169, 177
History of the Indians of the New Spain
  (Motolinía), 117–118, 122, 124
Hölderlin, Friedrich, 197–199, 202
Huanacauri (mountaintop and *wak'a*), 90–96, *90*,
  92, *94*, 100n13
Huarochirí, 78, 83, 97, 100n9
Huayna Capac (Emperor), 86–87, 97, 100n9
Humboldt, Alexander von, 146

I
Identity
  collective, 81, 100n11
  community, 5
  cultural, 156
  elite, 37, 90
  indigenous (local), 84
  national, 137
  Pan-Andean, 84
  political, 156
Idol, 60–63, 67, 80, 111–112, 120–122,
  126, 148
Idolatry, 62–63, 114, 117, 119, 121, 128
Imperialism, 31–32, 43, 78, 161
Inca
  administrator (*kuraka*), 86, 89
  ancestor, 90
  elite, 87, 90–91
  Empire, 72–98
  history, 75, 82–84
  imperialism, 78
  ruins, 74, 89, 95–96, 98, 212
incommensurability, 31, 34, 212
Indigenous archaeologies, 4, 15, 32, 35, 40, 50,
  61, 138, 152
Indigenous archaeologist, 35, 202
Inequality, 38–43
Informant
  Arab, 174, 214
  Bedouin, 170–179, 214
  European visitor as, 142
  local Mexican, 78, 115, 117, 122
  Samburu 35
Interaction, mode of, 2, 5, 8, 11, 186–188,
  206n3, 216
Ioannina, 145, 153–154
Iztac Mixcoatl, 110, 122, 124–126

J
Jesuit priests, 16, 99n1, 119

K
Kalahari San people, 39
Kant, Immanuel, 197, 204
Kastron Mefaa (*also* Umm er-Resas), 174
Khipu (*also* quipus, knotted cords), 66,
  80, 82
Khosrau II (Sasanian king), 167–168
Kin affiliation, 39, 78, 80, 86, 97
Klein, Frederick Augustus, 171, 174, 179n4
Knight, Henry Gally, 143–145
Knowledge
  classifiable, 76–78
  collaborative, 32–33
  colonial, 118
  forms of, 4, 31, 83, 114, 187
  epistolary, 51–53
  folk, 31
  local (indigenous), 51–54, 61, 100n13
  objects of, 76, 88, 114, 134
  production, 5, 31–32, 50–51, 128, 170
  regulation, 79
  repositories for, 64
  social, 36
Kore, marble, 143, *144*, 157n3
Kuraka (Inca administrator), 86, 89

L
*Land of Moab: Travels and Discoveries on the East
  Side of the Dead Sea and the Jordan* (Tristram),
  165–177
Las Casas, Bartolomé de, 124
Layard, Austen Henry, 165
Legends *see* Myths and legends
Leland, John, 79
Lieux de mémoire, 81
Lineage
  classical, 79
  genealogical, 39, 42, 65, 80, 110, 117,
    121–126
  history in terms of, 79–80
  noble, 176
Lisu people (Burma), 38–39
López de Gómara, Francisco, 125, 128

M
Maendeleo (modernity), 35–36
Maeander River Valley, 20
Mahmud Efendi, 154–155
Maldonado de Torres, Alonso, 88
Malquis (mummies), 80–82, 84
Mama Ocllo, 86, *87*
Manco (Inca ruler), 86
Mapmaking, 52–53, 66, 165
Maras (Peru), 87–88
Margarit, Joan, 79

Materiality
  enduring, 83–84, 96, 98
  multisensory engagement with, 202
  sacred, 62–63
  textual, 64
  vernacular view of, 139
*Memorials or Book of the Things of the New Spain
  and its Natives* (Motolinía), 117, 121, 125
Memory
  ancient, 13
  Andean, 76, 95–96
  archaeology of, 4
  aristocratic, 37
  Aztec, 111, 114, 119
  Bedouin, 176–177
  collective, 13, 36, 81, 100n11, 179n6
  cultural, 14, 42
  indigenous, 110
  oral, 128
  practices, 33, 37
  public, 88
  social, 81
  time beyond, 78, 86, 89, 96–97
Mena, Cristóbal de, 75
Mendieta, Jerónimo, 125–126, 128
Mesha Stele (*also* "Moabite Stone"), 171, *173*
Mestizo, 99n3, 119, 128
Metempsychosis, 23
Mexica (Aztecs), 110, 119, 122, 125
Mexico City (ancient Tenochtitlan), 111, 113, 122
Millenarianism, Franciscan, 115, 118
Mitla palaces, 59–60
Moab, 163, 165, 169, 175
Moabite Stone (*also* Mesha Stele), 171, *173*
Moctezuma II, 114
Mode of engagement, 32, 186–188, 191, 195,
  198–199, 202, 204; *see also* Interaction, mode of
Modernity, 32–33, 35–36, 38–39, 51, 179n1, 204
Momigliano, Arnaldo, 1, 6n1, 12, 109, 215, 217
Monnier, Joseph Gabriel, 201
Morea, 134–156, 214
Motolinía (Benavente, Toribio de), 109–128, 212
Mount Sipylos, 18
Mshatta 163, *164*, 165–168, 170, 176, 178
Mummies (*malquis*), 80–82, 84
Mycenae, 11, 134, 139, 140–145, 151–152, 155
Myths and legends
  Arab, 174
  Andean, 76–78, 83, 91, 97, 99n3, 100n9
  Aztec, 110
  Christian, 76
  classical, 79
  creation 37, 76, 78, 113
  European vernacular, 99n5
  explanatory, 36

flood, 76, 78, 95, 99n3, 123–124
foundation, 11, 37, 76, 110

N
Nahuatl (language), 118–120, 122, 125
Nationalism, 38, 84, 154
New Fire ceremony, 111–112, 117
Nicole, Pierre, 210
Nietzsche, Friedrich Wilhelm, 217–218
Niobe, petrified, 18
Noah, 79–82, 122–125
North, Frederick (Lord Guilford), 144–145, 150,
  153–154

O
Objects of knowledge, 76, 88, 114, 134
Odeion of Herodes Atticus (Athens), 189, 202
Offerings, 18, 23, 68, 93, *94*
Olfactory associations (*also* smell), 17–21, 188
Ollantaytambo, 85–89, *85*, 96
Olmecs, 113
Olmos, Andrés de, 116–117, 126
Olympieion (Temple of Olympian Zeus)
  (Athens), 189, 198, 201–202
On Marvelous Things Heard (Anonymous),
  17–18, 20
Ontology, 4, 8, 10, 34–35, 84, 98, 212
Oral
  history, 38–39, 42, 83, 178
  memory, 128
  performance, 82
  testimony, 174
  tradition, 140
Osirian Marble, 126
Other and Otherness, 5, 33–35, 37, 39, 43, 149,
  162, 206n2
Ottoman (provincial) elites, 138–140, 142,
  154–156
Ozolian Lokris, 19
Ozymandias
  Lightnin' McDuff's sculpture, 72, *73*, 74, 98
  Percy Bysshe Shelley's poem, 72, 74, 98

P
Pachar, 86, *87*, 88–89
Panopeus, 19
Paradoxography, 18
Parthenon (Athens)
  architect (Iktinos), 145
  apotropaic reuse, 178
  metopes, 203, 207n9
  mosque, 189, 192
  restitution of marbles, 22, 156
  sculptures, 22, 135, 151, 156, 205
Pausanias, 3, 11–12, 15–16, 18–19, 140, 153–154

Peiresc, Nicolas Fabri de, 215, 217
Performance, 37, 82, 91, 97
Pergamon, 171
Pergamon Altar, 22
Personified
    mountain (*apus*), 91
    place, 78, 80, 86, *87*
    thing, 82
Pheidias 20
Phenomenological approach, 214–215
Phigaleian Frieze (*also* Bassae sculptures), 149,
    151–153, 155, 157n5, 157n7
Philhellenism, Romantic, 197–198, 204; *see also*
    Romanticism
Philopappos, Monument of (Athens), 189, 202
Philostratos, 11–12
Phlegra (Campania), 18–19
Phokis, 19
Pictographic maps, 66
Pictorial codices, 110–111, *112*, 117–119, *123*,
    125–128, *127*
Pignoria, Lorenzo, 125–126
Pizarro, Hernán (Hernando), 86
Pizarro, Pedro, 82
Plague, 56–57, 62
Pliny the Elder, 19
Plutarch, 19
Ponce monolith, *77*
Postcolonial critiques, 31–33, 39–40, 138
Pouqueville, François, 145, 157n4
Procession, 91, 113
Prometheus, 19
Pseudo-Berossos, 123–126
Puchstein, Otto, 161, 177
Pulgar, Fernando del, 79
Puma Urco, *81*
Pythagoras, 22–24, 213

Q

Quipus (*also khipu*, knotted cords), 66, 80, 82

R

Reincarnation, 23, 213
Relaciones geográficas, 50–68
Relaciones topográficas, 50–68
Relics, 38, 67, 84, 109–114, 117, 119, 121, 154
Renaissance Europe, 49–50, 109–111, 114–116,
    119, 122–124
Repartimiento, 58, 66, 86, 88
Representations of the past, 89, 95, 110
Restitution of antiquities, 22, 156, 170
Revett, Nicholas, 6n2, 135, 186, 193–195, 198,
    203
Ricci, Matteo, 16, 210
Ríos, Pedro de los, 125

Ríos Codex (*also* Codex Vaticanus Latinus 3738
    or Codex Vaticanus A), 125–126, *127*
Ritual specialist, 42, *44*, 100n8
Romanticism, 186, 198–199; *see also*
    Philhellenism, romantic
Rome, 13–14, 19, 36–37, 50, 68n2, 111, 191,
    198
Ruination practices, 74–75, 85, 89–91, 95–96,
    98, 121

S

Saint-Non, Jean-Claude Richard de, 193, *194*
Saladin, 170, 177, 179
Samburu of Kenya, 35–36
Saqsaywaman, temple, 84
Sattam Al-Fayez (*also* Zadam), 170–179
Schliemann, Heinrich, 24, 142
Schnapp, Alain, 1–2, 16, 138
Schöne, Richard, 161–162
Shield of Euphorbos, 22, 213
Shirin (wife of Khosrau II), 168, 170
Sites of articulation, 74, 84
Sith Shwala people, 40–43
Sligo, Lord (Browne, Howe Peter, 2nd Marquess
    of Sligo), 140, 155
Smell (*also* Olfactory associations), 17–21, 188
Social distinction, 165, 170, 185
Society
    egalitarian, 38–39, 43
    Ethiopian Christian, 42
    hierarchical, 36, 38, 139, 185–186
    non-modern, 32
    preindustrial, 32
    pre-literate, 162, 213
    stratified, 184
    traditional, 32
    see also State societies
"Society of Friends", 145–146, 149, 152
Solipsism, 189, 199, 204, 213
Spolia, 60, 174, 176
Spon, Jacob, 216–217
Stackelberg, Otto Magnus von, 146, *146*, 152
State societies, 34, 36, 38, 42
Strabo, 13–15, 18–19, 79
Stuart, James, 1, 6n2, 135, 186, 193, 195, 198,
    203
Sudan, 39, 42
Sudanese-Ethiopian borderland, 39
Sun, cult of the, 86–87, 89, 91, 96
Superstition, 31, 138, 150, 174–175, 178, 206n2

T

Tecpantlayacac, 114
Tehuacan Valley, 125
Temistitan *see* Tenochtitlan

Temple
    Aphaea (Aegina), 145
    Apollo Epicurius (Bassae), 135, 145–150, *146*
    Athena (Lindos), 23
    Baalbek (Lebanon), 161
    depository, 23
    Great Temple (Mexico City), 113
    Olympian Zeus (Olympieion) (Athens), 189,
        198, 201–202
    Parthenon (Athens), 135, 145, 151, 156, 178,
        189, 203, 205
    pyramid of Cholula, 119
    pyramid of the Sun (Teotihuacan), 61
    Saqsaywaman, 84
Tenochtitlan, 111, 118–119, 122
Teocalme (temples), 119
Teotihuacan, 61, 113
Tepedelenli Ali Pasha, 135, 139, 149–151,
    153–154, 156
Thessaloniki, 186–187, 193
Thessaly, Veli Pasha's court, 150, 154
Thucydides, 10–12
Tiahuanaco, 76–78, *77*
Time immemorial, 78, 86, 89, 96–97
Titicaca, Lake, 81, 100n7, 100n9
Tiwanaku, 59–60, 68n2
Tlaxcala, 51, 119–121
Tlazolli, 111–112
Tomb of Absalom, 195, *196*
Torquemade, Juan de, 126
Tovar, Juan de, 119, *123*
Travel account
    Brønsted, Peter Oluf, 146–148
    Eighteenth century, 193
    Franciscan, 116
    Gell, William, 143
    Puchstein, Otto, 161
    Son of Charles Cockerell, 148–149
    Stackelberg, Otto Magnus von, 146
    Tristram, Henry Baker, 163, 165–175, 178
    Western, 151, 153
    Wood, Robert, 193

Treasury of Atreus, 134–135, *135–136,* 140,
    141–142, 142, 146, 155, 157n7
Trigger, Bruce, 2, 15–16, 23
Tripoli (governor's palace), 135, 140, 144–145,
    149, 154
Tristram, Henry Baker, 163, 165–178
Tupicocha, 82
Turdetani, 13–14
Tzocuillixeque (giants), 126, *127*

U
Umm er-Resas (*also* Kastron Mefaa), 174
Universalism, European, 154, 202

V
Varro, Marcus Terentius, 117
Vasilakis (Veli Pasha's agent), 147–148
Veli Pasha, 135, 137–156
Vernacular practices, 74, 80, 139,
    169, 178
Vilcas Guaman, 60–61
Von Humboldt, Alexander *see* Humboldt,
    Alexander von
Von Stackelberg, Otto Magnus *see* Stackelberg,
    Otto Magnus von
Votives, 18, 23, 109, 111, 113,
    117, 143

W
Wak'a, 59, 72, 78–98, 206n4
Wild museography, 39, 42–43
Wood, Robert, 193

X
Xiuhtonalamatl, 119

Y
Yucay Valley, 97

Z
Zadam (Sattam Al-Fayez), 170–179
Ziza, 171, 176–177